Myrtle Fillmore
Mother of Unity

By Thomas E. Witherspoon

UNITY BOOKS
Unity Village, Missouri 64065

Cover: Portrait of Myrtle Fillmore
By Pam Preciado

The photograph on page 254 is used with permission
of The American Magazine. Thanks are extended to
various photographers who have contributed to the
Unity photographic library, from which the remainder
of photographs in this book have been borrowed.

Acknowledgments

Sincere thanks are extended to the Board of Directors of Unity School of Christianity for authorizing and supporting the author in writing this biography. Gratitude is also expressed to Harold Whaley, Unity's Library Director, and Irene Fortney, Heritage Room Archivist, for granting the author complete freedom to use library facilities and examine historical documents and letters. *The Story of Unity* has been invaluable as a resource, and grateful appreciation is made to James Dillet Freeman, its author.

This book is dedicated to the more than 500 persons who are employed by Unity School of Christianity; to the more than 300 Unity ministers who carry the Truth message to people all over the world; to the hundreds of licensed teachers who work with study groups and classes; and to Truth students everywhere who are learning and living the Jesus Christ principles as interpreted and taught by Myrtle and Charles Fillmore.

Contents

Preface

"If only you had time for writing Mama Myrtle! If only you had!"

Pleas such as this poured in by the hundreds during the lifetime of Myrtle Fillmore, cofounder with Charles Fillmore of Unity School of Christianity.

People all over the world wanted to know more about her life, and about the work she was doing, but she was reluctant to share such personal information. When she was asked to write her memoirs, for example, she declared: "We have never cared to interest folks in our individual lives. It makes no difference who we are or what we have done. What is important is that we are doing what the Father has given us to do, according to our best light."

Mrs. Fillmore occasionally wavered a bit and said that someday she might write about her life and her work with Unity, but that if she did not get around to it Spirit would see to it that someone else would do it, if it needed to be done.

"There is no hurry," she would say. "There is all of eternity you know. There is a great deal in my heart, but it comes to me that I should *make* the Truths of living now rather than *write* about them. Sometimes I long to put into print the beautiful things which fill me. But I am not anxious about it!"

This book is an attempt to accurately and honestly record the life of Myrtle Fillmore. It was researched, written, and edited over a two-year period. The writer pored through thousands of documents, letters, and articles by or about Mrs. Fillmore; visited every area where she lived—from Ohio to Missouri to Texas and Colorado; and talked to many persons who knew Mrs. Fillmore personally. The end result was thousands of fragments of information which, when pieced together, became: MYRTLE FILLMORE: MOTHER OF UNITY.

It has been a great joy to chronicle the life of this amazing person, this overcomer, this woman who knew God and who lived a lifetime of service to humanity.

There has been no attempt to deify her. Instead, every effort was made to keep her life in human perspective. She grew and unfolded spiritually throughout her life; she met and successfully worked through many challenges; and she could well be a model for any person seeking to find the Truth of his own being.

T.E.W.

I

The Golden Days of Youth

The first rays of the light of a new day were visible in the eastern sky and there were stirrings within the log cabin, but Mary Caroline was content in her warm bed and she pulled a heavy comforter up and over her head as if to hide from the outside world. Her mother knew well, however, the button to touch to set aglow all the expectancy of the little girl's life. She knelt by the bed, pulled the comforter back, and gently kissed the child's brow.

"If my little girl would get Aurora's kiss this morning, she will have to be stirring."

Quicker than it can be told, Mary Caroline bounded from her resting place, hugged her mother about the waist, and dashed outside to get the beauty kiss that Aurora, goddess of the morning, shares with early risers. There she spoke to the sunrise, as she did most mornings.

"My, you are beautiful, with your lovely garments trailing all over the sky, and your dewy summer kisses scattered all over the grass and trees. My soul springs forth to meet you. A day can never be dull or unhappy that begins with your kiss!"

Later, after breakfast with the rest of the family and after chores were completed, Mary Caroline would retreat to her favorite place, a shaded nook along the banks of Big

Walnut Creek, where she could rest beneath the willows and oaks and watch the small animals and listen to the warbling of the birds.

Mary Caroline would tuck her hands under her head, with her face turned skyward, and soon she wasn't there at all. No, she would be way up among the fleecy, changeful, melting clouds. She would be among the swaying branches of the green trees, among the birds that sang and soared—among whatever there was up there to be among. Somehow, she would seem to be one with all that was. Then suddenly her soul and body would be reunited and she would be aware that the process had taken place.

Mary Caroline wondered how she got out of her body and how she got back in and why she could not always be "up there" mingling with it all. When she thought about her body and how it was so often filled with pain, the trees, the birds, and the clouds would seem to lift themselves away from her, and she would feel all lonely and shut in. But, when she thought of herself as free from her body, and how she was both without *and* within *it, and how she was undoubtedly one with the All, sharing life with all things living, sharing beauty with all things beautiful, sharing joy with all things joyful, how glad and happy and how* free *Mary Caroline became. And then her soul soared again, free and unfettered, and she consciously blended herself into the One.*

Mary Caroline Page was born on August 6, 1845, in Pagetown, Ohio, according to birth records. She died, known as Myrtle Fillmore, on October 6, 1931, at Unity Village, Missouri, according to a death certificate. But the truth of the matter is that the soul which inhabited the bodily manifestation is timeless and ethereal, without beginning and without end. The impact she left upon the earth is still keenly being felt and will be for centuries to come, perhaps forever.

As a child, Mary Caroline was known as a dreamer, a funny and peculiar little girl with a head full of air castles. As a woman, Myrtle Fillmore lived many of her childhood dreams into reality, and, with her husband Charles Fillmore, cofounded Unity School of Christianity, an internationally-known institution for the study of life and religion as demonstrated by Jesus Christ.

The little girl, known as Myrtle by her father, Mary Caroline by her mother (until she yielded eventually to Myrtle), "young-un" by her brothers and sisters, and "that funny red-headed girl" by most of the townspeople, was the eighth of nine children born to Marcus and Lucy (Wheeler) Page.

There are two versions of how the name Mary Caroline evolved into Myrtle, both of which have validity. Marcus Page loved to grab his children by the hands and swing them about. In doing so to Mary Caroline, he would shout, "My little Myrtilee!" The nickname stuck and as the little girl matured, the name was shortened to the more sophisticated Myrtle. A more esoteric explanation was offered many years later by Mrs. Fillmore. "Myrtle wasn't the name they gave me," she told friends. "It just came through and has stayed. I think my soul must have asserted itself and took its own name, rather than the one given by affectionate parents."

Myrtle's mother, Lucy Wheeler Page, was born June 2, 1805, in Luyenn County, Pennsylvania, a daughter of Thomas and Abigail (Newbury) Wheeler. Lucy's brother, James Wheeler, was one of the best known missionaries of his day and ministered to the Wyandot Indian tribes.

Myrtle's father, Marcus Page, was born September 17, 1805, in Broome County, New York, a son of Samuel Page. Samuel emigrated to Ohio in 1817 with his wife and children and settled in what is now northern Delaware County. He cleared land for a farm and erected a log cabin, but two years later, in 1819, his brother William and his family also moved to Ohio and Samuel sold his farm to him. Samuel took his family a few miles north into what is now Morrow County and bought another farm. Samuel died in 1839 and Marcus inherited the land his father had owned. Two years before, however, Marcus had purchased seven acres of land near Big Walnut Creek and laid out a town that came to be known as Pagetown. Located about thirty miles north of Columbus, Pagetown reached its zenith during the years Marcus and Lucy were raising their family—but it never became more than a village with limited business and industry, and only a score or so of dwellings.

Marcus and Lucy were married on February 16, 1830. The first child, Jane, was born November 22 the same year. Henrietta arrived May 17, 1832; Sarah on April 27, 1834; Thomas on August 11, 1836; Sophronia on June 29, 1838; David on July 26, 1840; Daniel on December 16, 1842; Mary Caroline on the 1845 date; and Frances (known also as Buena) on July 16, 1848. Sophronia and Frances died in infancy and Thomas died when he was twenty-nine. Two of the children, Jane and Henrietta, lived into their nineties.

The Pagetown of Myrtle's youth had a small hotel, a tannery to process hides of animals, a carding mill for wool, an iron foundry which turned out plow points and other implements for farming, a blacksmith shop and a nearby buggy shop, a post office, a general store, a tavern, and a school. Pagetown didn't have a church until about 1860, but townspeople, including the Page family, attended services in a nearby community or, when weather made travel impossible, church services were conducted in one of the village homes. Marcus and Lucy were deeply religious and were faithful Methodists. Myrtle, however, never became a member of her parents' church. When she came of age she decided not to join. Marcus Page never gave his children a choice about attending church as long as they were members of his household, but he did not force any of them to join a church.

Myrtle appreciated the services in the Methodist church she attended, but even at a very young age she found much of the doctrine unacceptable in her own life. Undoubtedly she was influenced by an elder sister, Jane, who left home because she didn't like Methodist practices. "I don't believe in hell," she had told her parents, "and I won't belong to a church that preaches it." Myrtle agreed with her sister, although she never made such a strong issue of her feelings. Instead, she simply affirmed the truth her soul could accept about Methodism and quietly denied that part she could not accept. She never spoke harshly concerning the religion of her parents. In fact, as an adult she fondly recalled her Methodist experience. Writing to a friend, she said, "I know my life must express many of the splendid ideas embodied in the Methodist faith. And I always have a warm spot in my heart for all Methodist people."

Marcus Page worshiped a stern and vengeful God, and he insisted on a puritanical life-style for every family member. He could be threatening at times in matters of religion and decorum, but more often he was a warm and understanding father to his children. Once when daughter Jane asked permission to go to a public dance, he roared, "Yes, but if you do I'll break both your legs." Then, moments later, as if to make amends, he would toss and twirl the children in the privacy of their home, and teach them dance steps he had learned many years earlier.

Myrtle's father was, in addition to being the founding father of the community, a leader in several capacities. Primarily he was a farmer, but he also served a term as postmaster and for a short time he operated a general store. He was known as an abolitionist, and he assisted many blacks in their journey to freedom along the underground railroad from the south to Canada. Perhaps most important, he was a leader in the church and was instrumental in having a church established in Pagetown in 1860. About two years earlier, when Myrtle was twelve, members of the community decided to have church services in the basement of a home. There was a well in one corner, and it was an object of curiosity to young Myrtle. Somehow she became convinced that the well was the "well of salvation" mentioned in the Bible. One day while a workman was building pews for the temporary structure, she could resist no longer, so she asked him: "Is that the well of salvation?" The remark haunted Myrtle for years to come because the amused workman spread the story far and wide. She shrugged off the laughter with the thought that nothing was impossible, and it *very well could have been* the well of salvation.

She recalled later that it often felt chilly and hard when folks talked about and laughed at her "funny ideas," but she knew there was nothing too good or too beautiful to be true and in her designing room she was determined to make patterns for a beautiful world. She was dedicated to helping build a world where people would not crystallize and stagnate or get stale and stiff. She envisioned a world that would be *alive!* "Things will hum," she told her friends, "when the new world comes out!"

There always was comfort for Myrtle in the arms of her mother Lucy, and when laughter or scorn had hurt her feelings, she sought solace there and received it. Often it came in the form of a little song:

Ye fearful saints, fresh courage take:
The clouds you so much dread
Are big with mercies, and shall break
With blessings on your head.

Lucy Page was as ardently religious as her husband, and she shared his beliefs about a God who, if He chose to, would punish and hurt His children. "I marvel," Myrtle said later, "that my wonderful mother, who loved so devotedly, could have worshiped a God who punished, or took the lives of His children."

Myrtle was passionately in love with God and with nature, and she spent many happy hours in splendid isolation along the banks of the little stream behind her home or high on one of the rolling hills surrounding the village. Her relationship with nature was very satisfying, and although she may not fully have known it as a child, she knew later that she was feeling and responding in those golden days of youth to the omnipresence of God. The abundant life of God poured out to her from everywhere, and her hungry soul and body drank it in and rejoiced in expressing it.

Myrtle was afflicted at an early age with a disease which doctors determined to be tuberculosis. She grew up with members of the family saying: "She is delicate. She must be protected. She must not overdo." Not until many years later, and after much suffering, did she learn the truth about herself, that she was God's child and as such she was not subject to ills of the flesh.

Second only to her love of God and His creation was her love for education. School days for Myrtle opened wide vistas of excitement. She was an eager pupil and she always

wanted to read material that was more advanced than her
years, or books that educators said were not suitable for
young girls. As a result, she would secrete her brother's
books one at a time, and when no one was observing, she
would steal away to her secluded place by the stream and
read them. She could never understand why her parents
felt those books were unsuited to her active mind. They
told her of wonderful things, and they opened her mind,
making it possible for her to think through many of life's
complexities.

She raced through simple mathematics and pored
deeply into algebra, geometry, and trigonometry long
before she had advanced officially into such subjects in the
little one-room Pagetown school building. Science, as
taught at the elementary level, failed to hold her interest, so
she read her brother's books about chemistry and physics,
and also became avidly interested in astronomy. At a
tender age she could identify many of the constellations.
Homework was rarely a problem, but occasionally a
teacher would try to challenge Myrtle's alert mind and
momentary consternation would result. But Myrtle had a
system! After the reading lamp was extinguished or the
last candle flickered out, she would take the problem the
teacher had posed and go to bed with it. She recalled many
years later that invariably when she awakened the next
morning the whole solution to the problem would be clearly
in her mind. During the night the workers in that realm of
mind called the subconscious had taken hold of the
problem and had worked it out.

As a teenager, Myrtle had read every book in the Page
household, a rather large number of volumes for any home
to contain in those pioneer days. Included were works by
Shakespeare and Josephus, the latter the historian of the
Jewish people; "The Life of Watson," "The History of All

Religions," "The Life of Luther," "The Life of Wesley,"
"Plutarch Lives," "Gold and the Gospel," "Home Truths,"
"Mason's Spiritual Treasures," the Bible, and dozens more.

Young Miss Myrtle had little time for boys, and even
less time for girls who did have time for them. When she was
in high school, she had a very close friend who shared her
interest in God, nature, and serious study. One day a boy
came between her and her chum, and the happy and
carefree times she and her girl friend had enjoyed abruptly
came to an end. "I can't see what she finds in fixing herself
up and going out with boys," she declared to her mother.
"You will," Lucy replied. "You will." Myrtle didn't know it at
the time, but her illness, her interest in education, and her
family circumstances were all pointing her in the direction
of her life's love interest, Charles Fillmore . . . but that day
was many years away.

When Myrtle completed high school the Civil War was
under way, and a short time later, while the nation was
mourning its fallen leader Abraham Lincoln, death also
visited the Page household. Marcus Page died on August
23, 1865, to be followed a few days later, on September 13,
by the death of Myrtle's brother Thomas. Two Page
children already had been placed beneath the ground in the
burial plot just north of the village. Sophronia had died in
1839 and Frances in 1850. It was the sad duty of the family
to gather twice again in 1865 to bid farewell to a father and
his son. Thomas was twenty-nine years old at the time of his
death, while Marcus was just under sixty years of age. A
stone about nine feet tall, which still stands, was placed on
the plot with four names inscribed on it. Eleven years later,
in 1876, the name of Lucy Wheeler Page was added, the last
of five Page family members to be buried there.

With Marcus Page gone, the responsibilities of helping
maintain a home for Lucy and seeing to family affairs fell

largely to Myrtle, who still lived at home, and to the brothers David and Daniel. David, the eldest, was named administrator of the Marcus Page estate. The death had been rather sudden and there was no will. The estate totaled just over two thousand dollars in assets, including seven hundred dollars in cash. Marcus Page had been a hard-working and honest man and had accrued few debts, save those of a doctor during his last days and the cost of having a coffin built. In addition to household furnishings and clothing, Marcus Page left his family a red cow valued at forty dollars, a smaller red cow worth thirty dollars, a black mare priced at thirty dollars, two fat hogs with a total value of sixty dollars, nine tons of good hay at thirty-six dollars, forty-seven bushels of wheat at forty-seven dollars, and three swarms of bees, five dollars each. He had disposed of all land he had owned, even the land upon which his log cabin rested. Raising a large family and costly business setbacks in an effort to make Pagetown prosper had eroded most of what had been a fairly sizable estate.

While probate was under way, Lucy was granted a yearly support sum of four hundred dollars, part of which was in livestock and grain.

Myrtle decided to take a job during this period and moved for a brief time to Columbus, Ohio, where she was employed as a writer with a newspaper. Although she had never legally changed her name from Mary Caroline to Myrtle, she used the latter in signed articles for the newspaper in Columbus. In 1867 she took another important step in her development when she enrolled in "The Literary Course for Ladies" at Oberlin College, Oberlin, Ohio. Her studies lasted only one year because women were not eligible for the regular four-year college programs. Upon graduation she was licensed as a teacher.

She returned to Pagetown where she joined her mother
and her brother David and his family, and together they
made plans to go west. David had earlier attended
Wesleyan University and then had moved to Philadelphia
where he was a clerk in a wholesale warehouse. In 1867 he
was passing through Pagetown on his way to a new life in
Illinois.

Myrtle had secured a position as a school teacher in
Clinton, Missouri, so in 1868 she traveled west with her
family to Marshall County, Illinois, where David had settled
with their mother Lucy. A sister, Henrietta, lived in the
town of Lacon, the county seat. Myrtle traveled on, and
David and Lucy followed her to Clinton, Missouri, three
years later and settled there. While in Illinois, David worked
in a store, but in Clinton he engaged in the coal business
and started a nursery. Later he owned a cooperative store
in Clinton, Page & Hopkins.

During part of the time that Myrtle was in Clinton she belonged to an organization known as "The Amateurs" and participated in plays, readings, and choral events performed by the group. A Clinton newspaper mentioned that she gave many creditable performances and said she had "decided talent." Occasionally the group would travel to neighboring communities, sometimes as far as thirty or forty miles away to present plays for large crowds.

Myrtle loved Clinton and she was much loved there by both the townspeople and the children she taught, but the specter of tuberculosis continued to haunt her and her life force seemed to be slowly ebbing away. Doctors in Clinton advised her that if she wished to survive, she would have to leave Missouri where dampness and winter's cold complicated the symptoms she endured. It was recommended that she depart as soon as possible for Denison, Texas, known at that time as a resort area for comsumptive patients. The community was located two miles south of the Red River in North Texas. The site was considered healthy because the prevailing winds were from the south, and thus diseases common to river-area residents were believed to be blown away to the north. Denison business interests advertised all over the nation that "not more than ten days a year is it cold enough for a wrap to be worn and few residents ever catch cold." The air in Denison was fresh, and this is a vital part of any tubercular victim's recovery.

So it was that in the mid-1870s, Myrtle Page left Clinton and moved toward better health, little suspecting that her future husband and spiritual co-worker also awaited her in Denison. Upon her arrival in Texas, she busied herself with activities in the local Methodist church, did a small amount of private tutoring, and joined the Denison Literary Club which held Monday evening meetings above a drug store. Doctors had forbidden her to resume her teaching career.

Charles Fillmore, who had come south from Minnesota to seek his fortune, was also a member of the literary club. He and Myrtle were attracted to each other immediately, although Charles was much more sure that marriage was a part of their respective destinies. Myrtle was so busy with her activities that she simply did not have time to think of men—until Charles made his presence felt so strongly.

Charles first saw Myrtle on the occasion of her delivering an original reading at a literary club meeting. When he looked at her, something within him said, *"There's your wife, Charles."* He always thought he had chosen her, but many years later she confided to him that it had only seemed so. "The woman always does the choosing," she told him, "even though it only be to insist upon the man living up to her high ideals." But she added, "You were splendid, dear, or I wouldn't have chosen you."

She often recalled that day of decision, and told friends and family members about it:

"When he saw me, he decided he was going to have me for his companion! Of course, he hadn't consulted me, but apparently I didn't have much to say about it. But he was awfully nice, and I suppose I was a little hungry to have a home of my own, and my very own boys to help me as I'd like to do."

As a young girl, when she had criticized her friend for discovering boys, she had thought interest in male companionship would detract from her happy pursuit of knowledge in the form of books and from her love of God and nature. But she immediately recognized that Charles could enhance her devotion to these matters, for he shared many of her interests. His spiritual unfolding was in its earliest stages, but she saw the great potential there.

Denison was a railroad town wherein the Missouri, Kansas, and Texas Railroad (MK&T or "The Katy") terminated. Charles was a freight agent at the time he met Myrtle. The little town of Denison was caught in the throes of progress and every day those ladies known by townsmen as the "fairest flowers of the prairie" and by the clergy and the women of the community as "excessively soiled doves" arrived to ply their trade. In addition to prostitution, Denison boasted of a multitude of drinking and gambling places. There was very little law, and that which did exist was essentially the "Law of the Colt," which made every man the same size. Yet by frontier standards Denison was a relatively tame town, superior to many others in the West. But it was a far cry from Pagetown, and even Clinton, for the genteel Myrtle Page.

In 1878, in an effort to put an end to some of the drinking problems in the city, the church which Myrtle attended decided to have a temperance rally. Each night of the session, Myrtle read from her own poetry to appreciative crowds. The Denison Daily Herald watched the temperance meetings closely and informed its readers that there was always "loud applause for the young lady's efforts, Miss Myrtle Page." Following her reading, a minister spoke each night on the evils of drinking and then asked those so moved to come forward, take the pledge against alcohol, and "don the blue ribbon." Within the first five days, more than three hundred individuals, mostly boys and girls, had pledged.

On April 17, 1878, a special person was in the audience, and Miss Page gave him special attention as she recited. It was her friend Charles Fillmore, who had on occasion imbibed of the spirits. He listened carefully that

night, both to his friend Myrtle and to the minister, and at the end of the session he went forward to take the pledge. Liquor had never suited him anyway, he said, and Myrtle and the minister had given him the courage to quit it altogether. The next day the Daily Herald excitedly reported the news that Charles Fillmore, recently promoted to cashier of the "Katy," had donned the blue ribbon of temperance.

Less than a month later, with Myrtle Page at his side, Charles Fillmore himself was leading temperance sessions, speaking on "Temperance, from a New Viewpoint."

In all, more than five hundred persons took the pledge during the various temperance sessions that spring and summer of 1878. Some of them wore their blue ribbons proudly, but others took their personally inscribed ribbons and nailed them to the town hall notice board. Charles Fillmore was among the latter. He had made a decision, and he wanted everyone to know it. He encouraged others to don the blue ribbon too, as the children of Israel were instructed in Numbers 15:37-39:

*"The Lord said to Moses, 'Speak to the people
of Israel, and bid them to make tassels on
the corners of their garments throughout their
generations, and to put upon the tassel of
each corner a cord of blue; and it shall be to
you a tassel to look upon and remember all
the commandments of the Lord, to do them,
not to follow after your own heart and your
own eyes, which you are inclined to go after
wantonly.' "*

In addition to her work in temperance, Myrtle decided
in 1878 that she was well enough to return to full-time work
as a teacher. Memories of the Civil War were still quite
vivid, however, and when the children found out that she
was from the North, she quickly received the nickname
"Yankee." At first this appeared to be a barrier to her
success in teaching young Texas children, but her love and
understanding and easy way with youngsters soon
overcame the stigma. Many of the students in her school
were quite large and some of them had reputations for
being "bad." But Myrtle did not treat them as "bad"
children, so they soon started behaving more properly. "I
liked them and I expected them to like me, and to be good
to me, and they were," she told friends in later years. "The
man who came, and took me away, has never taken the
place in my heart which is given over to my own dear boys
and girls of those other schooldays."

While she was teaching in 1878, she stayed with a
family which included several young children. The young
girls of the home embroidered pillows and bath towels for
Miss Page and filled her room with lovely things. The
mother confided to Myrtle on one occasion that her tiny
daughter had patted Myrtle's pillow one evening and kissed
it, saying, "A golden head will rest on this pillow tonight."

Such was the extent of the love "Miss Page" generated among the children in Denison.

When Myrtle opened her private school in Denison in January, 1878, the Denison Daily Herald noted the occasion:

> "Miss Myrtle Page, a lady of culture and refinement, and a practical and experienced normal teacher in the public graded schools of the north and east, will open a subscription school next week. This will afford an excellent opportunity for parents to put their children in a good school where they will receive the attention which is impossible in a crowded school room."

In an adjacent advertising column, Myrtle pointed out that the school would be located on Burnett Avenue, near Gandy, first door west of Sam Hanna's—at two dollars per student per month.

The school attracted a sizable number of pupils and the Herald kept a close watch on the situation, reporting its progress from time to time. On March 4, 1878, the editor observed:

> "If it were generally known that Miss Page is teaching one of the best private schools in the state of Texas right here in Denison, many more of our people would avail themselves of this opportunity to school their children. She is a thoroughly competent teacher for beginners as well as more advanced pupils. Patrons of Miss Page's school are well pleased with the progress her pupils are making."

Still later, on April 22, 1878, the editor practically glowed in reporting that the pupils in Miss Page's school had started a newspaper. He indicated he was "favorably struck by evidence of wit, thought, and thorough mental training in pupils so young."

If the editor was surprised at such goings on in school, one can only imagine the attitudes of mothers and fathers who were sending their children to such a progressive institution. It was an unusual school indeed, and indicated that Myrtle Page was far ahead of her time in the field of education. In still another newspaper account, the editor reported: "Miss Page possesses a happy faculty of instilling into the minds of her pupils the necessity for independent thought upon all matters connected with the regular school exercises. The books are used as texts only, and the child is permitted to frame the idea in his own language, which is the best evidence of the degree of understanding attained."

However, in June, after the school had operated only six months, Myrtle announced to the community that she was closing its doors and that she would return to Clinton, Missouri, where she would teach in the public schools. Many sad citizens read of her decision in the Herald:

> "Miss Myrtle Page, who has a private school on Burnett Ave., has been elected one of the teachers in the Public Schools of Clinton, Mo., at a larger salary than any other lady teacher in the school. She unquestionably is one of the best teachers Denison has ever known, as the progress and efficiency of her school indicates. It is a pity that she could not have been retained in Denison."

When the school closed on June 14, 1878, she was confronted by a number of parents who insisted that she spend the rest of the summer in Denison and promised that they would pay her if she would teach them how to tutor their children privately with her system. She bowed to the pressure and announced that classes would begin the following week for all who were interested in reading, elocution, and related subjects. She taught this special program for two months, then said good-bye to Denison for good, and to her dear friend Charles Fillmore for a few years. She taught in Clinton for three years, at a starting salary of thirty-five dollars a month, until 1881, when Charles reentered her life.

The contacts Myrtle made with children as a teacher in both Clinton and Denison followed her the rest of her life. One highly valued letter from a former student arrived just a few days before her death in 1931. Portions of it read:

"My dear Mrs. Fillmore, or dear Miss Page, as I shall always think of you. I always think of you as you were in the 1870s, a slim wisp of a girl, with beautiful brown eyes and titian hair, done high with two adorable curls cuddling around on the right side, with a wonderful complexion that goes with that rather unusual shade of hair, and last of all, that sweet smile, that was so infectious as to work wonders with a lot of 12- and 14-year-old boys and girls, no matter how serious the escapades had been. One glance at the sweet face of our dearly beloved teacher would bring penitence and contrition. In retrospect, I never fail to see you with an indescribable charm of manner that made us think we would be your slaves forever—all is indelibly stamped in memory."

Mrs. Fillmore replied, also quoted in part:

"You turned not time, but memory, back to the seventies and the picture you made of Miss Page was very attractive, but rather overdrawn. You see, dear, it was your love painting Miss Myrtle into a beauty. I think she never quite earned the adjective beautiful, although she was alive to the needs of her boys and girls.

"We did have funny, good times in those blessed days. But haven't we kept on believing in the Good all these years? And my blessed girl, though they haven't always been rose-tinted, still we have wrung from them the true

values of life. I'd love to see you. I wonder if the dear little girl that has a place in my memory garden is anything at all like the blessed friend of today? I think you'd find some changes in Miss Page. The titian curls have changed to what, I've been told by some of our dear friends here at Unity, is now the latest mode of color of hair—not silver, but platinum. It's rather nice, don't you think so, to be right in style, without having to put forth any effort to be fashionable?"

During the time Charles and Myrtle lived in Denison, they became very close friends, and although Charles did not say this in so many words, both of them presumed the relationship would ultimately result in marriage. Charles, as a matter of fact, may have intended to marry Miss Page in Denison had she stayed there. Two days after she opened her private school in early 1878, Charles bought a large corner lot in the city and announced plans for a brick residence to be erected upon it. A month later he was promoted from freight agent to cashier, an important position in the railroad town, an elevation in rank that drew the attention of the newspaper. It called the promotion "proper and deserved" and said, "Charles Fillmore is thoroughly qualified and esteemed." By the time spring arrived, the brick home was completed, but Miss Page had announced her departure. Charles lived in the home with his mother for less than a year, and he too left the area and set out for Colorado's gold and silver mines.

Many years later, after their marriage, Charles and Myrtle reminisced about their days of friendship in Denison and agreed that the time spent together there, usually in the company of good friends, was among the most idyllic of their lives.

They took long walks together in the outdoors that both

of them so dearly loved, and they told each other of their hopes and dreams for the future. They exchanged essays that they had written and they read to each other from the Bible, Shakespeare, Lowell, and their favorite, Emerson. Often they wrote poetry to each other and recited it aloud. They attended worship services together and participated in virtually all church activities. After Myrtle departed for Missouri, there was a great void in Charles' heart, but he wrote to her and asked if they might correspond. She replied:

"I was pleased to find, when I returned from my visit in the country Thursday, among my other mail, a letter from you. Such correspondence would prove rather a treat than a burden to me. I shall ever feel grateful to you for contributing so much to my literary enjoyments and for new thoughts and suggestions, yes, and for a kind of sympathy I seldom meet.

"I have learned many lessons in the past year.
What the world teaches profits to the world.
What the soul teaches profits to the soul.
Which then first stands erect with Godward face,
When she lets fall her pack of withered facts,
The gleanings of the outward eye and ear,
And looks and listens with her finer sense;
Nor truth nor knowledge cometh from without.

"You question my orthodoxy? Well, if I were called upon to write out my creed it would be a rather strange mixture. I am decidedly eclectic in my theology. Is it not my right to be? Over all is a grand ideal God but full of love and mercy. And dear to my heart is Christ, the perfect man, who shared our earthly sorrows, yet ever lived blameless, and taught such sweet lessons of patience, forgiveness, and tolerance. Outside of ourselves must we go for a

strength to trust and rely on. Trusted, that strength proves a help. Call it by what name you choose, the soul understands it.

"Last Sabbath I had a glorious time. They sent for me to visit down in the country among my old Fairview friends, and Sunday there was a 'basket meeting way off in the woods.' I went. The sermons were quite good, and the spot was divine. Near the preachers' stand rose a great ledge of rock that overhung a small stream. It stretched for a half-mile or more. Oh, it was grand! I went up to the top, gathered ferns and mosses—the most beautiful mosses. One's foot sunk down among them, green and silver and gray they were. And the most picturesque nooks and grottoes. O, to me the messages came then, from the Divine Spirit, more direct than through His human messengers!

"The good, simple-hearted country folk enjoyed seeing me enjoy it so and confessed, 'It was mighty nice.' They saw rock and moss, listened decorously to the man of God, while I, in a kind of charmed life, was a part of all I saw—and a part of God. What have I said? But you understand me, you know there are times when we go out and seem to become a part of this great Spirit of the Universe. Now, I seldom dare confess this foolish (?) other life I keep within myself, but I couldn't live without it. And when I try to choke it out, I am the most miserable creature on earth."

The relationship grew and strengthened as Myrtle and Charles corresponded. It was obvious to both of them that it would blossom into a proposal of marriage, but that day was to be years away.

II

The Man of Her Life

Charles Fillmore was born in 1854 in a log cabin near St. Cloud, Minnesota. His parents, Henry and Mary Fillmore, christened him Charles Sherlock Fillmore, but he never used the middle name. His family got its start in North America when John Fillmore jumped from a pirate ship in the 1700s in Boston harbor. He had been captured by the pirates when he was thirteen years old and was forced to work for them until his escape at eighteen years of age.

Charles Fillmore's mother was Welsh and his father was English. The word *Fillmore* was derived from the English: Philmore—Philip who lived on the moors. In response to many questions through the years about a possible relationship to President Millard Fillmore, Charles was able to report honestly that his father and Millard were cousins and playmates in their youth. In later years, Charles was often asked by astrologers to provide specific birth information. He replied on one occasion:

"I am not positively sure of the time and place, as no records were kept officially in northern Minnesota in the early days. However, I am certain it did happen. Mother says it was 4 o'clock on the afternoon of August 22, 1854. Father placed his guess as a year later. I don't know; but I favor mother's judgment as she was there at the time."

Charles' father migrated to Minnesota from New York. His mother, the former Mary Georgianna Stone, a daughter of a Nova Scotian millwright, moved to the Minnesota area with her family when she was a small child. When Henry and Mary were married is unknown, but in 1861 when Charles was seven, they decided to separate and they did not live together again. Charles had a brother, Norton, two years younger than he. They were the only children.

Mary Fillmore was left alone with the boys in the wilds of the Minnesota frontier, while her husband Henry relocated his furrier business ten miles north. The two boys were shuffled back and forth during the first few years of the separation, but eventually they made a permanent home with their mother and lost contact with their father altogether.

It was a primitive existence in the north woods, with Indians, often hostile, outnumbering the white settlers. The Indians were frequently on the warpath against each other and occasionally against the white intruders. One day a band of Sioux Indians kidnapped two-year-old Charles, but late the same day they returned him to his parents. He always believed he had been used in some kind of tribal ceremony; but, of course, he never knew for sure.

When Charles was ten years old, he was severely injured while ice-skating. His right hip was dislocated and it refused to respond to any kind of medical treatment. The doctors of that time, and especially those on the frontier, were inept and used crude techniques such as lancing and bleeding and placing leeches on open sores. Infection set in and for more than two years Charles lay between life and death. The hip socket seemed irreparably damaged; the right leg stopped growing and started to wither. Finally, when the infection had run its course and the crisis ended, his right leg was four inches shorter than the left one, and it was necessary for his right shoe to be fitted with a lift. Young Charles was on crutches for a time, but his spirit would not permit this kind of artificial assistance any longer than necessary, and soon he was getting about by himself, albeit with great difficulty.

When he returned to school at the age of twelve, he found himself hopelessly behind his former classmates, and he soon realized he would be unable to resume any kind of normal educational or physical activity.

In addition, his mother needed his assistance to help support the family; Norton was then ten years old. Charles abandoned school and took his first job—as a printer's devil. As an apprentice he learned the fundamentals of a trade he would put to good use later. He also became acquainted with banking and business practices while employed by a grocery store and a bank.

Young Charles Fillmore

Deep within him, however, he knew it was necessary for him to acquire an education, and his soul directed him to the one who could provide it. The result was that a direct link to Myrtle Page was established, at the tender age of twelve.

Edgar Taylor, an army officer stationed in St. Cloud, had a son of Charles' age. The officer's wife Caroline was devoted to her son and personally tutored him in literature, grammar, writing, philosophy, and many other subjects. The boy was not an eager student, but his friend Charles Fillmore was intrigued and begged permission to sit in on the tutoring sessions. Soon Charles became practically a permanent fixture in the Taylor home, and he thirstily drank in all the knowledge that Mrs. Taylor could impart to him. Without knowing it at the time, he was beginning a deliberate and certain course toward his meeting many years later with Myrtle Page and the ultimate life partnership which would spiritually touch millions of people through the formation of Unity School of Christianity.

Caroline Taylor had graduated from Oberlin College in Ohio, and so it was that her student Charles Fillmore received virtually the same education that his future wife was receiving. At almost the same time, Myrtle studied directly at Oberlin, and he, indirectly through a tutor. There is little wonder then that Charles and Myrtle found so much in common when they later met in Denison, Texas. Another ironic twist in Charles' life was that the two women who had the greatest impact on his mind—before Myrtle—were Mary Fillmore, his mother, and Caroline Taylor, his tutor. Mary and Caroline. And then came Mary Caroline Page into his life, even though she preferred the name *Myrtle*.

Charles left St. Cloud in the spring of 1874 when he was nineteen years old, determined to make his fortune in

Caddo, Oklahoma Territory. He had a cousin there who had regaled him with what turned out to be exaggerated accounts of prosperity in that area.

Charles told his mother he would send for her as soon as he struck it rich. Norton had run away from home several years earlier, so Mary Fillmore was alone. She well knew Charles' ambition, though, one he had voiced many times and in later years he heartily admitted:

"I want to go out on the wild prairies, wear leather breeches, break wild broncos, sing, and be an honest-to-goodness cowboy."

He had no idea, however, how rugged frontier life could be, so when he arrived in Caddo he was ill-prepared for the wild activities that routinely took place there. Cowboys, rough and often mule-tempered, rode into the settlement virtually every night and shot at anything that moved; rode their horses into stores and demanded liquor, and that their steeds be fed and watered, and generally raised havoc. Caddo, Charles quickly concluded, was purely and simply a mistake, one he immediately corrected by moving south a few miles into a North Texas town called Denison. He secured a position with the MK&T Railroad as a freight-car counter and, true to his word, sent for his mother when he could afford to do so. There he met, wooed, and eventually won his life's love, Miss Myrtle Page.

Charles lived in Denison only one year after Myrtle returned to Missouri. He was discharged from his position as cashier of the railroad when he defended a fellow worker who was falsely accused of improper activities. Since cashiering had not been his idea of success anyway, he was relieved to be free. He set out for Colorado after hearing of the fortunes that were being made there in mining. After less than a year, in 1880 he wrote to a friend of his disillusionment:

"I have not struck anything yet, and the prospects are not good for doing so either. These gold mining camps are mighty uncertain, and this one is especially so. With the exception of Leadville, I have not seen a place since leaving Texas where as much business was done as in Denison. This is a most desolate, barren region. Nothing grows but sage brush and cactus. Advise your friends to stay home if they wish to be happy."

The apparently unhappy Charles Fillmore was making the most of a bad situation, anyway. He worked in a variety of positions, finally settling on being a mule-team driver, or what was more commonly known as a "mule-skinner." One of the towns on his freight route was Gunnison. It was a boom town in 1880 and Charles decided to end his precarious occupation of driving and settle down there. At first he did a little mining on his own, then he learned the assay business, and finally he entered into the real estate arena.

Gunnison was booming, but it was almost as primitive as Caddo had been. Almost everything centered around mining. There were the Red Jacket Mine, Pandora, Maid of Athens, Golden Fleece, Nest Egg, Silver Bell, El Capitan, and dozens more. All promised quick fortune, but they attracted not only the hard workers—such as Charles Fillmore—but also undesirable types. Street gunfights were common and stagecoaches routinely were held up. One stage driver alone complained that he had been held up six times. Despite the shootings, holdups, lynchings, and general boisterousness, the town had grown from one store in 1878 to more than two hundred businesses by the end of 1880. Charles felt he could profit in real estate with such growth under way, so he found a partner and took out an advertisement in the Gunnison Review:

"Hall & Fillmore, Assayers. Real Estate and Insurance Agts.—Tumitchi Ave., West Gunnison, Colo. Assaying done, taxes paid, rents collected, and other business attended to for non-residents. Remittances made promptly, first class references furnished, correspondence solicited." The editor, in an accompanying story, called attention to the advertisement and remarked, "They have their assay, real estate, and insurance office in full blast and solicit a share in the patronage."

Charles Fillmore had *arrived*. He had put down some roots, and he now shared in the ownership of a business that seemed destined to prosper. So he mustered his courage and wrote to Myrtle Page in Clinton, Missouri, and told her that when the winter snows melted in the spring of 1881, he would like to travel to Clinton and have her become his wife. She was delighted with the proposal and accepted it.

In March of 1881 a friend wrote in Charles' autograph book: "As the coming years glide swiftly down the stream of time, may these be recorded on each PAGE of your life's history—volumes of advancement and success, and may MYRTLE wreaths of love and happiness daily crown your life with all that is bright and beautiful."

A few days later, in Clinton, Charles stood beside the bright and beautiful Myrtle Page, and the vows of marriage were repeated. Both Clinton newspapers recorded the event for posterity.

"FILLMORE—PAGE—In Clinton, Tuesday evening, March 29, 1881, at the residence of Mr. J. G. Vinson by Dr. S. Jones—Mr. Charles Fillmore of Gunnison City, Colo., to Miss Myrtle Page of Clinton.

"The ceremony was witnessed only by a few friends of the high contracting parties, and the bride and groom left at 9 p.m. for Colorado, their future home. Mr. Fillmore is an exemplary gentleman, widely and favorably known in the West. Miss Page is one among the most promising young ladies in Henry County—intellectual, beautiful, and accomplished. She was a teacher in our Clinton Public Schools and in her departure society has lost one of its most gifted ornaments."—The Henry County Democrat.

"FILLMORE—PAGE—On the evening of the 29th of March, in this city, Charles Fillmore to Myrtle Page, Rev. Samuel Jones officiating. They expect to make Gunnison City, Colorado, their future home.

"May the Myrtle which he hath enshrined in his heart with her gentle entwinings keep sacred that treasure; and Fillmore completely each possible part than ever could be from an otherwise pleasure."—The Clinton Advocate.

If readers were confused by the second paragraph of the Advocate story, they were no more so than the fifty-three children in the former Miss Page's intermediate class. School was out for spring planting and other farm chores, but when it resumed in late summer their beloved Miss Page would be gone. Charles Fillmore was not a very popular fellow in Clinton the day the vows were spoken. One of Miss Page's students wrote years later to sum up the situation, "We did not like Mr. Charles Fillmore then at all!"

Myrtle's friends and family gathered at the railroad station the same night of the wedding to see the couple off. The Fillmores traveled all night, and when the sun rose on their first full day of marriage, they were speeding through Kansas toward the end of rails at Poncha Springs, Colorado. Upon arrival in Poncha Springs, the Fillmores relaxed a few days until April 4, when they set out for Gunnison by stagecoach. The stage took them to within ten miles of a mountain pass over the continental divide, and there it was necessary for them to board a horse-drawn sleigh to carry them through the pass. It was a perilous yet terribly exciting trip for Myrtle and can best be described in her own words in a letter she wrote later to her sister Jane:

"This is the first work my pen has done since I crossed the 'delectable mountains.' (Charles smiles at my name for the continental divide.)

"Of the three weeks since the day, one was spent on the road, one in resting, and this last one in taking in the situation. Gunnison, like all rapid growths, has not stopped for the extras. We all live in one dooryard fenced in by the mountains. Children and burros seem to have spontaneous growth here and belong to no one in particular, but rove 'round over the unfenced wastes, creating a melody that makes one unconsciously shield his ears.

"Three weeks ago, we left you. I seem to have an unsorted jumble of mountains, snow, and strange experiences in my mind to fill up this space between now and then. Our journey was delightful—I might fib a little to include our trip over the range. We remained at Poncha Springs, the end of the rails, two days, resting for our stagecoach trip. We left Poncha in a stagecoach at seven in the morning (Monday). At eleven we had a layover at a ranch till eight o'clock at night, waiting for the snow to freeze on the mountains. We had Mark Twain's typical driver, by name 'Jack.' When we were finally transferred to sleigh runners, such an experience as we had. There were eleven men, I the only lady.

"The roads or passes were in such fearful condition that the men were obliged to walk the greater part of the way up. It was grand. The moon hung above, the stars seemed to crown the higher peaks. Constant changes seemed to be taking place, mountain on mountain piled on one side, water pouring down in cataracts among the pines far, far below. Again fields of snow would rise till the stars seemed to have them for background. On the other hand one misstep would have landed us hundreds of feet below where the snow was pierced by the dark needles of the pines.

"It was a very dangerous ride. We were two days and one night getting through and had to contrive all manner of ways to get through at all. We had several breakdowns. Sometimes the men had to use all their strength to steer the sled clear of some steep precipice.

"I enjoyed it the first day and night, it was all so new and sublime. We reached the summit at midnight. Old Mount Ouray lay at our right covered with snow and crowned with stars. The moon, that had seemed to us to set two or three times, rose again and gave us light. We commenced our descent. The roar of the waters that seemed to make the road their bed gave a new touch to the sublime.

"I wasn't aware at the time that I was doing anything remarkable by keeping cool during all this journey of hairbreadth escapes, but 'Jack' seemed to have conceived a great respect for me and laid aside all his adjectives and even compromised himself enough to enquire after the comfort of 'the lady.' I learned that I gained quite a reputation for bravery among the masculine part of our adventurers, who seemed to have discussed the subject and agreed that 'not one lady in a thousand would have shown such coolness and bravery.'

"We got into Gunnison about six o'clock Tuesday afternoon. The Halls had been worrying about us, having heard fearful reports of the treacherous mountain roads. And it was fortunate we got through when we did, for almost a week passed before the next coach got through."

The Review, Gunnison's newspaper, noted the arrival of the Fillmores and remarked about the stage and sleigh trip necessary to make the mountain passage: "The trip is anything but a pleasure with ten passengers crowded into a sleigh going over the backbone of the continent." It added that a woman who had made the passage a year earlier under similar conditions had said, "I didn't know whether to be more frightened at the prospect of an Indian attack in Gunnison or going back east on that sleigh and stage!"

The Review hadn't overlooked social amenities while Charles Fillmore was away to get married. On April 2, 1881, it reported: "Charles Fillmore was married at Clinton, Mo., March 29 to Miss Myrtle Page. He will be here with his bride in a day or two." The following issue, April 9, 1881, reported that "Charley Fillmore arrived with his wife last Tuesday, April 5."

During the first two months the newlyweds lived in Gunnison, the economic situation in the area slipped drastically from boom to near bust. The Review, trying to bolster sagging spirits, raved on each week about the city's great potential. In one two-and-one-half-column story, nine headlines ranged from "Gunnison, the Great Metropolis of Western Colorado" to "Enough Wealth Within Twenty-Five Miles of Gunnison to Pay the National Debt" to "Gunnison to Be the Great Railroad Centre West of the Range" to "Machine Shops, Round Houses, Stamp Mills and Smelters Will Soon Follow the Railroads." But these weren't to come true. And Charles Fillmore, astute businessman that he was, knew it. He began thinking of leaving Gunnison.

On June 4, 1881, the Review printed a tiny story which undoubtedly caught the eye of Charles Fillmore. It read: "Pueblo was never before in so prosperous a condition as it is at present. The Chieftain (the Pueblo newspaper) says if the town keeps on spreading it will soon become necessary to lay out several more additions."

Less than a month later Mr. and Mrs. Fillmore were on their way to Pueblo, back east over the "delectable mountains" to the far eastern slopes. Left behind them in Gunnison were only memories and a tiny newspaper account: "Charley Fillmore has gone to Pueblo where he will engage in the real estate and assaying business. Mr. Fillmore is a first class assayer and the Review wishes him success."

When the Fillmores arrived in Pueblo it was obviously booming. More than two thousand persons were living in tents on the outskirts of the community because not enough buildings had been erected yet to house the giant influx of humanity into the area. Charles found lodging for his new bride and almost immediately set himself up in a real estate and insurance operation in the corner of a grocery store. Within a few months he had prospered to the extent that he could take on a partner, Charles Small, and open his own office. Small was a brother-in-law of Nona Brooks, who later founded the religious movement known as Divine Science. The partnership advertised in the Chieftain: "Small, Fillmore & Co. Real Estate Agents and Notaries Public. No. 60 Union Ave. S. Pueblo, Colorado (Old Office of Parsons & Small). Houses and lots for sale and lease. Rents collected, deeds drawn, insurance effected, loans negotiated." By April 27, 1882, the Chieftain was reporting on the success of the new firm: "Messrs. Small, Fillmore & Co., the real estate dealers, report business lively and increasing every day. They sold several lots for business purposes yesterday."

Another item the same day almost certainly caught the eye of Mr. and Mrs. Fillmore and it just as certainly caused them a degree of sadness, for it concerned their beloved Ralph Waldo Emerson. The headline blared: "R. W.

Emerson! Very Ill! His Life Despaired Of."

The following day the headline completed the sad report: "Finished! Death of Concord Sage! Ralph Waldo Emerson!"

The building season of 1882 was a good one, and a suburb known as Pueblo Gardens was developed by Small, Fillmore & Co. Population continued to increase in the city. It had gone from 3,217 in 1879 to 24,588 in 1880. By 1882 the estimated population was more than thirty thousand, a sizable city by western standards. The steel mills that had been forecast to function in Gunnison had brought prosperity to Pueblo instead, and business couldn't have looked better. The Fillmores prospered and established themselves in the community, both on the social and business levels.

The names of the happy couple appeared occasionally in the Chieftain, most often in social or church context. Mrs. Fillmore was quite active with the ladies' guild of the Trinity Episcopal Church and was frequently hostess for parties and teas for the ladies of that organization. She also arranged for readings and music recitals in their home. The Chieftain complimented her on her good taste and decorum in serving as hostess for such events and pointed out the attendance was "large, yet select." The Fillmores had attended the Methodist Church in Denison, and Myrtle had attended various Methodist churches all her life, but for some reason they chose to attend Episcopalian services while in Pueblo.

Real estate entered a period of decline in 1883, and in 1884 the recession worsened. Charles and Myrtle knew what they had to do, so they packed again and moved. This time they headed for Omaha, Nebraska, but they spent only a few months there before traveling eastward to

Kansas City, Missouri. It was to be their last long-distance move.

They could look back at their experiences together in the West and see much that was pleasurable and some that was painful. But the two things they could see every day while they were in Kansas City that would most remind them of their western life were two little boys. Lowell Page Fillmore was born January 4, 1882, and Waldo Rickert Fillmore was born June 1, 1884. Myrtle finally had the boys she had always wanted, and another was to join them soon in Kansas City. Charles faced the challenge of supporting not only his mother, his wife, and himself, but also the two little namesakes of Ralph Waldo Emerson and James Russell Lowell.

 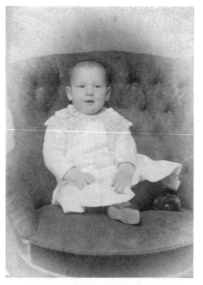

Lowell Page Fillmore   **Waldo Rickert Fillmore**

III

Unity Emerges from Myrtle's Healing

Life in Kansas City for Charles and Myrtle Fillmore in 1884 was not easy. They had brought little with them from Colorado in terms of prosperity, except the determination to succeed. Kansas City was in the midst of a building boom, so Charles immediately opened a real estate office. In a very short time he was more prosperous than ever before in his life, and the prosperity challenge was met and surmounted, at least temporarily.

Health was another matter. Neither of the Fillmores was very strong, and Myrtle's condition was deteriorating rapidly. The thin, clean mountain air of Colorado had been good for her respiratory difficulties, but a return to the Middle West and its dampness had resulted in a flare-up of tuberculosis, complicated by the fevers of malaria. Myrtle did not have the spiritual awareness then that she was later to develop, so she placed her faith in doctors and medicine rather than in God. Lowell Fillmore recalled many years later that his mother was constantly dosing herself with medicine and that she inflicted the "foul stuff" on others in the family, too. Ultimately, doctors said that they could do nothing else for her, and she was told she had only a short time to live.

Charles and Myrtle talked about returning to Colorado, thinking her health might improve there, but

Charles had a dream at about this time that convinced him they should stay in Kansas City. He dreamed he would do some kind of great work in the Kansas City area and that the destinies of the Fillmores depended upon their staying. After the dream, he recalled that he had had a similar dream earlier, also telling him Kansas City was to be their home and the place for a great work of some kind.

By the spring of 1886, it appeared that the end of life for Myrtle Fillmore was near. She clutched at any straw in the wind that might give her more time. Together, she and Charles attended virtually every health-oriented lecture given in the area. And then, she, too, had a dream. In it she heard voices calling to her and she saw hands beckoning to her, apparently from another realm of existence. But she felt a strong force on this earth plane holding her in the visible realm. Shortly after this experience, a lecturer by the name of Dr. E. B. Weeks from the Illinois Metaphysical College came to Kansas City. Dr. Weeks, trained by Emma Curtis Hopkins, one of the foremost metaphysicians of her time, brought a great truth to Myrtle Fillmore. As she left his lecture that night, one sentence illumined the very depths of her soul: *"I am a child of God and therefore I do not inherit sickness."* Slowly she let this Truth sink into her conscious mind and take hold. It was her last straw, and she grasped it with both hands and all her strength, and she would not let it go. All her life she had been told that she had inherited tuberculosis from her parents and that she was born to be ill, and suffer, and die prematurely.

She took within her this new Truth she had learned, and she talked to her body. Days, weeks, and months went by, and gradually she noted improvement. She closed herself in a room, with Charles' blessing, and studied the Four Gospels. She sat next to an empty chair and she *knew* that the Spirit of Jesus Christ occupied that chair and was supporting her and encouraging her in her quest. She read the gospels meticulously, especially studying the words of Jesus Christ concerning healing.

She read and re-read from John:

"Truly, truly, I say to you, he who believes in me will also do the works that I do; and greater works than these will he do, because I go to the Father."

And she read from Mark:

"Therefore I tell you, whatever you ask in prayer, believe that you receive it, and you will."

And, also from John:

"Do you want to be healed?"

She believed. And she accepted. Charles was startled and remarked that her health appeared to be improving. She was more adamant: *"I am healed and you are, too, for we are one!"* Together, they began a period of intensive prayer and study, and Charles soon noted an improvement in his own health, but his healing was to come later. The seed, however, had been planted.

Myrtle wrote of her healing:

"I was ready soil for the first teaching of this wonderful truth. I could not explain what the change that came over me was like—I only knew that God had gotten into my mind and heart to make of me what I really was in Him. I was supposed to be dying, or very close to it, of tuberculosis, a disease that was supposed to belong to my father's family. My first teacher spoke the word: 'One is your Father, even God. He is your heredity parentage— only what belongs to God belongs to you.' The truth came to me—a great revelation, showing me that I am a child of the one whole and perfect mind, created to express the health that God is."

By the time she was healed completely, about 1888, Charles had discovered the Truth, too, and they were preparing to launch into the spiritual work that would eventually be known as Unity School of Christianity.

It was about this time that Myrtle Fillmore remembered still another dream. It had taken place when she was a schoolgirl and was much impressed with the study of geology. The dream had meant little to her then, but now, with her healing complete and her future assured, it meant all the world. She shared the vision from her past with her loved ones in this manner:

"There was a bed of a stream that must have been active at some time. It was beautiful, with white, sandy bottom, but all the water it held was in a few bowls of white rock—apparently a dried-up stream. Stopping to investigate, I could find no source. A very high ledge of rock crossed its bed at the south, and looking to the north I could see only a continuous bed of like character as that before me. In my astonishment, I voiced the question, 'From whence the source of this stream?' And for answer there came a sudden voice, more of waters than anything else, 'I will show you.' And over the ledge of rock came pouring a regular Niagara. I had to get back further into the woods, away from the spray. It ceased when the bed was filled. As I stood looking at the clear water of the stream, beautiful flowers sprang up. This is one of my many dreams, the meaning of which was to be made plain afterwards, although at the time Scripture verses came to me about the rock of salvation and the waters of life. When my life stream was low, and I was about to lose it, and then there came pouring into me this truth, I saw more clearly the meaning of the dream. I remembered the source of my life (where the source of my life was and how it came over

the rock that was higher than I). Where there had seemed to be lack and low pressure of life, there was now free-flowing, more abundant Christ life, made fruitful unto good works through His power, wisdom, and love."

It was not enough, however, for Myrtle Fillmore to believe in and accept her own healing. She wanted to share it with Charles, with the rest of the family, and with friends. Finally, she shared it with the world in an article which she wrote entitled, "How I Found Health." Since its first publication in UNITY Magazine, it has never been out of print. Countless thousands have read it in pamphlet form and have been inspired by it:

"I have made what seems to me a discovery. I was fearfully sick; I had all the ills of mind and body that I could bear. Medicine and doctors ceased to give me relief, and I was in despair, when I found practical Christianity. I took it up and I was healed. I did most of the healing myself, because I wanted the understanding for future use. This is how I made what I call my discovery:

"I was thinking about life. Life is everywhere—in worm and in man. 'Then why does not the life in the worm make a body like man's?' I asked. Then I thought, 'The worm has not as much sense as man.' Ah! Intelligence, as well as life, is needed to make a body. Here is the key to my discovery. Life has to be guided by intelligence in making all forms. The same law works in my own body. Life is simply a form of energy, and has to be guided and directed in man's body by his intelligence. How do we communicate intelligence? By thinking and talking, of course. Then it flashed upon me that I might talk to the life in every part of my body and have it do just what I wanted. I began to teach my body and got marvelous results.

"I told the life in my liver that it was not torpid or inert, but full of vigor and energy. I told the life in my stomach that it was not weak or inefficient, but energetic, strong, and intelligent. I told the life in my abdomen that it was no longer infested with ignorant ideas of disease, put there by myself and by doctors, but that it was all athrill with the sweet, pure, wholesome energy of God. I told my limbs that they were active and strong. I told my eyes that they did not see of themselves but that they expressed the sight of Spirit, and that they were drawing on an unlimited source. I told them that they were young eyes, clear, bright eyes, because the light of God shone right through them. I told my heart that the pure love of Jesus Christ flowed in and out through its beatings and that all the world felt its joyous pulsation.

"I went to all the life centers in my body and spoke words of Truth to them—words of strength and power. I asked their forgiveness for the foolish, ignorant course that I had pursued in the past, when I had condemned them and called them weak, inefficient, and diseased. I did not become discouraged at their being slow to wake up, but kept right on, both silently and aloud, declaring the words of Truth, until the organs responded. And neither did I forget to tell them that they were free, unlimited Spirit. I told them that they were no longer in bondage to the carnal mind; that they were not corruptible flesh, but centers of life and energy omnipresent.

"Then I asked the Father to forgive me for taking His life into my organism and there using it so meanly. I promised Him that I would never, never again retard the free flow of that life through my mind and my body by any false word or thought; that I would always bless it and encourage it with true thoughts and words in its wise work of building up my body temple; that I would use all diligence and wisdom in telling it just what I wanted it to do.

"I also saw that I was using the life of the Father

in thinking thoughts and speaking words, and I became very watchful as to what I thought and said.

"I did not let any worried or anxious thoughts into my mind, and I stopped speaking gossipy, frivolous, petulant, angry words. I let a little prayer go up every hour that Jesus Christ would be with me and help me to think and speak only kind, loving, true words; and I am sure that He is with me, because I am so peaceful and happy now.

"I want everybody to know about this beautiful, true law, and to use it. It is not a new discovery, but, when you use it and get the fruits of health and harmony it will seem new to you, and you will feel that it is your own discovery."

In the same year that Myrtle Fillmore declared herself completely healed, Charles Fillmore also reached a turning point in his life. In 1888 the economic pace in Kansas City was slowing considerably. Not only weren't the Fillmores prosperous, they even had trouble paying normal household debts. Although Charles had always been a student of religion and philosophy, he was not "religious" as such. He was a good man, but as Myrtle Fillmore was to explain to many persons in future years, "Charles didn't always have the light that he has now." He was a businessman first and all else came second in those early days.

But God had greater work for Charles than selling real estate and insurance, and his business decline could be taken as an indication of this fact. He began to take far more notice of Myrtle than in the past. He saw her sitting in prayer, or in the silence. He saw her health improving. He saw their friends coming to her for prayer and going away with visible results in healing and in attitude. The light which radiated from his wife began to intrigue him. He did not

Myrtle Fillmore

know quite what was happening, but he knew that it was remarkable and that he should become a part of it. He talked with Myrtle, he prayed with her, and he studied with her. He was skeptical, yet he wanted to believe. But after all his effort, he was still not healed of his own infirmities.

Finally, in a calculated and businesslike manner, he decided to take charge of his own life and go directly to God. He maintained that if there was anything at all to prayer, it had to be a two-way proposition. There must be communication between God and the person doing the praying. He sat in the silence alone with God for many hours every day for weeks, then months. Long after he was almost convinced that it was foolishness, the breakthrough came. He reached God and God reached him. Somehow his sitting in the silence, his dreams, his thoughts, and certainly intuitive guidance worked together to open a communication channel with the Father. Charles proved to

Charles Fillmore

himself in his businesslike approach what Myrtle had demonstrated by her simple and childlike acceptance. The Truth of God was never to be a stranger to these two persons from then forward.

Now that they had received the illumination of God, the Fillmores felt they needed a teacher. Emma Curtis Hopkins filled that need. They attended classes conducted by this "teacher of teachers" in Chicago, and they also studied her courses by correspondence in Kansas City. On at least one occasion she visited Kansas City to teach them personally. Mrs. Hopkins had earlier been associated in Boston with Mary Baker Eddy of orthodox Christian Science, but she had broken away over doctrinal points and personal policies, and she had established her own school in Chicago. Mrs. Fillmore often said of Mrs. Hopkins, "I know of no other writings which mean so much to me as hers do."

Neither Charles nor Myrtle Fillmore ever studied under Mrs. Eddy, nor did they formally study orthodox Christian Science, although both of them read much of the literature. Mrs. Fillmore acknowledged the Truth in the Eddy brand of Christian Science, saying somewhat with tongue in cheek: "We gladly give Christian Science credit for any discovery that Mrs. Eddy may have made. It is claimed by many that Mrs. Eddy got most of her truth from Dr. Phineas Quimby, and Dr. Quimby got his from Saint Paul, and Saint Paul got his from Jesus, and Jesus Christ got His from God." Both Charles and Myrtle denied Mrs. Eddy's claims that Christian Science was hers and hers alone. They believed the words *Christian Science* to be generic and in the public domain, as did many other metaphysicians of the time. Mrs. Eddy strongly protested to the contrary.

In 1889 when economic conditions in Kansas City and the Fillmores' own situtation looked their worst, and with a third child, John Royal, joining the family, the Fillmores stepped out on faith and started a publishing venture. Charles had checked out his wife's "discovery" to his satisfaction and had found it valid. He had made his own peace with God and was beginning to see healing taking place in his body. His chronic pains were easing, his hip was growing stronger, and most importantly, his withered leg was beginning to fill out and lengthen. Both he and Myrtle felt that it was time to share the Truth.

The first issue of their magazine *Modern Thought* appeared in April 1889. The ten-cent, sixteen-page publication was labeled as "Devoted to the Spiritualization of Humanity from an Independent Standpoint." It was pointed out that the magazine would be a mouthpiece for all honest souls earnestly seeking spiritual light. The Bible, it was stressed, would be the guidebook to uncovering

Truth. Actually, the magazine was a collection of metaphysics and the occult, with articles from the pens of Theosophists, Spiritualists, and Christian Scientists. It was obvious to the few readers of that first issue that the publisher was very open-minded and interested in Truth in all its forms. Lecturers and healers were invited to send in their names and addresses and were promised that a directory would be published. The response was immediate and wide-ranging. So many persons wanted to be listed that the small amount of space for articles was threatened.

Within a very short time it became obvious that the magazine was doomed to failure without major policy changes. *Modern Thought* had no direction, no primary thrust. The answer was to restructure and develop a goal. Mr. Fillmore eliminated the dross, so that the magazine might emphasize more eternal Truth. He omitted spiritualism, occultism, astrology, palmistry, psychometry, mesmerism, hypnotism, and magnetism. A distinct move was made in the direction of the kind of practical Christianity taught today at Unity School. Quite likely Mrs. Fillmore's influence was great in eliminating many of these subjects. She had looked into Spiritualism as a young woman in Ohio and for herself had found it wanting.

On the occasion of *Modern Thought's* first anniversary, April 1890, the publication's name was changed to *Christian Science Thought*. Mrs. Hopkins glowed, saying: "We welcome with great rejoicing *Modern Thought* of Kansas City to the ranks of Christian Science literature. Mr. Charles Fillmore, its editor, has not heretofore wholly committed himself to the highest teachings, but now comes out with uncompromising boldness and dedication, all to Christian Science." Two months later, Mrs. Hopkins was even more elated: "There is no editor in the field of metaphysical literature whose heart is kinder and whose pen is more healing than Mr. Charles Fillmore. Success and prosperity attend the *Christian Science Thought.*"

In contrast to Mrs. Hopkins' joy, there was consternation in Boston. Mrs. Eddy complained sharply about the renaming of *Modern Thought,* claiming once again that the two words *Christian Science* were her property. Mrs. Eddy said that if the Fillmores or anyone else were to use the term *Christian Science,* they must teach her philosophy and her doctrine. The Fillmores refused such demands, believing that the teachings that were evolving out of their efforts were of the Spirit of Truth. But they renamed the magazine again, this time, *Thought.* Charles explained years later why the change was made:

"We have studied many isms, many cults. People of every religion under the sun claim that we either belong to them or have borrowed the best part of our teaching from them. We have borrowed the best from all religions, that is the reason we are called Unity . . . . We studied Christian Science, as all the religions. We were also called New Thought people, Mental Scientists, Theosophists, and so on, but none of these sufficiently emphasized the higher attributes of man, and we avoided any close affiliation with them . . . . Unity is not a sect, not a separation of people into an exclusive group of know-it-alls. Unity is the Truth that is taught in all religions, simplified and systemized so that anyone can understand and apply it. Students of Unity do not find it necessary to sever their church affiliations. The church needs the vitalization that this renaissance of primitive Christianity gives it."

Neither Charles nor Myrtle considered the name

Thought to be entirely appropriate for the Truth they wanted to impart through their magazine, so they contemplated a number of other possibilities.

One night in the spring of 1891, while the two of them were praying with some other Truth students, the word *Unity* suddenly flashed into Charles' mind. "That's it!" he cried out. *"Unity."* So, Unity was born, an appropriate name because the Fillmores had indeed taken the best from the many religions they had studied and had always emphasized that all religious orders should work together for the common purpose of oneness with God.

In the first years of publication, *Thought* had readers numbering in the hundreds. The circulation list was handwritten and hung on a door. At first all the work was done by Charles and Myrtle, but soon Lowell was old enough to take an interest and assist in the operation. The magazine was published from the old Journal building at the corner of Tenth and Walnut in downtown Kansas City. Charles wrote under the name *Leo Virgo,* as his birthday was on the cusp of those two astrological signs (August 22) and because he wished anonymity at first. Myrtle signed articles in the magazine *M* or *M.F.,* including the famous "How I Found Health," which was first published "by M, Your Happy Friend" in March 1897.

Mrs. Fillmore later signed her full name, and Charles dropped his pseudonym when it suited him to do so. After the first five months of publication, the magazine was moved to the Deardorff building at Eleventh and Main. Just before a disastrous fire struck this property, the Fillmores moved their publishing office to the Hall building. By September of 1890 the magazine had reached some degree of permanency, was usually published on time and distributed when promised. Many issues were late, however, and on at least one occasion an issue was omitted, only to be "made up" in the next edition. During all this time, Mrs. Fillmore helped at the office as much as she could and met family responsibilities at home too. Mr. Fillmore continued his real estate business until it was possible for him to earn a living with his Unity work.

Harry Church

While the Fillmores were in the Hall building, a man came to them who was to be a major influence in their lives—Harry Church, a vegetarian and Seventh Day Adventist who became their first printer. He was the primary reason that the Fillmores were to become vegetarians five years later. He talked to them often about the inconsistency of spiritual people taking animal life for food, and eventually he convinced both of them to eliminate meat from their diets.

The eight years in the Hall building marked a period of great success for Unity and the Fillmores. *Thought* began counting subscribers by the thousands instead of hundreds, and merged in 1895 with UNITY, a magazine that had been started to serve members of the Society of Silent Unity. Under the name UNITY, the publication was

issued twice monthly until 1898 when it settled into a
monthly format.

In August of 1893 the first issue of *Wee Wisdom*
appeared, a magazine primarily designed for children and
edited by Mrs. Fillmore.

1315 McGee Street

In 1898 the printing operations were moved into a large
house on McGee Street. Two women employees joined the
Fillmores and Mr. Church; and Lowell, who had graduated
from high school, was hired for five dollars a week. The
Unity Book Company also was established during this time
and still another phase of communicating Truth was
created.

The influence of Emma Curtis Hopkins on the
Fillmores during the last few years of the nineteenth
century cannot be overstated. After Dr. Weeks spoke his
healing words to Myrtle Fillmore in 1886, eleven other
speakers from Mrs. Hopkins' institution spoke in Kansas

City. Undoubtedly, the Fillmores attended most if not all of
these sessions. It is known that they were in the audience
when the great teacher herself came to Kansas City for a
two-week series of lectures. Both Charles and Myrtle
addressed the students, some eighty-seven of them, during
that course, and they became well acquainted with Mrs.
Hopkins. Right after she spoke in Kansas City, Mr. and
Mrs. Fillmore enrolled in a study course in Chicago with
Mrs. Hopkins. This course, which entailed several visits to
Chicago, led to their ordination as ministers in Christian
Science. Mrs. Fillmore described one Chicago visit with
Mrs. Hopkins in a letter to a friend:

"There are so many things I wanted to tell you about
our Chicago experiences. I got my black dress made up so
that it is very stylish and becoming with velvet sleeves and
collar, and the front of the waist is velvet. The Rays fixed me
up a velvet hat out of that velvet of your bonnet; they
furnished a wing and trim. There were lots of beautiful
dresses there but one didn't think much about such things.

"Of course we met all those whose names are so
familiar in the literature: Ida Nichols, Nellie Anderson, Julia
Twinchester, and so forth. A finer set of people I never met.

"We were fortunate enough to have a room under
Mrs. Hopkins' roof. She is just lovely to be with. There were
over a hundred at the Review and all ate at her tables. It was
the happiest, most harmonious family meeting on earth—
for that's what it seemed—everything seemed as free and
natural as air.

"You can see from the program how we spent most of
our time. Tuesday was a day off, for they were getting the
seminary ready for ordination services. Charles and I
wandered about the city, went to see 'Jerusalem on the
Day of Crucifixion.' It is a wonderful cyclodrama.

"At night, we all went over to C. I. Thacher's—and

such a time. Never was there such a jolly, happy set. He cleared out the basement and decorated it and had an orchestra down there as a surprise to the party. You ought to have seen Doctor Gibbons and another old minister there trip the fantastic toe. Can you imagine John Thacher, Sullivan, and Barton dancing? I laughed till I could hardly stand up, it was so funny. As they closed about the fourth set, Charles rushed into the middle of the floor and shouted out: 'I can't dance, but I can sing. Let's sing "Praise God from Whom All Blessings Flow." ' And before the orchestra could change its tune to fall in, the house trembled with the old hymn; it was powerfully sung. Then followed a healing song, and next the dancing was resumed. The musicians looked funny. I suppose they thought they had struck a lot of lunatics. A nice supper was served about eleven o'clock.

"Charles and I were invited out there on Sunday before dinner. Doctor Gibbons, Miss Rix, Miss Austin, and several others were there. I tell you, they have an elegant home and things are served up in grand style. They keep three servants all the time, two girls and a man. And after our eight o'clock dinner, we sat in silence, and such a wonderful power came over us. We gave it direction, and those we have heard from were wonderfully benefited. It was then our baby was named and blessed." (Previously the child had been known only as "Baby"—but at this party he was christened John Royal.)

The first class of ordained ministers was graduated in 1889 from the Hopkins Metaphysical Institute in Chicago (the name was later changed to Christian Science Association). Most of the twenty-two graduates were women, and a Chicago newspaper reported that "women were ordained by a woman." The Fillmores read about the ordinations in the pages of the Christian Science Magazine published by the Institute, and both Mr. and Mrs. Fillmore enrolled as students, taking some courses in Chicago and others by correspondence from Kansas City. Both became contributors to Christian Science Magazine, which had a circulation of some ten thousand copies. Mrs. Fillmore wrote at least three articles, including one about labor reformers and temperance advocates, suggesting some changes in their approaches to the problems. In addition, the Fillmores advertised in Christian Science, offering their magazine and other related literature.

The full name of the study course the Fillmores entered into in Chicago was "Theological Seminary for the Preparation of Students for the Christian Science Ministry," which was presided over by Emma Curtis Hopkins, 2019 Indiana Avenue. The first course was devoted to instruction in the principles and practice of Christian Science healing, while the second concentrated on theology and practical ministry. The motto of the seminary was: "We give ourselves to the ministry of the world."

On June 1, 1891, both Mr. and Mrs. Fillmore were ordained into the Christian Science ministry. As the ordinations were made, Mrs. Hopkins spoke these words to each ordinand: "It is finished. Now your demonstrations are instantaneous."

The course of study had cost the Fillmores fifty dollars each, a large sum of money in those days, but the investment was to prove sound. In addition to their own prayer and study efforts, they had been exposed to one of the most thoroughly organized Truth teachers of all times, Mrs. Hopkins. What she, in turn, said of the ordinands at the session proved spectacularly true of the Fillmores:

"You have been tried and not found wanting. You have spoken and thereby received that fullness of power

Emma Curtis Hopkins

for which the devout in all ages have prayed. You can heal the sick by the word of your speaking. You can cheer the fainting. When hearts are cast down, you shall say, 'There is lifting up.' You are the springing forth of that ministry prophesied by the devout of old. The Lord Himself shall guide you continually and you shall want for no good thing."

By the time of the ordination into Christian Science, the Fillmores had omitted the words *Christian Science,* from their magazine. They stressed in the pages of their publication that they still felt they had a right to consider themselves Christian Science students. Within a few years, however, they virtually stopped using the words *Christian Science* because so many persons were confused about it. Unity began to take on its own particular identity, and as with other religions the Fillmores had studied, they took what they considered the best of Christian Science and blended it into their own philosophies of Truth.

As they drifted out of Christian Science and into the Truth that Unity teaches today, they never parted personally with Emma Curtis Hopkins. She was their ideal as a teacher, and they were two of her most prominent students. Mrs. Hopkins wrote to them often, addressing them as "My two blessed friends." She said of them: "God is pouring great prosperity through you all the time. I hear more and more about your work in the magazines." She often asked the Fillmores for prayer help with patients she was treating. The contact between Mrs. Hopkins and the Fillmores was maintained for more than thirty years, until Mrs. Hopkins died in the 1920s. As late as 1923, Mrs. Hopkins was singing the praises of the Fillmores and Unity: "I am so glad in your great success and worldwide influence. Everywhere the newer ways are gaining converts."

Two of Mrs. Hopkins favorite affirmations were used by Mrs. Fillmore throughout her ministry. She spoke the words often, and she passed them along to hundreds, perhaps thousands, in letters and in conversations. The affirmations were her constant companions. They were:

"O countenance! Beholding me, looking toward me through the ages. Breath of the everlasting life in me, and manna to my fadeless substance, Thy name, which folds me 'round with tenderness, and lifts me high above the pitfalls of my earthly destiny, is Jesus Christ."

"Nothing can injure the immortal principle of the soul."

In drifting away from Christian Science and emphasizing their own ideas as Unity, the Fillmores found themselves more and more interested in what other New

Thought leaders were doing and teaching. They attended a congress of New Thought people in 1893 in Chicago, and returned in 1895 to the congress of the International Divine Science Association. In 1896 the Fillmores attended the congress in Kansas City. This organization was later to evolve into the International New Thought Alliance. Mr. and Mrs. Fillmore were actively involved in it until 1895 when they decided they could not continue. Charles explained why in an article in UNITY:

"So far as the Unity Society of Practical Christianity is concerned, we must candidly say that its teachings are widely different from those of the majority of New Thought doctrines, and we do not feel at home in the average gathering under that name, although we try to harmonize with all Truth seekers."

Mrs. Fillmore added, "Instead of thinking and saying New Thought, it would be better to think and speak God Thought. To identify oneself with the Jesus Christ standard of thinking keeps one poised and free and filled with light."

Although friendly relations were retained with the New Thought group and many of its top spokesmen spoke to Unity audiences, an official separation was maintained until 1919. At that time Unity rejoined the Alliance, only to drop out again in 1922. On an individual basis, however, many Unity ministers and teachers are now members of the INTA.

In 1892 only a few months after their ordination and the birth of the name of the organization *Unity,* an event took place in the lives of the Fillmores that sealed their commitment to Truth and indelibly etched into their consciousnesses the task that lay ahead of them. On December 7 of that year, Charles handwrote what was called "Dedication and Covenant." He and Myrtle signed it and lived by it the rest of their lives. It read:

    "We, Charles Fillmore and Myrtle Fillmore, husband and wife, hereby dedicate ourselves, our time, our money, all we have and all we expect to have, to the Spirit of Truth, and through it, to the Society of Silent Unity.

    "It being understood and agreed that the said Spirit of Truth shall render unto us an equivalent for this dedication, in peace of mind, health of body, wisdom, understanding, love, life and an abundant supply of all things necessary to meet every want without our making any of these things the object of our existence.

    "In the presence of the Conscious Mind of Christ Jesus, this 7th day of December, A.D. 1892."

The "Dedication and Covenant" was not made public during the Fillmore's lifetime, although the results of it were evident in everything they did. The document was discovered in their personal effects, after their deaths.

The first few years of the Unity movement were devoted largely to the development and expansion of Silent Unity, the publication of UNITY and *Wee Wisdom*, establishing a Sunday School and classes for teaching Truth, and publishing the most important book in the history of Unity, *Lessons in Truth*.

Dr. H. Emilie Cady, a practicing physician in New York City, wrote for Mrs. Hopkins' Christian Science Magazine and other Truth magazines and newspapers of that era. One of her articles, "Finding the Christ in Ourselves," reached the hands of Mrs. Fillmore. She found it exciting so she wrote to Dr. Cady and told her so, and received permission to reprint it in UNITY. As early as 1892, Dr. Cady's writings were appearing in the pages of UNITY and receiving considerable attention from readers. In 1894 the Fillmores urged Dr. Cady to undertake the task of writing a series of simple lessons which might help the novice Truth student better understand what Unity was espousing. Mrs. Cady replied, in part:

"Yours, asking me to write a consecutive course of lessons for Unity, received. These are the words given to me in reply: 'Now therefore go, and I will be with thy mouth, and teach thee what thou shalt speak.'

"So, there is nothing left for me to say, but yes . . . . I shall not give any stilted or set form of lessons, but just the utter simplicity of the gospel in words that the wayfarer, 'though a fool,' may understand; for I believe that to be the need of the hour. . . . "

The first lesson appeared the following month, October 1894, entitled, "Statement of Being," now the second chapter of *Lessons in Truth.* About 1.5 million copies of the book have been distributed since that eventful day of its first publication. After the series was published in UNITY, it was decided to prepare it in book form. It has remained the most popular book in Unity history.

Myrtle Fillmore and Dr. H. Emilie Cady carried on a correspondence for the rest of their lives. Dr. Cady was well-paid through royalties for *Lessons in Truth,* another book—*How I Used Truth,* and many articles through the years, but best of all, in Dr. Cady's estimation, was the love that she received from the multitudes who read her works and so much appreciated them. Mrs. Fillmore was among that number. She told Dr. Cady that *Lessons in Truth* "is a foundation stone and we feel that the students who build on it shall be safe and secure in their ongoing. You have developed the teaching of Jesus Christ and have made it so real and have pointed the way so clearly."

As late as 1929, Mrs. Fillmore wrote to Dr. Cady: "I feel like writing you often to tell you the good news of the ever-increasing reach of the Truth. But you always seem so near that I think you surely must know as we do what your own blessed contributions to Truth literature are doing."

H. Emilie Cady

After a trip Mrs. Fillmore made to New York to visit Dr. Cady in 1926 and their first face-to-face meeting, Dr. Cady wrote: "The time was all too short—and the weather too hot—to say half I wanted to. How could we in an hour's time cover a period of thirty-five years, even touching the high points? One thing I wanted to say was that I deeply appreciate the never-failing 'free gift' which comes without care or anxiety on my part at a time of life when it is most acceptable. I am yours in love."

By 1900 the one-hundred-seat chapel the Fillmores used for classes and services was too small for the crowds that were being attracted. One of the most successful series of lectures Unity has ever enjoyed, called the "No Name Series," was conducted in the 1890s. No one except

Charles and Myrtle knew who would speak at these sessions until starting time. Charles sometimes spoke, and Myrtle usually offered prayer or meditation, but the main speaker often was just someone from the audience, or a Truth speaker from Chicago, or someone from one of the other Kansas City metaphysical groups. The Fillmores were not interested in personal acclaim, and they turned over the spotlight to many other persons who had Truth to offer.

Church services were held on Sunday and Wednesday afternoons at first. The intention was to avoid conflicts with established churches. The Fillmores never intended to start a church, but to provide a place for religious and spiritual education for all people, regardless of their creed. Eventually the demand for Sunday morning services was so great that the Fillmores yielded; likewise, they established a Wednesday night prayer meeting.

During the first few years of their ministry both Charles and Myrtle taught classes in addition to the Sunday and Wednesday meetings. A typical class lasted twelve sessions, and no charge was ever made. Early in their work, the Fillmores decided to trust God, not man, for their prosperity, and He never failed them. At times He may have *seemed* to be failing, but they always knew He would help them and support them.

One class which Mr. Fillmore taught with Mrs. Fillmore's assistance brought in a total of $9.59 during the last two weeks of November 1897. The highest love offering at that session was $2.45 on December 1, and the lowest was four cents on November 29. Mr. Fillmore kept meticulous records of attendance and income. Many of the early ledgers still are preserved. The records show that some two-week courses brought Unity as much as eighty dollars.

Whatever the classes brought in, there was never a doubt by either Mr. or Mrs. Fillmore that they were on the right and proper course in teaching Truth, and they looked to the future of Unity with assurance. They were filling their chapel every Sunday, Silent Unity was growing so rapidly that more and more assistance was necessary to meet the demands of those seeking prayer, the magazines UNITY and *Wee Wisdom* were flourishing, and perhaps most important of all, expansion of the work was no longer a dream, but an absolute necessity.

As the new century approached, Mr. and Mrs. Fillmore and the workers of Unity knew that they had much work ahead of them, and much prayer, to see that the expansion became reality.

IV

The Expansion of an Idea

By 1902 it was clearly evident to Charles and Myrtle Fillmore that the work they had started was truly a divine idea, because enthusiasm for its expansion was contagious among Unity students and friends. The Fillmores knew that action had to be taken to find more suitable quarters, but as had often been the case, the money simply was not available. This had never stopped them before, and it wouldn't this time either. They knew that God was their Source and that if they held to that idea, they could not fail in anything they sought to do.

A building committee was appointed, and the first contribution was a penny. Although the donor meant it as a joke, Charles Fillmore did not take it as one. He blessed the penny and *expected* it to grow. It did . . . but ever so slowly. By the end of 1903 there were twenty-five cents in the building fund. But, in addition to the twenty-five cents, there was something else—the Unity Society of Practical Christianity. The society was incorporated on July 29, 1903, not as a church, but as a "society for scientific and educational purposes, for the study of universal law." Despite this action, contributions to the building fund came in slowly, with the total in 1905 at only $601.

With typical Fillmore determination, however, one hot Sunday afternoon after church services, a building site

913 Tracy

inspection was conducted. Charles, Lowell, and Royal
Fillmore walked along with Jesse I. Wallace, the building
fund chairman, while Mrs. Fillmore, Mrs. Wallace, and her
little daughter Tesla rode in a carriage to 913 Tracy Street.
The eight-room house on the spacious lot excited all of
them, and it was decided instantly that on this site Unity
would stake its future and plant seeds for growth. Mrs.
Fillmore was especially pleased that it was near the family
home, and also near a streetcar line. Within a few weeks the
house was moved to the back of the lot, and excavation for
a new building was started.

When it was necessary to pay for anything, the money
became available. God worked through one member of the
Unity Society to mortgage his home and loan the proceeds,
some ten thousand dollars, to the building program. Many
readers of Unity publications responded with love offerings
for Unity's expansion, and the friends and students of Unity

in the Kansas City area were generous. On July 29, 1906, services were conducted in the new three-story brick building. Dedication services took place August 19 to 25.

It had been twenty years since Mrs. Fillmore received the spark of Truth that had started her toward her healing, and now she and Mr. Fillmore could look around them and see manifest evidence of God's good. They had started the Unity work on little more than faith, but their faith had been rewarded. They had their magazines spreading Truth all over the country and into many other lands; they had Silent Unity effectively working with thousands of persons in prayer; they had expanded from tiny, cramped quarters into a spacious new building with a seating capacity of more than two hundred; and they had a loyal following of students. But there was something lacking, and they had talked about it often . . . and many Unity students had discussed it with them. The Fillmores were ordained *Christian Science* ministers. Shouldn't they be ordained as Unity ministers, they wondered?

After much thought and prayer and careful preparation, Charles and Myrtle decided that they wanted Unity ordinations, and they also wanted to ordain loyal Unity students into the ministry to assist them in starting new works in other cities. On August 31, 1906, a special ordination meeting was conducted. W. G. Haseltine, president of the board of Unity Society of Practical Christianity, announced that seventeen students had taken the Unity ordination examination, and twelve had passed. Of those, nine had committed themselves to the Unity ministry on a full-time basis and would be ordained. The nine were: Charles Fillmore, Myrtle Fillmore, C. E. Prather, Edna L. Carter, Jennie Croft, May D. Wolzak, Cassius A. Shafer, J. Gilbert Murray, and Mrs. E. Dodge Carson. The three who passed the examination but asked

for later ordination, when they were ready to go to work in
the ministry full-time, were: Carl Gleeser, Laura Custer,
and Mrs. S. B. Quigley.

Charles Fillmore wrote the ordination test of sixty-
eight questions, so perhaps it is not surprising that he
scored 100 percent. Mrs. Fillmore was given a mark of 98.5
percent, because she overlooked one question and Mr.
Fillmore adjudged another question as less than perfectly
answered.

Mr. and Mrs. Fillmore were ordained by W. G.
Haseltine, and afterward they both responded to their
renewed commitment.

Mr. Fillmore said: *"We are what might be called a
young child in this matter of ordaining ministers, this being
our first experience. And we desire to be especially careful,
that we shall send forth only competent workers in our
cause. We want to build on a firm foundation."*

Mrs. Fillmore remarked: *"My life, my health, all that I
am I owe to this blessed Truth, and for many years I have
given myself with all the strength of my understanding to
the ministering. I am called again to make an
acknowledgment of it. It has been sixteen years since we
got our diplomas from the Christian Science Seminary in
Chicago, but I never felt like looking back. It is all that I am
interested in and so I am glad to dedicate myself again to
this Truth. I will go where You want me to go, dear Lord."*

Apparently the ordinations of 1906 were "in spirit"
only, because no ordination certificates were issued. This
was rectified twelve years later in 1918, when Lowell was
ordained on September 8. Both Charles and Myrtle were
presented at that time with ornate ordination certificates,
signed by Frank Whitney and Lowell Fillmore. Charles also
signed Myrtle's certificate, and struck the word *him*
throughout, writing in the word *her* where appropriate. It

was a man's world in those days, but Myrtle was determined to help change that.

When Royal went to the University of Missouri in 1907, Mrs. Fillmore wrote him these prophetic words: "By the time you and Rick are ready to help with our publishing, we'll cover the ground from Ninth and Tracy to Tenth and Tracy. Our growth will be more rapid from now on." Between 1906 and 1916 Unity's growth was substantial. In that ten-year span ten workers expanded to 130; eight times the floor space was added; typewriters increased from three to fifty; and three desks evolved into eighty.

An informal Sunday school had been started by Mrs. Fillmore in the 1890s, but she didn't have time to supervise and organize it, so Jennie Croft was assigned that responsibility in 1902. From a handful of students in the 1890s, the average attendance grew to 105 each Sunday by 1909, and by 1916 it was more than 140 each Sunday. For many years Mrs. Fillmore retained an active interest in the children and taught classes, usually at the infant level. Lowell Fillmore recalled many years later the philosophy of Unity's Sunday School when it was formed: *"The little ones needed to know how to control their thoughts. We regard this as one of the most important branches of the work, as a little child is naturally more impressionable than an older person, hence the sooner it is started along the right road of living and thinking, the better off it is, and the world as well, for the child of today is the man of tomorrow."*
Another development that led to more Unity growth took place in 1909 when *Weekly Unity* was born. Lowell Fillmore was its editor, and the first of his "Things to Be Remembered" columns stressed Sunday school. "Remember," he wrote, "that Sunday school at 10 A.M. is for little folks and big folks." His mother, with her work

among the children as editor of *Wee Wisdom* and in
Sunday school, had proved to be a great influence on
Lowell's work. Another idea Lowell had, this one in 1910,
also came out of his mother's experience—that of
prosperity and the need for it to be taught to Truth
students. Lowell devised a "prosperity bank," a technique
for saving and investing that thousands have learned to
appreciate since its inception.

Silent-70, a formalized system of distributing literature
free to those who desire it, was born during this time period
also. The Fillmores had always given away their magazines
and literature to those who felt they couldn't afford them,
but now a distribution system was set up that provided
materials to hospitals, schools, prisons, libraries, and other
such institutions.

The Fillmores had decided that they would not charge
for their prayer treatments, depending instead upon free-
will offerings. They reasoned that God was their Source
and they would depend upon Him. Mrs. Fillmore never
wavered in that resolve, but Mr. Fillmore, by his own
admission, weakened on occasion when debts were
especially pressing. He said: *"Encouraged by my wife, I
persevered when almost at the point of failure; and if there
comes any universal success out of this continuous effort,
she should have the greater share of the credit. Had I been
alone I would have more than once thrown the whole thing
over and gone back to my real estate business."*
Mrs. Fillmore recalled how destitute they seemed to
be that first year after she and Charles had begun
publishing their magazine. But God provided then, and she
knew He would at all times. Concerning Christmas of that
first year, she wrote: "I had about decided that we must go
without buying the children Christmas presents when a

neighbor we have been praying for walked in and gave me a check for five dollars and insisted upon my keeping it. I got Lowell a two-dollar tool chest, and Rick had commanded me to get him a drum and a gun. I got the drum, a sword, and a military hat, so he is fixed for marching. A friend gave each a book, so all fared well."

Almost as soon as the first Unity building was occupied in 1906, it was too small. Within four years an even larger building, next door at 917 Tracy, was being erected. By September of 1910, the printing department was transferred next door, opening up considerable space in the 913 Tracy property. Expansion seemed necessary almost continuously, however, and in the next four years, the 917 Tracy building was remodeled and enlarged twice more. In 1916 a new auditorium was finished, and on April

917 Tracy

23 it was dedicated. Every seat was taken for the dedication, and many persons were turned away. Mr. and Mrs. Fillmore, seated on the platform for the service, were almost hidden among tropical foliage and flowers that covered the area. Mrs. Fillmore's blessing came first that day, and it was a simple one:

"Truth! The understanding of the Truth shall be imparted by the Spirit of Truth to all who enter here."

Many other buildings were erected at the Tracy location over the next few years, until Mrs. Fillmore's prophetic utterance proved true: Unity *had* covered the ground from Ninth to Tenth Street. In addition to the structures already mentioned, there was a radio building and tower, a building for the heating plant, repair shops, a garage, and apartments. On the corner of Ninth and Tracy stood the Unity Inn, a vegetarian cafeteria that became one of the most popular eating places in the city.

On the opposite page is
the Tracy complex, showing
913, 917, and the house that
served as Unity Inn.

At right is a picture of
Myrtle Fillmore and a
friend, Lida R. Hardy, standing outside the new Unity
Inn.

Below is a picture of the
new Inn and the bus that
served as transportation to
it in the early twenties.

Much change had taken place in a short time for Unity, but Kansas City was changing too. The neighborhood that had seemed so desirable in 1906 for teaching and for ministering to spiritual and physical needs was not so acceptable as the 1920s came along. The Fillmores surveyed their present position, looked at where they would like to be, and determined that a move for Unity to a rural area was not only desirable but necessary. There simply wasn't enough room on Tracy for more expansion, and the noise and dirt of the city were considered hindrances to the advancement of Unity's philosophy. There was never a thought of moving outside the Kansas City area or from Jackson County in particular. Charles had noted, and Myrtle had agreed: *"That a peculiar psychic atmosphere prevails here is plain to everyone who has made any attainments whatever in the unfoldment of the spirit. Metaphysicians from all parts of the country have sensed it and observed its harmonious effect upon them. We have carefully noted their separate testimonies as to its quality, and they all agree that they have here a sense of freedom and peace which they do not feel elsewhere."*

For Christmas of 1919, Charles Fillmore prepared a card which read: "Sop up your sorrows, blot out your woes; at dread tomorrows, turn up your nose. Rejoice. Sing a song and be gay, forgetting the past, be happy today." He had his name imprinted upon the card and sent it to his many friends. Myrtle Fillmore liked the card Charles had prepared better than one she had planned to send, so she added, "Me, Too, Myrtle," to each one of them and sent them to her friends. The message for the friends about "dread tomorrows" was appropriate for the Fillmores and Unity, for unless something was done now, Unity's tomorrow would not be all that it could be. On March 1, 1920, the future growth of Unity was assured with the first purchase of land near Lee's Summit, Missouri, just southeast of Kansas City.

Royal Fillmore excitedly announced to readers of Unity publications that fifty-eight acres of "country land" had been purchased and would be known as "Unity Farm." It would be fixed up with little houses, and there would be space for tents for vacationers. Acquisition of the first parcel of land was a demonstration of divine order. Charles Fillmore and his three sons had selected a piece of land to buy, but when they went to see the real estate agent about it, they found that the land had already been sold. The agent showed them another parcel of land, and they ultimately purchased it. Over the years, Unity Farm grew bit by bit to its present size of about fourteen hundred acres. Mrs. Fillmore commented in the 1920s on the land purchases:

"Surely we have been led in buying the Unity Farm land. And a few years ago, perhaps none of those landowners thought of such a thing as selling in the way that they did. If they could have seen what was to come, they might have raised their prices or refused to sell, thinking thereby to increase their gain. But the Father was managing, and the way was cleared for us to take over and to develop those hundreds of acres—for an inspiration and a practical demonstration of the hidden resources and the power of love to establish plenty and peace."

By 1921, the farm was comprised of 231 acres and included a golf course, a swimming pool, and several buildings. A country club was organized with dues of two dollars per year. One of the major problems at the farm was lack of water. Twenty-four attempts to drill for water failed! Each time either oil or natural gas was struck. Although the oil and gas were welcomed, there was far more of both than Unity could ever use. Silent Unity, led by Mrs. Fillmore, prayed almost unceasingly that water would be found, rather than oil, with each drilling. The Father, however, had another plan. He had decided Unity needed lakes, so as soon as the Fillmores stopped trying to find water *their* way and listened to the Father, two lakes were constructed, both adding to the beauty and recreational facilities of the farm.

The first gas well at the farm was also the first in Jackson County. It brought in 250,000 cubic feet per day of exceptional quality. But it wasn't the largest well. Another one produced 500,000 cubic feet, for example. One well was drilled with the intent to provide water for the pool. After oil came in, Rick jokingly advised would-be swimmers to wear oil-cloth suits if they wished to use the pool. Finally, a spring contributed its fresh, cool water for the pool, which then became one of the most popular places in the county.

Activity at Unity headquarters in Kansas City was brisk, with more and more persons subscribing to Unity magazines and ever-increasing attendance at services and classes, many of which were taught by Charles and Myrtle Fillmore. By 1928, for example, *Weekly Unity* had reached a circulation of 185,680, UNITY of 148,642, and *Wee Wisdom* of 52,805. But three more magazines were being published, one of which had already surpassed UNITY in readership. It was *Daily Word,* born in July, 1924. This daily devotional was destined to become Unity's most popular publication, surpassing the one-million circulation mark within its first fifty years of distribution. Unity's other two publications in 1928 were *Christian Business,* with a circulation of 23,784, and *Youth,* 27,623. In all, more than 589,000 persons or organizations subscribed to Unity magazines in 1928.

Charles and Myrtle Fillmore

Charles and Myrtle Fillmore had always worked hard, and now that they were in what was considered by many to be "old age," they were determined to continue their efforts—or perhaps even increase them—to spread the word of Truth. Because Unity was located in two areas, downtown and some twenty miles away at the farm, there was much shuffling between the two sites. Mrs. Fillmore, even when in her eighties, spent long days, and often nights in the work. She talked of Unity's expansion often, blessing it, yet somehow feeling not quite a part of it all as she had been in earlier days. *"I cannot keep a finger on all the work of the departments now,"* she said in a letter to a friend, *"as I could when the work was smaller, as far as numbers were concerned. But I can always hold to the principle and unify myself in spirit with all the work and the workers. We still hold that Jesus Christ is the head of our work and we praise and give thanks for His wisdom and love and power working in and through all. I am still at my job—'the power behind the throne'—I am not much in print anymore and don't do much writing—except the letters that need my kind of answers."*

A typical work week for Mrs. Fillmore in the 1920s would see her leave the city right after Sunday services, in which she participated by leading prayer and meditation, and go to the farm. She would rest and write letters Sunday afternoon in her little home, the Arches. On Monday and Tuesday she would handle correspondence and receive as many persons as possible for conversation and prayer. On Wednesday she would go back to the city, work in her office there all day, and participate in the evening service. She spent Thursday morning in her city office, then on Thursday afternoon she went to the farm where she taught a class, returning the next day to the city where she would work in her office until late Saturday. She liked to joke that she knew very little about the business side of the work: "The Father hasn't found me to be a really good manager of the business affairs here. Or, it may be that He is just giving others a 'chance' at it first."

Although Mrs. Fillmore loved the Tracy headquarters and the great consciousness of Truth there, she also loved the peace and tranquillity of Unity Farm, or as she liked to call it, "Unity City." In 1926 she wrote of the farming operation: "I wish you could see the fruit. Three hundred trees of wonderful peaches, beautiful beyond belief; a thousand bushels of grapes now and they can't be picked fast enough for the demand; one hundred and fifty acres of apple trees and small fruit; and everything overloaded. The rains came just in time to save the crops. They are just beginning the excavation of a twenty-three acre lake which will not only provide abundant water supply, but beauty and boating. When we get all our plans and school on the farm, we'll be providing for the pleasure and needs of the many who are desirous of coming to us for instruction and healing."

Rick Fillmore, the builder, was hard at work in the 1920s to see the dream come true—a haven of love and faith for instruction and healing. In April of 1923 a clubhouse was completed at a cost of $15,000. The chalet-type structure quickly became a favorite place for small gatherings and parties. Both Charles and Myrtle Fillmore taught classes and conducted prayer services there. The structure was well-built, for today it is just as comfortable and inviting as it was more than fifty years ago. Many Unity groups still meet in the building. In 1926 a large home was built on the farm and occupied by Mrs. Laura MacMahan. After her death it was found that the structure was willed to Unity, and it currently serves as a hotel. Shortly after the hotel was completed, the Silent Unity building and Tower

were started. Mrs. Fillmore liked to call the Tower "the
Lord's Tower of Prayer." All the improvements at the farm
were reminders of the grace and beauty and faith of the
Unity work that was started in 1889, and Myrtle never tired
of telling about the farm and its loveliness. The following
extracts from two of her 1929 letters are good examples:

*"I do want you to come and see with me the wonder
and loveliness of Unity Farm, with our workmen making
things happen right under our eyes, bringing order out of
chaos, beauty out of mere boards, plaster, and cement.*

*"And hurry, now, come with me to the east door (of
her Silent Unity office), which is really the back door, and
look out upon the wonder of God's kingdom. Surely, God
is everywhere—in such green fresh grass, in the sturdy
patience of a thousand trees, in the clear, bright sky
overhead, in the vast stretch of rolling hills and quiet
valleys. I can see so far, I feel one with all the world. Don't
you? It is as though the love of God has drawn us all
together, lifting us above every limitation—that we may
know only the beautiful, the joyous, the free.*

*"There is a quiet reverence in my heart, a holy joy. I
want to shout one minute, and be very still the next. And
my soul sings within me, 'Bless God for His mighty
goodness. Bless God, bless God, bless God.' Oh my dear,
dear friend. God is good, and His mighty blessing is upon
all His children. There is never a more glorious time than
right now, never more opportunities to let our light shine,
never more reason to be happy, never more cause for
rejoicing."*

*"I find great delight in all the improvements. I took
some friends down through the basement the other day to
see the new ventilating system for our building, then we*

went through the tunnel that connects the building with the Tower, and we had a trip in the elevator to the top—what a view we had! Then when I have an opportunity I love to watch some workmen who are making molds for the design of the fountain base and the little pillars that are being placed in a cement railing. While they are molding this rock, which has been ages in forming into its patterns, we are molding the substance of Spirit through thoughts and words into patterns of health and beauty and the temple not made with hands. And we know, too, they are building something beautiful in their lives in loving service."

Thousands of persons, Unity and non-Unity alike, flocked to the farm to enjoy its beauty and to purchase its fruits and vegetables. Many came for the concerts which the large Unity band performed several times a month in the outdoor amphitheater, often for crowds exceeding a thousand. Before and after the concerts many persons stopped in at the Tea Room, located in what now serves as an apartment building. Mrs. Fillmore especially enjoyed a patio at the Tea Room "fixed up out-of-doors with tables and beach parasols where one may enjoy the out-of-doors along with meals."

One day in 1929, after most of these improvements had been made on what once had been farmland and woods, the Fillmores thought it would be nice to have the owner of the original fifty-eight acres visit Unity Farm and inspect the changes that had been made. After he accepted the invitation, a car was sent for him, and Mr. and Mrs. Fillmore and Rick accompanied him on a tour of the farm. They saw the Tower, or companile as it was more formally called; the beautiful Silent Unity building; the underground passageways; the oil and gas wells and the new lakes; the clubhouse, golf course, tennis courts, swimming pool, and other recreational improvements; and all the other wonders that had been accomplished. The guest said very little during the tour, and the Fillmores were curious about the apparent negative reaction. Finally, Mr. Fillmore could stand it no longer, so he blurted out, "Well, what do you think of all this?" The man considered the question, thought for a moment, and replied, "You sure have ruined a good cornfield!"

In August of 1928 one of the greatest events in Unity's history took place: the Sixth Annual Unity Convention. The ten-day session was held at Unity Farm with the following biblical quotes as its slogan: "Old things are passed away," and "Behold, I make all things new." A tent city was erected to house hundreds of Unity teachers, students, and friends from all over the country and from some foreign countries. August normally is a dry month in Missouri, but in 1928 it rained. And it rained. And it was cold. One of Mrs. Fillmore's special guests came from California, forewarned that Missouri in August could be torturously hot. Before she had left her sunny clime, she had asked her sister to pray for cool weather in Missouri. The traveler arrived in Missouri without so much as a coat and found cold rain and mud at the site of the tent city. She immediately sent a wire to her sister asking that the weather prayer treatment be stopped!

The rain did let up a little and some sunshine fell on the muddy earth, but generally speaking, the weather was not as cooperative as planners had hoped. There were few complaints, though, for the joy of togetherness in the name of Truth and the good Father was enough to overcome any possible negativity.

Convention-goers were told in a souvenir program about Unity's growth and present status:

—Unity has 432 employees, ninety of whom are Silent Unity workers.

—A five-minute silence for *Daily Word* is observed by workers each morning.

—At 10 a.m. workers go to chapel for a half-hour service.

—At 11 a.m. workers stand in reverent attention while the Lord's Prayer is spoken over loudspeakers.

—About four thousand letters are received every day, more than half of which are requests for spiritual help.

—About six thousand pieces of mail are sent out each day, every letter blessed.

—Unity mails 1,065,000 magazines monthly.

—About three hundred centers carry a full line of Unity literature.

—There are about twelve hundred acres at Unity Farm.

Most of the convention meetings were conducted in the new Silent Unity building, and meals were also served there in what was then the dining hall. Food was strictly vegetarian. Charles and Myrtle Fillmore played major roles in programming, while C. M. Frangkiser, director of the Unity band, planned the entertainment. Speakers were among the most famous of their day, including H. B. Jeffery, Georgianna Tree West, Ida Palmer, Francis J. Gable, Ernest Wilson, May Whitney (later to become better known as May Rowland), Irwin Gregg, Douglas K. DeVorss, E. V. Ingraham, Charles H. Watts, and many others.

On Sunday, August 26, 1928, at three o'clock in the afternoon, the Silent Unity building was dedicated and consecrated to the work of Jesus Christ and Truth. Charles Fillmore spoke on "The Dynamic Power of the Holy Spirit in Silent Unity" after Myrtle Fillmore led the group in prayer and a silence. Lowell Fillmore outlined finances for the many improvements the conventioneers were witnessing, and Rick Fillmore discussed architecture and landscape ideals. There was much singing and praying and joyous celebration by the more than two thousand persons who attended this dedication and cornerstone blessing. The inscription on a copper tablet on the cornerstone read, "Jesus Christ, the stone which the builders rejected, is made the head of the corner." Many persons added their personal blessing before the stone was sealed.

Perhaps one of the most emotional sessions of the convention occurred on August 22. The day was dedicated to Silent Unity workers. Mrs. Fillmore said she and all the workers were prepared for the occasion with a special radiation of light, love, life, power, strength, and substance. They were prepared physically, too, with colorful garb and placards and banners. The workers filed into the meeting place with placards and banners held high, each with messages of Truth. They marched by twos, with Charles and Myrtle leading the way, singing and shouting affirmations. There weren't many dry eyes that day among the conventioneers, and many said it was the most beautiful sight they had ever seen. Afterward Mrs. Fillmore said, "Well, we felt a little on display, with our special clothes, and marching about and sitting on the platform— but we held steadily to the truth we were there to express and apparently our work was a success."

In 1930, when she was eighty-five, Mrs. Fillmore taught four weeks in the summer school. It was a strenuous time for her, especially in the heat of August, but she enjoyed every moment of it. In one of her lessons, she recalled an experience when she had tried very hard to overcome a negative condition: "It occurred to me," she told her students, "to imagine just how I'd feel if I were free from it. I entered fully into the imagination of freedom and wholeness, and lo! I discovered *I was in actual manifestation all that my imaging faculty declared me to be.*"

Mrs. Fillmore loved teaching and she loved her students who were being prepared for the ministry or for teaching careers in Truth. But she listened to the Father, and after the 1930 teaching experience ended, she said she was finished in that role. When the fall term for the school opened, many were surprised to see her name missing from the list of teachers. She explained it very simply: "I shall not give a course of lessons during the coming school—I just haven't received the Father's leading to do it, but whenever I am shown from within that it is time to do something more along this line, I shall be obedient."

Through the years literally thousands of persons came to Unity to seek work or to study. Many wanted to be ordained as Unity ministers, but few received such a distinction. Mrs. Fillmore discouraged all but the most persistent in such efforts. In response to one person who felt qualified for ordination, she wrote:

"We confer titles on no one. We use no titles ourselves and take no account of those other persons use. We are privileged to use the title Reverend if we so desire. Experience in the past has shown us we have been too free with our ordinations. There are those who have passed the examination intellectually and who have been given a

certificate for the work with us, and who have received the
baptism which we give and for whom we have prayed, who
have gone out and failed to measure up to what we really
expect of a Unity representative."

Mrs. Fillmore pointed out that the best ministers use
no frills. Their consciousness draws to them the students
they can help—not their names, their list of published
materials, or the lessons they have taken. "After
ordination," she continued, "we expect them to go out and
stand on their own feet, and build their own work. Those
who know the true purpose of this work are not so much
concerned about titles or positions. They are content upon
expressing the Spirit of Christ."

Even ordained Unity ministers who expressed their
great joy in the ministry were cautioned by Mrs. Fillmore.
One such minister wrote to her in glowing terms about the
peace and love in her service. Mrs. Fillmore answered:

"It is lovely to be associated with the fine types you
have drawn together. Now, if these happy folks, who have
much, don't just settle down and call it 'our center,' and feel
satisfied to have it reach only those whom they consider
worthwhile, and so miss the 'common folks' who need what
can be given them, 'the hem of the garment' will be there for
all to touch and be made whole. That's the greatest
temptation any of us has, perhaps at present—to draw
around us those whom we consider interesting, and to live
and study and work and enjoy with them, and to dislike to
be disturbed by those who clamor, and fumble, and insist
on having things Christlike, and fail to appreciate us, and
want something for nothing."

Perhaps a greater inclination among Unity devotees
was their feeling that they should give up their occupations,
and everything else, and travel to Kansas City to "work for
the Truth." For those who asked Unity for positions in

Silent Unity or other departments, Mrs. Fillmore asked: "What have you accomplished? What have you proved yourself capable of giving? What can you give (of self, not finances)? I want you to know that we can't guarantee to make heavenly conditions for those who feel that coming to Unity will solve their problems. It is a matter of individual growth; a learning to draw upon the individual's own inner spiritual resources and make practical use of them."

Even though such responses often discouraged would-be seekers, Mrs. Fillmore received strange reactions at times. One woman wrote to her in 1921, saying, "Tell Mr. Fillmore I am willing to invest me and all my savings in Unity and for him to please give me a job there." She sent a passbook with a sizable balance along with the letter. Mrs. Fillmore returned the passbook with this note: "We are returning your passbook. We have no place for you here at Unity, and we are sure that you would do wisely to stay there where you have the love, companionship, and help of your relatives. The only place you'll find happiness is within your own soul."

Somehow a lot of people felt they *had* to move to Kansas City to do Truth work. They *had* to be near Unity Farm and the Unity headquarters on Tracy. This was contrary to the teaching of Charles and Myrtle Fillmore. Mrs. Fillmore explained to many persons: "It isn't necessary for a person to be here in Kansas City, or in any Unity center for that matter, to do Truth work. In fact, we are doing all we know how to do to get folks everywhere to understand and to live the Truth just where they are. The more who get the spirit of our teaching and live it, the smaller number of workers we'll have to have here. Folks don't come here to get something, but to give something— something fine and powerful and far-reaching. Those who do come get something, but it is after they have given, with mind and heart and physical expression."

In March 1929, another giant step in Unity's continuing expansion took place. The first payment, five thousand dollars, was made on a piece of land in an area known as the Plaza in south Kansas City. Mrs. Fillmore eagerly told friends of the acquisition, and added, "It is the plan to build a new Unity temple there when the time seems right for it." That structure was some twenty years in the future, but as always, the Fillmores were planning ahead.

Unity had come a long way since the turn of the century. The change was dramatic, and the growth was something that the Fillmores surely must have seen as a dream in the early days of the movement. But they had a way about them—a way of making dreams come true.

Mrs. Fillmore described in a letter in 1929 some of the differences in the movement from the early days to the time of great expansion:

"We don't see all our Unity workers, sometimes for weeks at a time. We're spread out all over one side of a city block (and the Unity Farm). All of us are busy, doing the things we choose to call our own parts of the work. We are trying to learn omnipresence, so that whatever we have for folks, they may get, whoever they are and whenever they will take it. But some of this giving and receiving depends upon those who are seeking. They must develop the ability to tune in. Then, they won't care to come here and see us in our skins!"

V

Silent Unity—the Heart of the Idea

For more than forty years the names Silent Unity and Myrtle Fillmore were virtually synonymous in the minds of thousands of persons. In the beginning, 1890, Myrtle Fillmore *was* Silent Unity. She received the idea of such an organization, she nurtured it, and with her husband Charles she poured inspiration and effort into it. Their powerful and effective prayer work gave Silent Unity the start it needed to grow and evolve into the magnificent force for good that it is today. Until her death in 1931, Mrs. Fillmore maintained an active interest in Silent Unity and its prayer practice, and she kept in touch personally with hundreds of correspondents.

In April of 1890 Mrs. Fillmore announced the birth of Silent Unity in the pages of Unity's magazine, *Thought*. At that time she called the organization the Society of Silent Help. She wrote:

"All over the land are persons yearning for Truth, yet so dominated by the surrounding error that they find it almost impossible, without a helping hand, to come into harmony with the divine Spirit. To open a way for those and to help them overcome their sins, ills, and troubles is the object of the Society of Silent Help. The wonderful success of absent healing demonstrates that bodily presence is not necessary to those in spiritual harmony. Jesus

said, 'If two of you shall agree on earth as touching any thing
that they shall ask, it shall be done for them of my Father
who is in heaven.' Those who have had experience in asking
understandingly know that this is absolutely true.

"Hence a little band in this city has agreed to meet in
silent soul communion every night at ten o'clock all those
who are in trouble, sickness, or poverty, and who sincerely
desire the help of the good Father.

"Whoever will may join this society, the only require-
ment being that members shall sit in a quiet, retired place, if
possible, at the hour of ten o'clock every night, and hold in
silent thought, for not less than fifteen minutes, the words
that shall be given each month by the editor of this department. The difference in the solar time between widely
separated places will not materially interfere with the result, for to Spirit there is neither time nor space, hence
each member should sit at 10 p.m. local time."

The first words to be held in silent thought every night
from April 15 to May 15, 1890, were these:

*"God is all goodness and everywhere present. He is
the loving Father, and I am His child and have all His
attributes of life, love, truth, and intelligence. In Him is all
health, strength, wisdom, and harmony, and as His child
all these become mine by a recognition of the Truth that
God is all."*

Only a handful of people met in the beginning—Mr.
and Mrs. Fillmore and a few of their friends and neighbors.
The time, ten o'clock, soon proved to be too late for rural
followers of Unity, and it was adjusted to nine o'clock to
oblige those who pleaded for an earlier hour. The Society of
Silent Help grew rapidly as the idea caught on. All over the
nation and in some foreign lands, people joined the
Fillmores in the nightly prayer vigil. Letters containing
prayer requests soon started arriving in large numbers at
Unity Headquarters. The Fillmores might have been a bit

surprised at first, but pleasantly so, to find that many of the letters also contained a bit of money. Income at first was a trickle, but soon became a steady flow permitting modest expansion of the work. Never, however, was a price or a charge put on prayer.

The prayer requests were as varied as they were plentiful. They ran the gamut from healing to prosperity to illumination to guidance and everything in between. Nothing was too large or important and nothing was too small or insignificant to be prayed about. Farmers wrote to ask for rain or for sunshine, depending on the need; women wrote about husbands who mistreated them or who drank too much; prospective parents sought prayers for themselves and for those as yet unborn; people wrote about death and about life, about debts and about plenty, about hardships and about good times, about ignorance and about wisdom. No request was ever considered unimportant, and all requests were prayed over and held in the silence. Eventually, when expansion made it possible, virtually every letter was answered. Much of the work in the beginning—in fact almost all of it—was done by Mrs. Fillmore herself. Charles had his magazine and had not yet given up his real estate occupation, so his time was somewhat restricted.

From the beginning, prayer was almost constant in Silent Unity. Charles stayed on the job each day into the evening, not usually retiring until about 2 a.m. At that hour, Mrs. Fillmore would stir and stay awake into the morning, remaining in a state of prayer and meditation. Occasionally a volunteer would assist, but the Fillmores essentially were alone in those budding days of Silent Unity.

Silent Unity came into existence because the Fillmores believed without reservation in the existence of an omnipresent God. They reasoned that if it is true that

God is omnipresent, then it would not be necessary for persons making prayer requests to be in the presence of those doing the praying. They asked only three things of the one making the request: belief in God, belief in the power of prayer, and diligent use of the class thought. First there were a few dozen participants. Then hundreds. Then thousands. And now Silent Unity's measurement of participation is in the millions. From its humble beginning in the mind of Mrs. Fillmore, today (1977) Silent Unity has two-hundred prayerful workers, receives almost two million letters and four-hundred thousand telephone calls each year requesting prayer assistance.

Many persons have received "miraculous" healings, the poor have been prospered, and much wisdom has been imparted through prayers offered to God through Silent Unity in cooperation with those making pleas for help. How does Silent Unity work? Perhaps Mrs. Fillmore explained it best in one of her letters:

"It isn't that our prayers do anything magical. We simply hold you in the Truth consciousness and help you to remember and to place your faith in God, the omnipresent good, and to use your faculties in laying hold of and using this good. The moment you sense a need and ask for a blessing, you should have faith that God is responding and that the good will come forth. The daily repetition of prayers is not necessary to reach God, but rather to hold your own minds and hearts steady, until the thing you require is more real to you than the appearance to the contrary. It is your own constructive use of the power of mind, which lays hold of and molds the qualities of being to meet your individual demands, which determines your success, your satisfaction, and your freedom from all worry and anxiety."

An early prayer group. Myrtle is seated second from left; Charles and Lowell are standing behind her.

Mrs. Fillmore was the only Silent Unity letter writer in the beginning, and until her death she personally corresponded with many hundreds of persons. She wrote painstakingly by hand for many years, but then developed typing skills, and eventually Unity evolved to the point where secretaries were available for handling correspondence by dictation. Even then, however, she often added handwritten personal remarks to typed letters. Many correspondents begged her to write in her own hand, and she obliged some of them, but Silent Unity's growth was so spectacular that such letters were necessarily limited.

Silent Unity was born as a result of a healing—Myrtle Fillmore's—and its work stressed healing more than any other subject at its inception, as it does now, some eighty-five years later. Patience and perseverance were the two traits Mrs. Fillmore stressed most in the healing process of prayer. She knew from her own experience that healing

often takes time. Her healing certainly wasn't instantaneous, although such healings are possible. When
letter writers complained that they had tried and tried,
prayed and prayed, and there were no results, she could
understand their feelings and comfort them out of her own
experience. She, too, had prayed for most of her life. She
was always a religious person, yet she was sick, and in the
1880s, sick unto death. No matter how much she prayed,
her condition worsened. Finally, she had asked God what
was wrong, and the answer she received was passed along
later to hundreds of persons through Silent Unity:

*"The Spirit said to me, 'You have looked among your
faults; now look among your virtues.' I thought that
strange, but soon it came to me . . . that I didn't feel as
sweet and poised on the inside as I seemed outwardly. I
began to watch and to redeem this state of mind. As I
gained real poise and the ability to keep my thoughts and
feelings truly free, I was healed and restored to strength
and normal functioning."*

Here was the key to Myrtle Fillmore's healing and the
key to the success of Silent Unity in its healing work. Never
stress the sickness! Always look to the good in every
situation!

God revealed to Mrs. Fillmore that her body's cells
had intelligence and that powerful words of health affected
them. She learned that she could talk to her body in
positive, loving tones and that her body would respond with
health and life. Thousands of persons who have accepted
this concept have found new life and new health, as Myrtle
Fillmore herself had demonstrated.

Anonymity has long been the practice in Silent Unity
correspondence, but it didn't start that way. Mrs. Fillmore
answered many letters under her signature in the early

Myrtle at her desk on Tracy

days of Silent Unity, and even after anonymity became policy, she occasionally brought her personality to bear in answering letters. On one such occasion, she said:

"You will be wondering who this is, stepping out from the midst of Silent Unity to address you—not personally but as one of us; so I will make you feel comfortable and at home by telling you it is Myrtle Fillmore, who, in partnership with Charles Fillmore, founded this school of the wonderful Truth of the Real of Life; and finding what it did for us, we made a place in our message to the world for the sowing of the truth that should bring forth of their kind. Like the sower who went forth, we have kept up a continual process of scattering the seed of God the world over. This is the beginning of what we called the Silent Unity; and thousands and thousands have joined us. Though we are not the father and mother of this, we have kept close to the Law, and have done what we could in promoting the growth of these valuable words of truth— we are trying to have no false values but to always keep

this true secret—'It is not I, but the Father, He doeth the works.' "

Many persons through the years have asked for prayers from Silent Unity and at the same time have virtually apologized for not being able to "pay" for the prayer. Such letter writers received replies from Mrs. Fillmore that were as close to scolding as she was capable of writing. One such example:

"My dear, you spoke seven times about offerings to us, and your regrets that you didn't have one when you wanted to send it. It is our privilege to stand in this place and to offer ourselves to God, to do whatever we may to encourage and help those who are led to come to us. We truly feel that those who think of us, or who write to us, wire, or ask prayers, are in reality going to God, and making known to the Holy Presence their hearts' desire. We know the Father's countless blessings, and it is a great joy to help others to look for them and to call them forth for use. But surely we have never expected you to accompany your requests or your reports with offerings!"

Despite Mrs. Fillmore's insistence that offerings were not necessary for Silent Unity's prayer work, grateful persons by the thousands sent gifts, large and small, to advance the work. Prosperity was an idea Mrs. Fillmore could accept, and accept completely—both for Silent Unity and for the many who wrote for such prayers. When the Fillmores had started publishing their first magazine, they had experienced financial difficulties. Foreclosure of their type and printing equipment was threatened because of debts they had incurred. Mrs. Fillmore had turned to God and in meditation received inspiration to include prosperity in Unity's teachings. She approached Charles with the idea but he was somewhat reluctant, believing instead that health and spiritual growth were sufficient focal points for the budding movement.

"I talked to Mr. Fillmore until he, too, saw the way of God with men. It came at a time when failure seemed inevitable, to the senses—the only thing we owned, a little type, was being attached. It was surely a time to prove that the Truth for which we stood would work for us—and it did!" Mr. Fillmore was so convinced that from that point on never again did he hesitate to stress prosperity, and some of his greatest writings are on the subject—writings which have helped many persons to overcome the "poverty idea." One of Unity's most loved stories involves another situation in which the Fillmores were faced with fore-closure. Mr. Fillmore reportedly told the sheriff, *"I have a rich Father, and He'll get me the money I need."* The sheriff is alleged to have replied, "Oh, in that case you may have some more time." Indeed, Charles and Myrtle Fillmore both knew the truth of the statement, and the Father provided for their needs.

"Money is all right," Mrs. Fillmore said many times. "It serves us splendidly if we know how to use it. It is the evidence that others have faith in us and that we are doing that which they feel to be helpful, or that we are giving that which they feel the need of."

Prosperity was not a one-way street with the Fillmores, however. They shared too. Often Mrs. Fillmore's heart would be touched by a letter and she would enclose "a bit of green" with her reply, usually with a caution "to look to God, and not others, for your rewards, and you will never be disappointed in receiving." On one occasion, a woman who apparently was quite poor received a blessed one-dollar bill from Mrs. Fillmore. The recipient deposited the money in a bank and added to it from time to time until she had saved $4.26. Then she sent it back to Mrs. Fillmore for Silent Unity use. Mrs. Fillmore sent her five dollars in the return mail and told her to use it for food and clothing for her children. A woman with six children told Silent Unity about drought problems, mentioning that water had to be carried a half-mile from a creek. She asked for prayers for rain, and Silent Unity obliged, but Mr. and Mrs. Fillmore did more. They sent ten dollars and asked for sizes of clothing so that they might send boxes of garments to the family.

In contrast, when a woman wrote that she needed $100 because her husband had been fined that amount, Mrs. Fillmore responded: "Well, now I wouldn't bother about that! The Father is rich, and the only Power there is. Let's leave it with Him to manage this little affair." And when a woman wrote for prayers for a new automobile, Mrs. Fillmore started the prayer work, but did more—she sent the woman an automobile blessing card to be affixed to the dashboard of the car she would soon be manifesting.

Prosperity was vital in Unity's teachings then, as now, and Myrtle Fillmore can be credited with seeing just how important the idea of substance is in God's creation. She recalled those early thoughts about prosperity in a letter written during the depression:

"I can remember in the early days of the work, when it seemed my lot to receive only the cast-off clothes that were given me. I went to the Father about it. I said, 'Now Father, I am looking to You for my pay, for my provisions, for my clothes. If this is all I have earned in making myself ready to receive and in doing that which has come to me to do, well and good.' I wrote little notes of praise and thanks for needs met, before the supply was visible. And the good increased. And I set not my heart on the increase, but more lovingly on the Giver, and the increase continues."

The oldest known letter in Mrs. Fillmore's own handwriting is dated September 7, 1891. It was written to a woman and reflected the kind of thought that Silent Unity and the Fillmores were to stress through the years to come. It said, in part:

"My dear, you ask why you do not enter into the understanding you so desire. I will tell you. You are already in it, but think you have some great thing to do to get there. The kingdom of God is within you! The key to that kingdom is acknowledgment, or affirmation . . . . You have only to open your eyes to the sunlight and your lungs to the fresh air provided by the ever-present supplier of all . . . . Let consciousness lay hold of its boundless supply of life, love, wisdom now! It is your birthright . . . . All you need to do is 'Be still and know.' "

One of Mrs. Fillmore's most interesting and most helpful letter-writing techniques included the use of "The Prayer of Faith," written by Hannah More Kohaus. A typical response to a correspondent who asked for prayers for a variety of life's challenges was this one, written by Mrs. Fillmore in 1929:

> *"God is your help in every need."*
> Let the past be gone and wipe out all fearsome, worried thoughts for tomorrow with the joyous realization of the presence of God fulfilling your every need.
> *"God does your every hunger feed."*
> His presence fills you and infolds you, fully satisfying every hunger of your mind, soul, and body. Open the channel of your mind and wait upon God that you may receive the blessings which He has prepared for you.
> *"God walks beside you, guides your way*
> *Through every moment of the day."*
> With His hand in yours, He is leading you onward and

upward into all things which are for your highest good. His
Spirit has gone before, preparing and making smooth the
way, and He is guiding you that you may not stumble and
fall. Trust God unwaveringly.

"*You now are wise, you now are true,*
Patient, kind, and loving too."

With His love filling your heart, with the Christ Mind
expressing through your mind, you become a channel of
blessing to all whom you contact. You have no fear of what
others may do, but rather you place them in the care of God
and fully trust Him to lead them in wisdom, love, and good
judgment into all things which are for their highest good.
You are conscious of the divine presence infolding you and
you dwell in perfect assurance that all is well, for God
the good is with you.

"*All things you are, can be, and do,*
Through Christ, the Truth, that is in you."

In the constant realization of the Christ presence, all wisdom,
strength, and understanding are given unto you, and you
are shown the way to solve every problem and to meet every
obstacle that comes into your path.

"*God is your health, you can't be sick;*
God is your strength, unfailing, quick."

God within you is the ever-flowing fountain of eternal life.
As you contact this life through silent prayer and meditation,
all inharmonious appearances of mind and of body are
dissolved and the expression of perfect life and health is
brought into manifestation in you and through you.

"*God is your all, you know no fear,*
Since God and Love and Truth are here."

Praise God for His loving presence that reveals the truth of
being to you and wipes away all fear. In God there is only
love, peace, and perfect assurance, and for the one who
knows God there is no place in his whole being for a single
fear thought to find lodging.

Beloved, the Prayer of Faith is mighty. Think on these
things. Be still and know God. Be still and have faith in
God. Be still and trust God. In the consciousness of the
presence of God infolding you, we bless you, we bless your

husband, we bless your son, we bless all of your environ-
ment and all of your affairs. We have faith in God through
Christ Jesus.

Meditate on the thoughts in this letter until you get a
clear realization of their truth. Know these truths for yourself
and also for your husband. Know that God is with you both
and He is leading you in wisdom, love, and good judgment
into all things which are for your highest good. You are both
His children, and He loves you and will never forsake you.
In His name, I am Myrtle Fillmore, Your friend in Christ.

No problem was too embarrassing or too humiliating
for Silent Unity correspondence. Mrs. Fillmore or another
Silent Unity worker graciously received all letters,
telegrams, and telephone calls on all subjects. One such
poignant problem dealt with a child that had been born out
of wedlock and its ostracism from community life. "Tell
me," the writer pleaded, "is this the unpardonable sin? If
God can forgive, why can't the human? No prison door was
ever socked so hard against anyone as it is against my little
child and me. We are poor, very poor. It is seldom I ever see
a human. They seldom speak when I do, I am deaf, and deaf
people are always shut out. My baby loves children and
wants other children to play with. Her one happiness is
listening to me read. So far I have taught her nothing but
what is good and beautiful of people. But she has begun to
notice that not all of what I teach is true of people. At
church there are taunts and coldness."

Mrs. Fillmore's compassionate answer, from her
mother heart, surely warmed the sad writer: "We lovingly
extend to you and your dear little daughter the helping
hand of our spiritual ministry. The sin you mentioned is not
the unpardonable sin, so be at peace. Your body is the
temple of 'Christ in you' and you can worship Him in Spirit
and Truth without going to church. Place yourself and all

that concerns you lovingly in the hands of the Father and pray for His wisdom to guide and direct you. He is your friend, your guide, your help in every need."

If no problem was too intimate, likewise no problem was too trivial. A case in point was a young singer who asked for help because his collar bothered him during singing performances. Mrs. Fillmore replied: "Mr. Fillmore solved this same problem by wearing a kind of collar that gives freedom to the throat. He wears the Lord Byron style and stays with it regardless of what fashion may try to dictate. So your freedom lies in your wise selection of just the right kind of collar that will not touch your chin or any sensitive portion of your neck. If you take this advice, you will be able to concentrate entirely on the inside, where your voice has its throne of power."

In another case, Mrs. Fillmore showed her willingness to deal with the occult side of life when she replied to a woman who was hearing "voices" and receiving guidance from them:

"As you no doubt know, it is not an uncommon thing for those who are living spiritual lives and keeping close to God and the Christ standard of expression to have guidance from a realm of mind which is beyond the intellect and not always comprehended by it.

"Those who understand the soul to be the total of consciousness—the fruit of the individual entity's experiences in unfolding and expressing what the Creator has given—and who know that it is ever in touch with God Mind, which is its Source, realize that these leadings, or voices, which they intuitively know to be right and dependable, come from the innermost realms of the soul itself . . . . I, of course, do not know just what you believe about the psychic voice or force which directs you. But you do not need anyone, or anything, or any voice, outside of

your own consciousness, to guide you."

Weather was, and still is, another topic of interest to thousands of correspondents. Whatever the request—whether for sunshine for a weekend picnic or rain for a farmer's crops—the prayer is the same, and that is for divine order and God's will. Occasionally, however, Silent Unity prayer is more specific. During long periods of drought, for example, specific mention of the need for rainfall may be made in Silent Unity prayers. Once after prayers for rain had been spoken for two weeks during a drought, precipitation began, and Mr. Fillmore ran shouting through Silent Unity, "It's *our* rain!"

Silent Unity under Mrs. Fillmore's direction—and since—has prayed for princes and paupers alike. Late in Mrs. Fillmore's life, a correspondent from England thanked Silent Unity for prayers: "Your splendid healing work for King George of England was perfect . . . a perfect manifestation." King George may never have known that Silent Unity was praying for him, but someone, perhaps many people, had asked for such prayer, and it was done. From kings to presidents to common people, millions of names have been submitted to Silent Unity for prayer over the years.

Mrs. Fillmore often brought her own experiences into situations posed by letter writers and offered her own techniques of overcoming as examples. She told of her healing and of Mr. Fillmore's, she talked of their decision to dedicate their lives to God's work, and she told how joy, prosperity, health, and happiness became a part of their lives as a result of the decision. If someone suggested he had been working too hard and needed a rest, she might respond as she did on one occasion: "I know how it goes. Sometimes He gives me a hint that I need to take a rest, and frequently I do not take the hint—and when we don't take

the hint, we are given the *kick*. So it pays to be receptive
and obedient, always."

Still again, when someone asked about her healing and
the happy life she led, she confided this very personal story:

*"It was about twenty years after my healing that I was
downtown in one of our department stores purchasing
some decorations for our home, when a woman, a gypsy,
came along and showed a great deal of interest in me and
asked to read my palm. I explained that I did not put much
confidence in palmistry and such things, but I humored her
and let her read whatever she saw written upon my hand.
She was greatly amazed when she saw the life line and said
that I'd outlived my time many years, and she seemingly
could not understand it."*

At times, it was necessary for her to be firm with
certain letter writers. Once Mrs. Fillmore tried to comfort a
mother who had lost a child. The woman wrote back after
receiving Mrs. Fillmore's loving letter and said, "You just
don't understand the extent of my loss." Mrs. Fillmore
wrote again, including these words:

"You feel I do not understand what you have gone
through. Yes, I feel I do understand, in great measure
anyway—for I, too, had to give up my youngest son in death
after he had served in the war and came back to us to
devote himself to service for others here in Unity. And just
a short while before his going, I had seen his dear young
wife give up her life and leave a newborn babe, and the dear
husband, and the joys that life would have given her. I am
still doing what I may to help the dear baby, who lived and is
growing beautifully, to know the peace and joy and love
which are her birthright.

"You see, dear, we don't talk of these things or give in

to them. We really have faith in God and His omnipresent good, and do trust that all is well, and that life is all there is, and that every soul is dear to the Father and will have the opportunity to grow into the full consciousness of sonship."

Letters by the hundreds poured into Silent Unity every year addressed specifically to Mrs. Charles Fillmore, Mrs. Myrtle Fillmore, or some derivative thereof. Many were directed to "Mama Myrtle," "Precious Mother of Unity," "My Very Dearest One," or "Beloved Mother." Correspondents thanked her for helping them sell stores; for helping them better understand themselves and their goals; for helping them to find better health; for illumination in matters of wisdom and judgment; and for better jobs and brighter prosperity. They told her: "Your beautiful letters cannot come too often. They are such an inspiration and a help. They seem to lift me way up, to where I know I truly belong, and in this consciousness, I bask for a while under this influence of your beautiful and high ideals." She was befriended: "I wonder if ever a girl had a friend like you?" She was thanked: "Thanks for the wonderful work you and Mr. Fillmore are doing for humanity." And she was virtually idolized: "You are my spiritual inspiration and the Christ is my leader and my teacher." To this last remark, she replied: "I am trying my very best to manifest in all my ways the perfect ideal you have of me, and I am sure that you are expressing the 'image and likeness' the very best that you can."

Mrs. Fillmore was much loved by the scores of persons who wrote to her personally, but perhaps she was loved even more by those who worked with her in Silent Unity and in other Unity departments. She received literally thousands of gifts from co-workers, from delicate handkerchiefs to expensive items of art, from flowers and

fruit and vegetables to exquisite gourmet gifts. She shared
the good that she received with her family and also with the
Unity workers.She kept few gifts for herself, and many
that she did keep were retained only temporarily. After she
had enjoyed an item for a time, she would give it away.
Once she received a valuable and quite elaborate toilet kit
from an admirer. When the donor visited her and found it
nowhere in sight, she inquired about it. Mrs. Fillmore told
her that she had passed it along, explaining, "I wanted to
enjoy the same thrill of giving that you had when you
lovingly gave the gift to me."

Mrs. Fillmore liked to grasp the hand of a co-worker
and leave behind her "bit of green"—usually a five-dollar
bill. She saw and knew the needs of those about her, and
when she could, she helped fill the needs she recognized.
Usually she arrived at the office quite early, and often she
brought with her a huge bouquet of flowers. She walked all
about the office, stopping at each desk to deposit a flower.
One worker still associated with Silent Unity as this is being
written said: "She seemed to walk a few inches off the floor
and almost floated about. She seemed weightless and without a care or concern in the world. She was lovely and we
loved her."

Christmas was always an especially happy time in
Silent Unity, and Mrs. Fillmore liked to surprise the
workers with special gifts. One year she had prepared
baskets of food for each worker, and when she started to
distribute them, the workers had a little surprise for her. In
unison they shouted: "What's the matter with Myrtle?
She's all right! First in love, first in peace, first in the hearts
of the healing ones!"

The name Myrtle might well have become the most
popular name among Unity families had Mrs. Fillmore not
quietly discouraged it. She was always proud, but also a bit

embarrassed, when a worker named a new daughter Myrtle. The workers recognized this tendency to shyness on the part of Mrs. Fillmore, and the Myrtle-naming practice was quickly dropped. Not so, however, with more distant Unity folks. The Myrtle name craze grew rapidly with the formation of a motherhood column in UNITY Magazine which was written by Mrs. Fillmore. Charles was not left out either. Many letters arrived each year telling of blessed events named Myrtle, Charles, or some variation of these names. Many named their children Faith, Love, or Joy, also because of Unity's inspiration in their lives. It was not unusual for letter writers to ask Mrs. Fillmore to name their children. One wrote: "Mrs. Fillmore, I want you to name my son. If it had been a girl I was determined to call her Myrtle. I have picked Samuel as a middle name." Mrs. Fillmore responded in this case, as she always did, that it would be better for the parents to name the child.

Almost from the day it was born, Silent Unity was an idea whose time had come. After the few months of the Fillmores' going it alone, it seemed that new employees for prayer work were necessary every few days. By the end of the first thirty years of operation—years of often incredible results—the work force had reached two hundred fifty persons. In addition to the letters and telegrams of the very early days, the telephone was coming into its own, and hundreds of persons were calling Silent Unity each month. Mrs. Fillmore confided to a friend: "It is beyond belief how the folks keep crowding more desks into the space allotted them, which seemed full long ago. But more workers are required and they must have space for typewriters. Talk of multiplying fishes and loaves—we must stretch our buildings, or get better with this work of God that we have started."

The obvious answer was expansion, and an addition at Ninth and Tracy was deemed to be unwise. The Fillmores started looking to the rural suburban area, and son Rick started designing just the right kind of building for Silent Unity purposes. Once the site was purchased in 1920, at what is now Unity Village, work got underway in earnest to erect a building that would serve Silent Unity well for many years to come. Meanwhile, workers persevered in their cramped quarters.

On May 10, 1929, the great day arrived when the new Silent Unity building was ready to be occupied. On that day files, typewriters, desks, and everything else necessary for the Silent Unity work were moved to Unity Farm. Letter writers worked right up until the time their desks were removed. Three buses took workers to the farm at the beginning of each shift and returned them to the city at the end. Ralph Rhea, currently co-director of Unity's Radio and Television Department, was responsible for determining routes each day for employee pickups.

The transfer was generally smooth, but the Silent Unity workers and their consciousness were sorely missed at headquarters. The lonely feeling was especially voiced by Charles Fillmore, who arranged for all of the workers on the day shift to meet at the Tracy auditorium each Wednesday at 7:30 a.m. for a prayer session. The usual meeting lasted thirty minutes, but occasionally Charles would be so excited about the presence of the Silent Unity workers that he would "forget" and keep them in the chapel for as much as an hour. On one such day, he excused his tardiness at dismissing them by leading a session of group singing, then remarking: "When a giant tree is hewn down, it leaves a lonesome place in the skyline; and that was the way it seemed at headquarters with you gone. There was a

**Myrtle and Charles Fillmore seated on the platform
at a Silent Unity worker-prayer meeting in 1929.**

lonesome place." May Whitney responded: "Charles
Fillmore was right about the new Silent Unity building,
though. It is heaven, and heaven is right here with us now."
May Whitney Rowland became Silent Unity Director in
1916 and was succeeded in 1971 by James Dillet Freeman.

Even though there was sadness among workers for
the separation from headquarters—because all other Unity
business remained at the Tracy location, including
publication of the magazines—there was much joy too.
Rick Fillmore had simply outdone himself with the beauty
and the practicality of the new Silent Unity offices. "We are
learning to appreciate Rick more and more," Mrs. Fillmore
wrote, "and so are some of the other folks for all this that
has been created through his precious soul."

Mrs. Fillmore loved the new quarters and explained to a friend that she felt almost omnipresent going back and forth every day from city to farm and farm to city. Often she would make several trips a day as her appointments demanded. She glowed as she talked about, or wrote of, the loveliness at the farm and especially the new Silent Unity structure. "I love to have the doors [to her office] that open out upon the East Balcony open wide. They are glass. From them are views that would invite the skill of an artist or poet—the sweep of orchard and the valley. The dam, too, can be seen through the trees." But the more that she talked about the new building, the more her friends and correspondents wanted to know about it. She had so many requests for information that she finally wrote an essay entitled, "Tour of Silent Unity, Unity City." From that day on, this essay was made a part of many letters that left Mrs. Fillmore's office. It follows:

> "We shall start at the Arches, my fairy home. We shall pass the tennis courts and the golf links, cross the foot bridge over the swimming pool, pass the clubhouse, and enter the driveway that gives us views at the left of Lowell's home, the apartment house and tea room, the amphitheater, the greenhouses, and the homes of those who are helping us grow things and build homes.
>
> "On the right, we see the pond, the hotel, Rick's, and Mr. Boileau's and Mr. Gable's homes.
>
> "Ah, you are right, the building we are approaching is the Silent Unity building, the east wing of which Mr. Fillmore and I occupy. The tall structure is the campanile from which there is a tunnel to the Silent Unity building. The colorful foliage and flowers that border the winding walks about the building are from the greenhouse on the farm.
>
> "The pillars in the cloisters in the north wing of the building give just the right touch as one approaches the building. We'll look into the auditorium and then take a peep at the busy workers on the first floor—God's garden

room—the division of beginning Silent Unity letter writers, and the files division. Then we will make our happy way up the wide stairs to the second floor. We shall not stop to accept the invitation of the tempting chairs that are at the head of the stairway—there is a table there, too, with litera-ture placed attractively upon it, for visitors—but we will go into the healing room in its quiet beauty, and look into the telephone room on our way back through the north wing. Then we pass through the spacious room occupied by Silent Unity letter writers in the cloister, with its arched ceiling supported by columns capped by Italian corbels, from which we enter my office on the left. The door at the right leads to Mr. Fillmore's office. The two rooms in between are for our respective secretaries. Nothing seems to have been left undone that would add to the beauty and comfort of our surroundings.

"Each office has a fifteenth century type fireplace. The woodwork is of wormy chestnut. The furnishings are lovely, Mr. Fillmore's a bit more elaborate than mine, but not prettier. The bench in front of my fireplace is upholstered in tapestry as are the love seat and the armchair. The colors in the tapestry blend with the tints in the frieze that borders the ceiling. Each office has an elegant Persian rug.

"There are most comfortable leather chairs at our hand-carved desks. Leading from my office to the secretary's and the cloister are book coves. Our east doors open out on tiny Romeo and Juliet balconies.

"Shall we open the glass doors and step out to view the sweep of the orchard and valley? We may enjoy the view from the north window, too, and then have a heart-to-heart talk about all this wonderful gift of love, and the expansion of the work."

The joy of Silent Unity at Unity Farm was rather short-lived, however. The mood of the nation was not prosperous in 1929, and shortly after the beautiful new building was finished and occupied by devoted Silent Unity workers, the great depression struck with devastating force. Unity was among its victims. Mrs. Fillmore wrote of the times: "There seems to be a sweep of financial lack all over the land. The Lord is in it, to teach wiser ways and conservation of His gifts to needs of the work, and a bringing forth of a larger faith. I've felt for several years this test for a closer consciousness with invisible substance would be called for." At first, a few workers were laid off. Then bus routes carrying workers were shortened. Mail cars, which had made four trips from headquarters to the farm every day, were stopped. Finally as many as fifty workers were laid off, but the prayer work continued. "The glorious part of it," Mrs. Fillmore said, "was that they (the laid-off workers) immediately, or almost immediately, found other avenues of service open, and are happy and satisfied."

Finally, in mid-July 1930, Silent Unity operations at the farm were abandoned altogether, and the beautiful building that Mrs. Fillmore so loved to describe was vacated. Silent Unity returned to the downtown headquarters, and there it was to remain until the late 1940s when all Unity operations were transferred to the farm.

The return to headquarters was not considered a failure, nor was it done with sadness. There was joy, instead, because the workers knew that God was at work even in the nation's dismal-appearing financial situation and that nothing but good could come of the return to the city.

Although Charles Fillmore had been a very important part of Silent Unity and even had an office in the building at the farm, he had essentially been separated from the Silent Unity workers he so loved. The press of responsibilities upon him had kept him at headquarters most of the time, and he had been lonely with his beloved wife and the Silent Unity workers located at the farm. Even though finances made it possible within a short time after the return to the city, he and Mrs. Fillmore agreed that Silent Unity should remain at headquarters, despite cramped space. Both of the Fillmores knew that something had been missing with the two locations—the love and warmth and togetherness that are possible only with one central operation. So it was that they vowed there would be no further separation of Unity workers until *all* departments could be moved to the farm. Silent Unity occupied the third floor of the headquarters operation until 1949, when construction of a new administration building was completed at the farm, enabling a complete move of all departments.

VI

"Who Will Take Care of the Children?"

In the very first issue of *Wee Wisdom,* Myrtle Fillmore proved herself to be a real prophet. *"Wee Wisdom,"* she wrote, "makes a very humble beginning, but it will grow to be 'big folks' in time." It was August 1893, and the first issue of *Wee Wisdom* had just rolled off the presses. As Mrs. Fillmore held the eight-page publication in her hands for the first time, she may have recalled the vision that had led her to this point in her unfolding soul growth and service. When Unity was measured in months rather than years, in those very earliest days, Mrs. Fillmore had had a vision in which a huge crowd of people gathered about her. Many in the number were children, and most of them were quite undisciplined. Within her a voice asked, "Who will take care of the children?" The answer, too, came from within, and it was, "You are to take care of the children: this is your work."

Her first involvement with children was, of course, to have been a child herself; then she worked with children as a teacher; and then she became involved as mother of her own little ones. In 1893 Unity had grown and was a dynamic force for good in Kansas City and elsewhere. Many people were being attracted to Unity classes and services, but there was no place for the children. A Sunday school was the first step, one which Mrs. Fillmore took with enthusiasm, but *Wee Wisdom,* a magazine for children, probably has had the largest impact on youth of any project Unity has ever undertaken. Its birth marked the beginning of a ministry directed to children on a national and international scope. Today it is the oldest magazine for children in the world. Its circulation has ranged from a few hundred copies to more than two hundred thousand.

In the first issue of *Wee Wisdom,* Mrs. Fillmore stated the intent of the little publication quite clearly:

> "The mission of *Wee Wisdom* is not to entertain the children but to call them out. To be always entertained is to be dwarfed and dependent. To be 'called out' is to follow the harmonious law of the soul's unfoldment.
>
> "Who meddles with the rosebud? What fingers are deft enough to pry open that marvel of folded beauty? We are wise enough to leave it alone to follow the glad law of its own unfolding.
>
> "But our children! Have we dealt as wisely with these buds of marvelous possibilities? Have we always remembered that they, too, must quicken and unfold through the innate law of their own genius?"

It was not a good time for Unity to be starting a magazine for children. The new spiritual movement was struggling financially, even though Charles and Myrtle Fillmore were prosperous in the knowledge that God would provide for their needs so that the new publishing endeavor would be successful. Despite this, many challenges had to be met and overcome before the appearance of the first issue, which was a month overdue. It had been scheduled for July, but delays postponed its publication until August. Another challenge turned out to be a tiny article—an item so obscure and apparently unimportant that it didn't even carry a headline. It simply stated: "We know of a case of actual resurrection of the dead by a couple of children. The 'dead' was a frozen cat, and the little owners prayed over it until it came to life."

Mrs. Fillmore might as well have distributed a firecracker with each issue of the new magazine!

Readers gladly accepted part one of "Wee Wisdom's Way," a story penned by the editor, Mrs. Fillmore; they praised the poetry scattered throughout the first issue; they walked right into Mrs. Fillmore's "Wee Wisdom Reception Room," with her invitation to *"Come in, dear children, every one of you, I bid you loving welcome."* They studied and appreciated the Bible lesson; and they eagerly scanned items submitted by children who had responded to a UNITY Magazine request to do so. But many readers protested, some of them vehemently, the one tiny paragraph about the frozen cat. Many of them wrote angry letters, such as this one: "I can't see wherein the bringing to life of a frozen cat proves anything. Such signs are not necessary to prove truth. The spirit of a cat is not the spirit of a man. Please consider before publishing these Extraordinary things!"

In her typical "tell-it-like-it-is" philosophy, Mrs. Fillmore replied in the second issue of *Wee Wisdom* in an article entitled, "O Ye of Little Faith." She said some of *Wee Wisdom's* friends regretted that it should have doubled up its dimpled fists the very first thing and dealt unbelief such a ridiculously hard whack. What followed may be as close to sermonizing as Mrs. Fillmore ever reached during her many years as editor of *Wee Wisdom.* She wrote:

"It may be that the dear Father, whose love is so great that not even a sparrow falls on the ground without Him knowing, saw nothing *absurd* in the beautiful faith that

Myrtle Fillmore (*circa* 1900)

would not be refused a pet kitten's life. And maybe to Him
. . . there was no difference at all between the loving
confidence shown Him at the tomb of Lazarus and the
tender trust of those innocent children. 'Therefore I say
unto you, what things soever ye desire, when ye pray,
believe that ye receive them, and ye shall have them.' "

Not wanting to close the case for faith and confidence
until it was solidly made, she concluded her reply in this
manner: "The incident took place twenty years ago and I
know the two. One became a Baptist minister and if his
faith continues the same, he'll never have any funeral
sermons to preach."

It was months before the dead cat incident cooled down, but while it was simmering, circulation of the little magazine edged upward from a few dozen copies to a few hundred. Every new subscriber brought cause for rejoicing.

The third issue, October 1893, brought strong support for Mrs. Fillmore's adamant insistence that the cat story was true. The mother of the two boys involved wrote what amounted to a two-page account, with illustrations, of the episode. She said that the boys had found the cat outside after a blizzard and that it was frozen stiff. They brought it inside near the stove, and for three hours they prayed over it and rubbed its frozen fur, "never stopping to doubt or question." Finally the mother reported a pulsation, although her husband had said it was quite impossible. "That thing is as dead as a doornail," he remarked. But the cat began to breathe, and one of the boys closed the prayer meeting over the cat by saying, "Thank You, Father, for gimming us back our little kitty. Amen."

Immediately following this account, the letters criticizing *Wee Wisdom* for running the story about the frozen cat sharply diminished, and many who had believed all the time wrote in to say so. In fact, many readers began accepting Mrs. Fillmore's invitation to send in poetry, short essays, and letters of all kinds. Some of the missives from youngsters clearly indicated that the message of Truth was seeping into their minds.

A little boy wrote: *"Are you afraid of the dark? Isn't God just as much in the dark as in the light? You mustn't be afraid. I'm not afraid 'cause I know God's everywhere and God's good."*

A girl corresponded with an account of how everyone had given up on a man who was alleged to be dying, but she wouldn't: *"He forgot God and I remembered for him!"*

A child told of being punished: "I told her you can't hurt me. There isn't such a thing as 'hurt.' "

A youngster shared this occurrence: "One evening when our fire was burning bright and no one was thinking of evil, my little sister was playing on the chairs when she fell, oh so hard on the floor! Mama picked her up and she looked as if her neck was broken. Mama said, 'Oh, my child is killed!' I just closed my eyes to make sure I could see nothing but life and good, and oh, how I made the good words pass through my mind, and it was not long till I saw my sister open her eyes, and, oh, how grand I felt to know that I, only seven years old, had mastered an error."

Still another good report: "Well, the doctors are saying that we are going to have the mumps, and my teacher sent me home because my face was fat. Don't be afraid of the bumps for they don't hurt one bit. You just get fat for a few days, and that is all. Good thoughts never let anything hurt you."

And from Gracie: "*Wee Wisdom* has enjoyed my home so much and I would like to take it another year. I think it would be very nice to keep on knowing each other. The paper has made my home very happy for the last year, and how good it would be to make my home happy for another year. I do not want to be sick and this little paper helps me very much. I think I am God's child and cannot be sick. How well I would like for you to speak the good word so I can get my music lesson good!"

More than anything else, the truth that shone through in correspondence from young readers of *Wee Wisdom* resulted from a serial Mrs. Fillmore wrote entitled, "Wee Wisdom's Way." The project was started for the enjoyment of Lowell, Rick, and Royal, and they liked it so much that Mrs. Fillmore decided to share it with readers of the little magazine. It quickly found its way into the hearts of hundreds of other children, and they eagerly awaited each month's installment. The story line was simple, yet delightfully captivating. Aunt Joy came to visit her brother and found the household in despair. Her sister-in-law was sick and in bed; her nephew Ned was on crutches; baby Grace was afraid of the dark; and in general the other household members were disturbed and unhappy, despite frequent visits by both a doctor and a minister. Baby Grace was the first to take hold of Aunt Joy's Truth ideas, and she learned many things about nature and especially that the dark was friendly. Ned then began to see the light and was healed. Then sister Trixy overcame her anxieties, and then the rest of the family found health and happiness.

The Fillmore children were virtually the editors of "Wee Wisdom's Way," and, as their mother put it, "many tenderly budding pages of Ned and Trixy's doings were nipped by the early frosts of these boys' criticisms." They might say, for example, "That sounds pretty, mama, but boys don't do it that way at all." Mrs. Fillmore liked to tell her friends that if there was anything lacking in the story it was *not* lack of counsel or counselors.

The serial went on and on, with Mrs. Fillmore often writing the next chapter right up to the deadline for copy to go to the printer. She wanted to end it and get on to something of more interest to *her*, but the boys demanded that it continue. "Don't you do it, mama," they would plead. "Don't you stop that story. There's lots more to tell yet and nobody can tell it like Aunt Joy or Trixy can."

After about a year, however, she closed the story and told the boys: "If there are any more serials to be written in *Wee Wisdom*, you boys will write them."

Although she didn't say so at the time, she did reveal many years later that the characters in the book were drawn from people she had known and had watched unfold spiritually. And the little girl, Trixy, was Mary Caroline (Myrtle) Page—"the little girl in me, my soul which knows its oneness with God, the Father and the Source of all good."

"Wee Wisdom's Way" was such an overwhelming success in the magazine that it was published in book form, and many thousands of copies were distributed in several editions. Mrs. Fillmore gave away copies to children who wanted them but who didn't have any money, with a note saying that all the incidents written were true, but that names had been changed. "I've presented Truth principles in a way that's easy to grasp, and have had wonderful words of appreciation spoken to me by many who have read it."

The first year of *Wee Wisdom* was marked by a variety of difficulties, some financial, some technical. Because UNITY Magazine and other Unity printed materials were given priority on the printing press, *Wee Wisdom* was occasionally late in distribution and once was omitted altogether, to be published the following month twice the usual size. Circulation went up each month, but it did not reach expected levels. By the June 1895 publication date, *Wee Wisdom* again was omitted and was combined with the July issue. An announcement was made that the little magazine was in financial difficulties and that its size would be reduced in the future. Instead, however, *Wee Wisdom* went into exile, for all practical purposes, and became a very small department of UNITY Magazine. The apparent demise of *Wee Wisdom* was announced simply:

"This little corner [in UNITY Magazine] is reserved for us that we may meet here and keep astir the loving thought and good work which *Wee Wisdom* began. There has been a general lamentation because *Wee Wisdom* has ceased to go her rounds, and it looks as if her friends were legion and their intentions of such a nature to make her visits possible again someday."

Much of the space alloted in UNITY to *Wee Wisdom* during the next two months was given over to letters of protest from children that their beloved little paper was gone. One child wrote that she wanted the rest of her subscription "in good thoughts about my school tasks." A mother objected: "I am sorry to have the paper suspended. It was a lovely child's paper and I enjoyed it myself far more than I do what is called the advanced science. When we get too advanced in Truth we find ourselves removed from that child-like simplicity that is the door to its entrance."

Wee Wisdom stayed in its two-page format in UNITY Magazine until August 1898. UNITY was appearing bimonthly during the time it shared its pages with the children. The material consisted primarily of Bible lessons with an occasional poem or short Truth story. Mrs. Fillmore, who always called herself "Ye Editor," was often asked to reveal something of herself to the readers. Modestly she would reply, "What shall I say, only that we gladly do the work given us to do, and have never refused time or service to anyone who asked." Royal, as the youngest child of the Fillmores, was also a subject of much reader interest, since Mrs. Fillmore mentioned him from time to time. Once when a reader insisted that the editor tell more about Royal, Mrs. Fillmore wrote: "He is big and fat. One hundred pounds and seven years old. They call him baby elephant at school, and he wears clothes for a 13-year-old. He's never been sick and has never taken medicine."

Wee Wisdom appeared again in July 1898 in magazine form, but only as a supplement to UNITY. It was announced that the price for UNITY with the supplement was to be one dollar per year. Before the first subscription could be accepted, however, the U.S. Post Office Department ruled that the arrangement was against its regulations. So in August 1898 *Wee Wisdom* returned as an independent publication. It had only eight pages, instead of the sixteen it had previously boasted, but the outpouring of joy from children far and wide at *Wee Wisdom's* return assured its future success. During the entire existence of *Wee Wisdom,* income has never surpassed costs of publication and distribution. But the Fillmores knew that they must publish their little magazine for children at any cost because it was producing *results.*

The August 1898 issue of *Wee Wisdom* was a milestone in another respect, too. In that edition the most popular single item in the history of Unity publishing appeared for the first time. It was untitled and Mrs. Fillmore didn't know its author, but it was later determined to be "The Prayer of Faith," written by Hannah More Kohaus. It is:

> God is my help in every need;
> God does my every hunger feed;
> God walks beside me, guides my way
> Through every moment of the day.
>
> I now am wise, I now am true,
> Patient, kind, and loving, too.
> All things I am, can do, and be,
> Through Christ, the Truth that is in me.
>
> God is my health, I can't be sick;
> God is my strength, unfailing, quick;
> God is my all; I know no fear,
> Since God and love and Truth are here.

Hannah More Kohaus

It was not until 1905 that Mrs. Kohaus received recognition as the author of this now famous poem. Mrs. Fillmore was in Chicago that year and had a chance meeting with the author. Mrs. Kohaus explained that she had first written the piece for a Chicago Truth magazine, but it was then copied in a number of other publications and passed from person to person until the author's name was eventually lost. In time, she related, "A generous soul thought the poem good enough to own, so he put his name on it." She stressed to Mrs. Fillmore, however, that she indeed was the author and that it had been the very first output from her pen after she was born "into the Truth of being." She also told Mrs. Fillmore that Unity's *Wee Wisdom* mission was a splendid one, for 'Just as the twig is bent, the tree's inclined.' The new race rests upon the salvation of the children." Upon her return to Kansas City, Mrs. Fillmore wrote about her experiences in Chicago, particularly with Mrs. Kohaus, and said: "The Truth takes care of its own. The mistake has been corrected (about authorship), and now we love to know it was Mrs. Kohaus who clothed these mighty statements of truth in such simple, rhythmic garb that the tiniest tot can say them." Thus "The Prayer of Faith" was assured its place in what Mrs. Fillmore called "a part of the metaphysical scriptures." It has appeared countless times in *Wee Wisdom,* UNITY, and in tracts and pamphlets through the years. Thousands of *Wee Wisdom* readers made it their almost constant companion and memorized its words. Even today, the first thing taught in many Unity primary Sunday school classes is "The Prayer of Faith."

The year 1898 was marked by a third milestone in *Wee Wisdom* history, in addition to the first publication of "The Prayer of Faith" and the rebirth of the magazine itself. In December of that year, Mrs. Fillmore gave in to intense pressure from many young readers who implored her to "show yourself to us." She had refrained from personal publicity as much as possible and did not like such ego gratification, but she knew the insistent demands would not stop until she obeyed the commands. So on the cover of *Wee Wisdom* that month the faces of Myrtle Fillmore and her three sons smiled back at the readers. She wrote of the occasion:

> "On earth peace and good will to every living creature, is our Christmas salutation. We are glad to visit you, one and all, and meet you face to face in your homes and Sabbath schools. It seemed quite an undertaking when we planned this numerous visit. Part of a precious Saturday was cheerfully given to its preparation, though these boys do feel that it requires more courage to face a camera than a cannon, especially when the camera is pointed toward them and the cannon is not. But all obstacles are met and vanquished and here we are. As this roguish-eyed boy (Rick) at our right states it: 'The funny part of it is, mama, we'll be everywhere at once.' And so we are, which proves our omni-

Left to right: Royal, Lowell, Myrtle, and Rick

presence. We've had great times talking over this wonderful tour and what it means to visit all the way from the northern seas to the southern oceans; to find ourselves entertained in homes from Denmark to Australia, from Alaska to South America; to become guests in every state, country, and clime, even to far off Japan and the islands of the sea. The *everywhereness* of our visit means that in the joy of Christmas, we are *one*."

The three Fillmore children were involved in *Wee Wisdom* in varying degrees. Lowell, the oldest, was more concerned with business demands. Rick, a remarkable artist even at a tender age, often contributed drawings to the magazine. He tried his hand at writing for the little paper in 1899, but he didn't like *Wee Wisdom's* editorial policy. In the January issue that year he penned, "The Evolution of Santa Claus." Without his knowledge or *approval,* "Ye Editor" made several changes in his copy. In the following edition, Mrs. Fillmore remarked:

"He [Rick] objected to all the interpolations and changes, and said it did not mean at all 'that way' what he meant, and he wasn't going to own the story at all, and he wasn't going to write for anybody that meddled with his stories, either."

She beseeched her readers: "What do you think of that? What would you do about it if you were in the editor's chair? Won't you, dear Wisdoms, indulge your editor a little liberty with your spelling and English now and then, and love her none the less for it?"

Rick kept his word, however, and wrote little if anything for publication after his initial experience. But his brilliant artwork graced many covers and illustrated stories for years to come.

Royal also had a problem with writing. He took up his mother's challenge that if there were ever to be another serial in *Wee Wisdom,* the boys would have to write it. So, also in the January 1899 issue, he wrote:

"One day in autumn the wind was roaring and blowing leaves off trees. A little leaf said: 'Why are you blowing us off for?' The wind said: 'I am freeing you instead of hurting you.' And the leaf said: 'What are you freeing me from?' And then the wind tells all the story what follows."

Royal, ten years old at the time, ended his story with, "Continued next month."

The serial not only continued the next month, but it ended, too:

"You work all summer doing your task. Your task is making the little buds in the sunshine, which are to be little leaves like what you are next summer. And some of them are to be blossoms and some of them big branches. And I'm just going to give you a holiday for your work.

"I can't tell anyone about what the wind said, because the wind don't talk in words. And I've decided I will not write continued stories anymore, because you feel compelled when you write continued stories and I don't like to feel compelled!"

Royal was a child of few words, because it took him a year and a half to write another story for *Wee Wisdom*. And it was not continued: "We live in a nice home with a cornfield across the road, and flowers on all sides, and big lovely giant trees in the backyard. We have two summer houses and some of the prettiest flowers. I'm not one of those kids that are always talking."

Mrs. Fillmore enjoyed having the children make all kinds of contributions to the magazine, and as a typically proud mother of three fine boys, she liked to write about them too. In 1901 the boys caught what she called the "Kodak-craze." She explained to the readers:

"The three boys have new quarters. Yes, a brand-new, half grown-up house all their own—a kind of annex to the parent home with a little hallway (shute they call it) connecting the two. You would laugh looking at it a little way off, and wonder if it would ever catch up and quit tagging on that way. They've caught the Kodak-craze and have an ideal darkroom fitted up in one corner and are snapping everything in sight. You will hear of these quarters henceforth as 'the den,' and let us hope it will never be a den of growlers . . . only the Good has a place in the den."

As the new century unfolded, so did *Wee Wisdom*. Youngsters eagerly sent for their fifty-cent subscriptions in ever-increasing numbers. Indeed, *Wee Wisdom* had truly become an international children's publication, and Mrs. Fillmore so reported:

"Ye Editor forgot how big *everywhere* is! Why! Geography divides it up into *wheres* and puts Spring on

WEE·WISDOM

"Ye are of God, little Children. . . . Greater is He that is in you than he that is in the world."

Vol. 6.   KANSAS CITY, MO., OCTOBER, 1901.   No. 3·

one side and Fall on the other. So that while we are rejoicing in Spring, our Caroline 'way down in South Africa and our Wisdoms in Australia and New Zealand are having Fall. And you, dear Wisdoms, off there toward the North Pole, are just getting your first little gleam of Spring sunshine. But oh! Aren't we glad that there's no north nor south nor geographical division to Life and Love and Truth? Omnipresence is everywhere-presence, and that's why we can all be ever so close together when we are thinking the same true thoughts."

Mrs. Fillmore loved nature, and she enjoyed sharing her thoughts about it and its relationship to the loving Father. Holidays brought forth special words from Mrs. Fillmore's pen, too. Here are a few examples:

> "As we come together in mind and Spirit this month, eternally Ye Editor is sitting on a turned-over box under the branches of a soft-leaving-out shrub of some kind. Under her feet is the delicate carpet of the young Spring; over her head the undimmed blue of a perfect May day blends softly down till it fits the rim of the green and brown old bowl of earth. It is so delightful to have all outdoors for a sanctuary."
>
> ***
>
> "The birds! Dear-a-me! The Birds! It would seem what time they are not busy nest-building they stop and pour out this joy with ours. What is that sad, queer little 'coo' that comes from farther away than these joyous notes overhead? It must be what they call the mourning dove, but let's change her name to the 'rejoicing' dove and see if she won't catch up a more cheerful note."
>
> ***
>
> "Robin, don't stand there and coax Ye Editor from her pen, but tell her how she may give her Wisdoms the very essence of all this that so fills and glorifies this June morning—tell us the secret of all the joy and beauty and freedom that pulsate sweet life outside. Does the Robin speak? Is it the trees and the flowers that tell it, or is it the united voice of It all that speaks

so clearly this message: 'There is no without and within, there is no you and us, we are all the one glorious manifestation of gladness, beauty, and freedom. We are not separate, we are one in Om-Ni-Pres-Ence!'

***

"Suppose you each think over very carefully what you have to be thankful for. It would take a long time, to tell it all over, wouldn't it? Is it yours only for just the one day we call Thanksgiving Day? Well, then, why can't we *every day*, when we first open our eyes on a new day, count over all the good things we have to be thankful for, and give thanks? It would be like counting over gold to count over our good, and do you know, the more we count it the more it increases? The great storehouse of all there is, is mind and we must handle our good things stored there with our thoughts. When we see how the little fingers of our thought can reach in and take hold of the very things we have so longed for, shall we not understand how to train them, how to bring out our blessed good? We do this by being thankful for what we already find manifest in our little world." ***

"The great clock on this year turns its hands around to gift time once more, and everybody is planning some loving surprise for everybody else. What a time it is to forget self. What a time to live in loving remembrance of others' pleasures and needs. Someday we will all fall so into the habit of loving to remember others that it will be gift day all the year 'round.

"The more we keep seeing God's love and abundance everywhere, the more we grow Christmas joys. We must never give gifts because we think people are poor. We must never think of God's children in that way. *Poor* thoughts about people keep up the *seeming* of poverty. Give, but give because you love to show how bountiful God is. Don't ever call anyone poor. All that our Father hath belongs to every child of His. Then let us talk about plenty till it is showered upon all, and keep giving, because it is more blessed to give than to receive."

Ye Editor's column in *Wee Wisdom* was undoubtedly one of the most popular in the magazine, but two other features attracted a great deal of interest—"Pillow Verses" and Bible Lessons. The pillow verses usually occupied a full page, often the back cover. They consisted of seven drawings of fluffy pillows, each of which contained a truth affirmation such as, "Be gentle, be true, and loving, too," or "I am kind, I am good, and I do just what I should." Mrs. Fillmore recommended that readers use one of the affirmations each day upon rising and again upon retiring.

The Bible lessons employed scripture passages and commentary in the language of the children, simple yet accurate and practical. The story of Moses called by God to deliver the Israelites out of bondage, for example, was explained in this manner: "Everyone in the world is called of God to do the work of the Good. Some people know this and some do not, and those who know it soon find out the work they are to do and are taught how to do it. Moses knew he was called to a great work—the work of freeing his people from the bondage of Egypt, and for forty years in the wilderness, which really means in the silence, he was taught of God the wisest way to do it."

In the September 1901 issue of *Wee Wisdom*, while Mrs. Fillmore was away on a vacation, Lowell, Rick, and Royal took over the editorial duties, and unknown to Mrs. Fillmore, started a subscription fund campaign. The boys asked readers to send in any money they could spare, and it would be used to send *Wee Wisdom* to youngsters who did not have the money with which to subscribe. When Mrs. Fillmore returned to her editorial duties the following month she was forced to make a confession:

"I've already been sending many *Wee Wisdoms* to children not able to afford. Sometimes the publishers think Ye Editor is too givey, but you see it is this way: she gives her services free and it does seem as if love could take care of it all, and if a child is hungering for a book or a paper, *it shall have it* as long as one is left at headquarters. Now this is an honest confession, and one that some of the friends think will keep Ye Editor impoverished, but her idea is different. It is all the Lord's and we are but His stewards, and His treasury is always full."

The subscription fund was a success, nevertheless, and hundreds of coins poured into Unity headquarters to help out needy children. One child told Mrs. Fillmore that she had earned her contribution by sweeping porches, and another said he had sold his pigeons. The coins were accepted and put to work as *Wee Wisdom* subscriptions. Mrs. Fillmore said the youngsters who were helping others less fortunate than they were planting seeds of unselfish love which would bring forth its own kind.

As the popularity of *Wee Wisdom* grew, so did the number of contributions from children—poems, stories, and letters. Most of their offerings stressed the *good* because it was obvious that Mrs. Fillmore never permitted anything *bad* within the pages of the magazine. But occasionally, a child would test Ye Editor. On one such occasion a little girl named Anna penned a story called "Louisa's Accident." In it, Anna told of Louisa who was tortured by her father and stepmother and committed suicide by throwing herself off a cliff to get even with her parents. Mrs. Fillmore posted the article back to Anna as soon as she could find a stamp. "We would like to have Anna let Louisa come back and try it over again in a real, wholesome, delightful experience," she wrote. "What say you, Anna?" Anna reluctantly said yes, and rewrote her little tragedy into a happy adventure which Mrs. Fillmore accepted for publication.

On another occasion, Beatrice tested the market with "The Bad Boy." This article got the same attention—and a quick return. "Just think of it," Mrs. Fillmore wrote. "Here we are trying to lose the bad boy pattern so's there won't be any more bad boys made up. Say, Beatrice, suppose you tell us about the best boy you ever knew! You may not have to go far to find one. I guess there's one pretty near where you live."

Mrs. Fillmore was an editor, but more importantly, she was a teacher. She taught the children who read *Wee Wisdom* that everyone and everything are good. And she taught them not to fear hell but to enjoy heaven *now*. In answer to many inquiries about heaven, she wrote:

"The big folks have a place fixed up in mind so beautiful and so blissful they can never half describe it, and sickness and death, sorrow and want, have no presence there. They have fixed it up way off somewhere in the skies and expect some day, some way, to get into it, and stay there always. Now my Wisdoms, it is not one of Wisdom's ways to *expect*. That enchanting *somewhere* you have fixed with such grace and beauty is yours *now,* if you will throw away the ugly thoughts and skimpy patterns of life as it seems to the mortal of you. You are kings and queens in the realm of mind, and there is nothing too beautiful or too good to be true."

After the first ten years of *Wee Wisdom's* publication, it was obvious to both Mr. and Mrs. Fillmore that the magazine was a costly drain on other Unity operations, but they felt with deep conviction that the service *Wee Wisdom* was performing was valuable and that the magazine should survive whatever the cost. It was necessary for "Ye Editor" to remind the children of the need for their cooperation in the endeavor. She would write: "Now, if you are vitally

interested in the success of *Wee Wisdom,* you had better
be showing it; else Ye Editor will think she had better give
the time spent in trying to serve *you* to those who not only
appreciate her services, but sustain her, while she is
spending her time and money in trying to keep up this little
paper for her love of *you.*" Undoubtedly Mrs. Fillmore was
torn between the work she was doing for a relatively few
youngsters and the work she could be doing to expand and
improve the services offered by Silent Unity, her other
primary responsibility with Unity. Inevitably, however,
when Mrs. Fillmore was forced to jolt the children into
responding with articles, letters, and subscriptions—
results were forthcoming. Many of the children could
remember when *Wee Wisdom* went into exile and was out
of their midst for several years, so they poured out their
hearts in letters, articles, poems, and in subscriptions to
keep their precious publication coming their way. Some
took their copies of *Wee Wisdom* and went door to door
soliciting subscriptions, and others had their parents
advance them money so that they might purchase long-
term subscriptions for themselves. Mrs. Fillmore was
always touched by such outpourings of love and faith. In
1904, *Wee Wisdom's* eleventh year, she wrote:

"Some of these letters *Wee Wisdom* receives turn all
the world into joy, and really, I'm back in the little girl realm
again, where nothing was so real as the beautiful fancies
with which the little girl—me—painted the big world all over.
Folks said they weren't true, but I believe now they were
truer true than all the ugly shapes that come through the
hardening experiences of belief in time, toil, and trouble.
Sweeter than all else is the power to look through the un-
soiled, undimmed windows of the soul and see all this wonder
and beauty of the living Spirit, which is a real fairyland. And
greater than all else is the power to know and do the will

of this wonderful living Spirit, before whom all this unshapely, unhappy, unreal world passes from sight—like a dream of the night.

"You know how glad you are to wake up and find a bad dream is not true? Well, we are just beginning to wake up and find these miserable old conditions, called old age, and disease, and poverty, and sorrow, are nothing but mortal dreams. The swift and living Spirit lifts us out of them all. The real mission of *Wee Wisdom* is to keep you dear children from falling asleep in error and dreaming all these ugly dreams over again. Just think of dreaming you are old and wrinkled and helpless! Well, if you catch your grandma or anyone else dreaming such ugly dreams, you just wake them right up by telling them, *Spirit never grows old.*

"Maybe you will find somebody having a dreadful dream about sickness and pain sometime. Wake them right up with a good strong shaking like this: *Spirit cannot suffer. Spirit is whole and well. God is Spirit and you are awake in Spirit and Truth.* The true word will always destroy a lie, 'for the truth endureth forever.' God never made evil and you must not. People who believe in the hobgoblins of evil are really dreaming. Don't believe it true whoever tells you, 'I am sick,' 'I am blind,' 'I am helpless,' 'I am lame,' 'I am poor.' Wake them right up by telling them of the full, free presence of strong eternal life; of the power that never faileth; of the sight that can never be lost; of the swiftness of Spirit that is carrying them about."

By 1907, Mrs. Fillmore turned over primary responsibility for *Wee Wisdom's* editing to her young assistant, Blanche Sage Haseltine. Mrs. Fillmore retained the title of editor, however, and had final authority on content and style of the magazine. Her column appeared irregularly and, in fact, was missing altogether for about three years as Miss Haseltine quickly became accepted by the children. In the February 1910 issue, Mrs. Fillmore could no longer tolerate her position on the sidelines, and she penned a long column which filled all available space on the first three pages of the magazine. It was entitled, "Matters and Things in Which Ye Editor Gets in Her First Say." In part, she said:

"I've squeezed into small corners and cracks with my little say, till I've decided for once to push boldly to the front and say all I want to, and if there's any room left, the rest can have it."

She praised her Wisdoms for the support they had given to the magazine and pointed out the many changes and improvements that had been made. She said quite emphatically that from this point forward *Wee Wisdom* would not look backward at the days of seeming lack, both in income and in subscriptions, but forward in partnership with "Miss Prosperity, with nothing to do with Mis Fortune."

On the occasion of *Wee Wisdom's* sixteenth birthday, Mrs. Fillmore was heard from again, and she poured her heart out about the magazine:

> "The time draws near for *Wee Wisdom's* sixteenth birthday. She's getting to be a big girl now, and what shall we do about it? Lengthen her skirts, put up her hair, and make a debutante of her?
>
> "You are laughing! 'Oh, she isn't a real girl,' you are saying. To be sure. I had overlooked the fact that to you, *Wee Wisdom* is just a little magazine, visiting you at your homes and telling her little Truth stories. But to me she is a real, living Wisdom-child, almost as really my girl as these three blessed boys, that have grown up to manhood since her inception in type, are my boys. That being the case, you can understand how much Ye Editor loves *Wee Wisdom* and how glad she is to have her go into your homes and carry health and joy with her. Why! It is almost as if I were going myself, so interested do I feel in all our Wisdoms and their affairs."

By 1912, Royal had returned from the University of

Missouri and had assumed the title of managing editor of *Wee Wisdom*. From thirty-two to thirty-six pages were being published each month, but contributions from youngsters were so numerous that many "good" articles were being rejected or sharply condensed, and the same was true for letters. Two new departments were created— "Home," because more and more adults were reading the magazine, and "Youth," because many of the children who virtually had been weaned on *Wee Wisdom* were now teenagers and beyond, but wanted to continue receiving it. In 1913 Mrs. Fillmore yielded to pressure from those in this latter category and from her son Royal, and consented to a name change for the magazine. The "Wee" was dropped and the publication became *Wisdom*. Mrs. Fillmore explained it:

> "Since *Wee Wisdom* made her first bow to her wee readers and gave them her first Truth Pillows to rest their little heads upon, the three boys who kept 'Ye Editor' in sympathy with all wee folk have grown to manhood. Even Royal, the youngest, has been home from college for two years. This fact goes to prove that generations of wees have risen up and passed beyond the range of *Wee Wisdom's* ministry. So, upon this, her 19th birthday, Royal and I have decided to celebrate it through dropping the Wee from her name and broadening the scope of her ministry of Truth that it may include the Home and the Youth as well as the Wee, and all under the name, *Wisdom*."

The change was a mistake, and Mrs. Fillmore realized it almost instantly. The response from older children simply was not forthcoming, yet the younger children, who had so earnestly supported the magazine, now had less space of their own each month. The magazine's emphasis, almost certainly because of Royal's age-identification, shifted to

Royal Fillmore (*circa* 1912)

youth and away from the little ones. Within a few months the Home department was returned to UNITY, where it had been previously, a move made by popular demand. *Wisdom* became a one-editor magazine again, with the names of Mrs. Myrtle Fillmore, editor, and Blanche Sage Haseltine, associate editor, removed from the masthead. Royal had taken over sole responsibility and was the only editor listed (managing editor).

Circulation started dropping, old familiar bylines disappeared as writers stopped submitting articles designed for little children, and letters complaining about *Wisdom* began to pile up. "I long for the *Wee Wisdom* of old," one child lamented. "*Wisdom* is wearing calico. Let's put her back in Sunday clothes," another child insisted.

In July 1915 it was announced that *Wisdom* would expire in the following issue and *Wee Wisdom* would return. Mrs. Fillmore explained in an editorial note:

> "There came a time when *Wee Wisdom* herself felt grown up and wanted a larger house in which to entertain big folks, as well as little. So she put on long dresses and grown-up ways that didn't suit her one bit. But now she has learned that the years have no power to make her older, so she has decided never to grow up, but always to be *Wee Wisdom*."

The August 1915 *Wee Wisdom* had sixteen "rooms" or pages, instead of the normal thirty-two to thirty-six under the one-word title. Mrs. Fillmore reported that there had been a meeting of the butchers and bakers and candlestick makers, and it was determined that Miss Wisdom's extravagance would have to be curbed because she had spent more for her "traveling expenses" and for the entertainment of her young friends than had UNITY, her big brother. The Booster Club column, consisting of letters from youngsters, had previously been bylined by Royal and included an introductory remark or two. In this issue Royal's name was missing, and Miss Haseltine wrote: "We have all tired of being grown up, and are again little children, and shall remain as little children forever. I know for myself I like my little *Wee Wisdom* better than a big clumsy half-grown-up Miss Wisdom." Mrs. Fillmore explained in a note elsewhere in the same edition that Royal was pretending to be too big to preside over the *Wee Wisdom* Booster Club, but she reminded him in print, "It's not been so long since he was a Wee himself."

Royal apparently was deeply disappointed in his seeming failure to make *Wisdom* the successor to *Wee*

Wisdom and for several months busied himself with other duties at headquarters. But by late in the year he returned to his Booster Club secretary position and his mother decreed, "Hurrah, hurrah, Royal's with us again." He stayed on and helped with *Wee Wisdom* in any way he could until he was called into the Army in World War I. Mrs. Fillmore chose not to discuss the war in the pages of *Wee Wisdom* other than to report that Royal had put on the uniform, but she added, "In these days of world conflict between right and wrong we, dear Boosters and Wees, must mobilize for sustaining the principles of Truth and Righteousness through loyalty to God and to our country."

By 1919 *Wee Wisdom* had grown to thirty-six pages again, and its prosperity seemed assured with ever-increasing circulation. In that year Royal announced to its readers that Unity would soon purchase a farm near Lee's Summit, Missouri. He said: "It will be fixed up with little houses and the Unity workers will spend their vacations there. There are springs and big rocks and swimming pools and wild animals and wild flowers and big trees and birds and a whole acre of strawberries and just everything you dream about."

In response to the announcement, a child wrote about her mother's prophetic vision for Unity and the new land purchase:

"Mother has visioned Unity as a large place and says that the new buildings you are putting up are just the beginning of what you will have to build because you are going to be a mighty power for good in the world, and people are going to come to you from the very ends of the earth, in search of help and instruction."

In 1922, nine years before her death, Mrs. Fillmore turned over the editorship of the magazine to Imelda

Octavia Shanklin, a long-time contributor of articles for
Wee Wisdom. In 1930 Jane Palmer succeeded as editor
and served in the position for thirty-six years. When she
took the reins, Mrs. Fillmore sent her a copy of the first
edition of *Wee Wisdom* and said: "Always knowing the
Spirit that begat this form of touching the spiritual spark in
the Wees will always find a soul quickened and ready to
carry it forward. 'Great oaks from little acorns grow.' I have
great faith in your appreciation of being chosen to this child
ministry for this generation."

Since 1966 the magazine has had four editors—Anna
Thompson, Thomas Hopper, Jim Leftwich, and Colleen
Zuck. But the mark of Myrtle Fillmore has ever been on
Wee Wisdom, whoever the editor happened to be.

"The good is all that counts," she told her young readers for many, many years. Death was not a fit subject for
discussion, for life was the Truth. So, when Mrs. Fillmore
died in 1931, her death went unreported, as she would have
wanted it. After all, it was only the *appearance* of death
anyway. And Mrs. Fillmore, in *Wee Wisdom,* had left
behind her a living monument to Truth.

VII

Myrtle and the Family

What kind of wife was Myrtle Fillmore? What kind of mother? With all of her other responsibilities with Unity did she have sufficient time for her family? These and other similar questions have been asked about the cofounder of Unity through the years. It is known that she dedicated her life to God and His work through Unity School, but what of family considerations? In 1928, just three years before her passing, she replied to such questions in this manner:

"I have been companion to one man, and have had three others grow up calling me mother. And to know steadfastly beholding the Christ in these men, releasing them from what I might have felt they should do, that whatever the soul of them needed that I had would be called forth through love and wisdom, has given joy and satisfaction incomparable.

"I haven't always sat back and kept still. I have had my say; have insisted upon a high standard of thought and action. But it has ever been given in a great love and appreciation, and in the end, that which we all have wanted has prevailed. We have ever to make allowances for the experimental stages of the soul's unfoldment; these come in babyhood, in youth, in maturity—they keep coming, and are a sure sign of constant growth."

She loved Charles, she respected him, and she
believed in him. She stood beside him and grew along with
him through the lean years of their marriage. She saw him
unfold magnificently into what many consider a twentieth
century prophet. She watched him in his struggle in the
1880s to find God, and she prayed and meditated alongside
him. She watched him after her spiritual healing as he
began to take hold of the healing idea in his mind, and she
witnessed the change that came over him—mentally,
physically, and spiritually.

It may be that she did not love him in the "romantic"
sense of the word when she first met him in Denison,
Texas, in the 1870s. She never used the word *love* in
describing that encounter. But undoubtedly there was a
soul affinity in their relationship, and she saw in Charles the
potential that he would grow into in later years. But whatever her reasons for accepting in 1881 his marriage proposal, there can be no doubt of her intense love for him as
their partnership unfolded. She liked writing notes to him,
especially for his birthday, their anniversaries, and other
special occasions, such as Christmas. This one, directed to
him on Christmas 1910, perhaps best sums up her feelings:

*"To my husband. We go one way, dear: the same sun
that tints your morning sky throws wonderful rays into
mine and the shadows of your path are my shadows.
There is a thick wood on either side and even though we
hear wailings therefrom, we are happy because we are
together. We know our path leads to a deep pool whose
voice is silence, wherein every melody of the heart has
been sung and whose calm within and without is shadow in
which every color of the rainbow has been painted. And
we drink of its waters and are filled with song—song that
the world knows not and therefore it is the sweeter to us.
God bless you, dear."*

Myrtle was the perfect balance necessary for Charles' metaphysical genius, spiritual devotion, and mischievous humor. She always complemented him with her quiet dignity and dedication to the Jesus Christ standard of living. While he preferred giving talks and teaching Truth courses, she enjoyed leading in prayer and meditation. While he was reluctant to write letters even to close friends, she was prolific in her correspondence. She often told other family members that she didn't know what they would do without her, "their scribe." She mused that if she didn't do it, they would probably get around to it—but she *really* would not have had it any other way. One of the little tricks that Charles would employ to keep from having to answer some of his mail was to add an "s" to letters addressed to Mr. Charles Fillmore, thus making the salutation "Mrs." Charles Fillmore. "Sometimes," she charged him, "you do it with such care that the change is hardly visible!"

Charles' humor and practical jokes sometimes gave Myrtle cause for concern. One of Unity's legends has her gently tugging at his coattails to restrain him during a story. He liked proverbs—the kind he made up on his own. Once when he posted one in Unity headquarters, she demanded that it be removed, and he acquiesced. It read, *"Those who are not fired by enthusiasm for their work usually get fired."* Charles thought it was funny; she did not. She was more tolerant of some of his other proverbs, such as *"The reason people who mind their own business are so successful is because they have so little competition."* Once in a public session, she pretended great shock, but was really quite amused, when he pointed out that there could not possibly be any women in heaven. "Can't you see?" he asked. "Right here in Revelation it says that for a space of a half-hour there was perfect silence in heaven."

She would get even with him for his barbs on occasion. In response to some teasing, she once told a crowd that Charles had gotten a package from a composer wanting him to examine some music manuscripts. The composer had written, "I understand that you, too, are a composer of some note." Myrtle gleefully declared, "He's still trying to find out what note." Again, when Charles showed up in the office one day in the early 1920s wearing knickers, she remarked in a stage voice, "He's leading in advanced style as well as in advanced thought." When a laundry was burglarized, Charles was quite relieved that his suit had not been taken, and he returned home smiling as he told of how his garment had been under divine protection. Myrtle liked Lowell's account better. He said it was too old to steal.

Charles and Myrtle Fillmore had a life of adventure, love, personal growth, and satisfaction in doing the work God wanted them to undertake. They were married for fifty years. Among the happiest of these were the last five or six years when, despite their equally busy schedules, they were able to spend a great deal of time together at the Arches, their little home at Unity farm.

Perhaps the greatest tribute any woman could give a man were the five words Myrtle so often used to describe her husband, *"He is a great light."*

Charles and Myrtle Fillmore had three sons, but the daughter that she wanted never arrived. Instead she got three daughters-in-law of whom she said: "They all suited my sons perfectly, and that's the most important thing. They have treated me with every consideration." Myrtle recognized that good was at work, despite her disappointment at not having a daughter. "I have felt that had one of my children been born a girl, I should have had the joy of more of her companionship, but it isn't

The Fillmore Family (left to right): Lowell, Myrtle, Rick, Charles, Mary (Grandmother), and Royal (circa 1917)

Left to right: Lowell, Royal, Rick

always so. Many of our girls go away to make their homes so very young, and their busy lives absorb them. So perhaps we are blessed with having boys."

Lowell Page Fillmore was born in 1882 and spent virtually his entire life as a Unity worker, his duties ranging from errand boy to president. He was doing chores about the office for his parents before he was ten years old, eventually succeeded to manager, and then became president in 1948 upon his father's death. He didn't attend college after high school, but continued his education as his mother described it, "after work hours and in the doing of the work itself." Lowell was a steadying influence on everyone he knew, and he helped carry out the dreams of his mother and father. He was quite close to both of his parents, but especially so to his mother. The two of them would sit down, talk things over, and then go into the silence together. After one such session, Mrs. Fillmore told a friend: "The old, unhappy frame of mind let loose and passed away. Lowell helped me feel more like my Christ self again."

Many people asked Myrtle about her children and especially about Lowell, because he was so visible and active in the Unity movement. She replied on one occasion: "Lowell has always been ready to make the best of conditions. He spends some of his time in quiet, getting his ideas, and deciding just what he would do; then he works out the plans with all the confidence in the world—knowing the Father is backing him, and that there are those who will be willing to encourage and aid, where that is necessary, and that he can handle whatever is his to do."

On the occasion of his birthday anniversary on January 4, 1931, he received a gift and this note from his parents: "We want you to realize what a joy and blessing you have been to us all these years you have spent with us

Lowell Fillmore

in our close relationship as son. You came to us in the guise of a new babe—a gift from the hand of the infinite Father. We welcomed you gladly, for we felt dimly what we now fully realize. You are a great soul in the making given into our charge for a season for care and guidance in your unfoldment on this experimental plane we call living. You have been through it all with us, and we have never had reason to regret."

On February 14, 1926, Lowell married Miss Alice Lee, a good and efficient Unity worker. Myrtle, telling a relative about the wedding, wrote, "I trust she will appreciate the high ideals Lowell stands for." And she did. Alice, who survives Lowell, spent nearly fifty years at his side in the Unity work. Two years after their marriage, work was

Alice Fillmore

started at Unity Village on a lovely home for them. It included a large garden because Lowell was a master with plants and flowers.

In 1909 Lowell was responsible for the beginning of *Weekly Unity,* a publication which he edited until its merger with UNITY in the early 1970s. A few months after its inception, he initiated a column entitled, "Things to Be Remembered." That first column included the words: "Remember to smile. Remember to say a good word. Remember to remember only the good." The three suggestions Lowell made for others were literally three facts about himself. He always remembered the good as he carried out the spiritual plans he and his parents had envisioned.

Charles' and Myrtle's second son Waldo Rickert,
known to everyone as Rick, was born in 1884 and also took
an active part in the Unity development while still a child.
He had great artistic talent; his drawings graced the covers
of *Wee Wisdom* many times and accompanied articles in
other publications. Lowell directed virtually all his attention
to Unity, but Rick had other interests too. He loved to
tinker with gadgets, and sometimes the results were
surprisingly innovative inventions. In 1913, for example, he
so startled his mother that she wrote to her sister:

"Rick is turning out some inventions that are very
practical and promising. He is working on a folding bed
now. It seems like a fairy tale that a bed can hide itself and
furnish a room, and I could not get it straightened out in my
mind till I saw it there demonstrated. People who are building
flats and apartments are wild over it. It should bring in a
royal income. His brain seems to be teeming with all kinds
of new ideas, and he has about him those who are able to
carry them right into practice."

Rick was a student at the Art Institute of Chicago from
1906 to 1909 and traveled and studied abroad in 1910 and
1911. He worked as an artist and interior decorator from
1912 to 1915; served as a corporal in the tank corps in
World War I, and in 1923 became secretary of Unity
School, a position he retained forty-one years until his
death. He served the community of Kansas City in many
ways, including as general chairman of United Charities in
1932. He was a member of the Kansas City Art
Commission and president of the Kansas City Art Institute.
He served a term as president of the Kansas City Rotary
Club and later became district governor and traveled
extensively in this position. In 1928 he was the host
chairman for the Republican national convention, held in
Kansas City.

Myrtle was very proud of Rick and after he was appointed by the Kansas City mayor to head a committee to work out a ten-year improvement plan for the city, she wrote: "It was a wonderful thing for all these good people to rejoice with Kansas City in the outlook for property and improvement. Rick was given a big place in dividing and arranging, and we at Unity recognized that back of it all the dear Father was working out prosperity and good for all concerned."

When the first purchase of land for Unity Village was made, Rick's attention turned more to Unity affairs. He had studied architecture both in the United States and abroad, and he set out personally to design and construct every building erected at the farm. Even buildings constructed after his death bear his mark.

Myrtle saw the greatness in her son early, and on the occasion of his twenty-first birthday, she wrote to him:

"Sir W. Rickert Fillmore: When you came into the Fillmore family 21 years ago, from the point of observation you were 'small potatoes and few in a hill.' You were reticent as to your past and brought neither name nor wardrobe with you. The family bestowed upon you the above name, but finding it unwieldly for daily use have handled you by the name of Rick.

"The wardrobe has been a matter of ever serious consideration in as much as it has involved change and expense from the period of swaddling clothes to the time of swallow-tail coats. So today, as you mount the years of your majority, 'count yourself big potatoes and plenty to the hill.' With our blessings and congratulations, we enclose you *more* wardrobe. Your ma and pa Fillmore."

Rick, like his father, had the kind of humor that endeared him to many. In 1925 he boasted that he would be the first in the area to get an airmail letter. The next day at

Charles R., Harriet, Rosemary, and W. Rickert Fillmore

the farm a letter came floating down from a small airplane. It was addressed to Rick, much to the amazement of everyone. Realizing the joke that Rick had played upon them, one of the women workers gave Rick an exaggerated dirty look. "It's no use," he told her. "I've always had one."

Rick was married on September 5, 1919, to Harriet Collins, who passed on in 1939. Two children resulted from the union: Charles R., current president of Unity, and Rosemary Fillmore Rhea, now co-director with her husband Ralph of Unity's Radio and Television Department.

Charles and Myrtle Fillmore delighted in their two adult sons, Lowell and Rick, both of whom made wonderful contributions to Unity. But there was a third son of whom little is known because of his early death. John Royal Fillmore was born on July 16, 1889, and he died on September 9, 1923. The only monument to this son, known as Royal, is the love of everyone who knew him and the love he had for life and every living thing. Mrs. Fillmore was completely unabashed in her affection for Royal, and his death was a severe challenge for her.

Royal worked closely with his mother in the early days of *Wee Wisdom* and was its managing editor for a short time. Royal, who weighed three hundred pounds as an adult, was known for his good nature. A teacher said of him: "I never knew him to have the blues. He was happy in everything he undertook."

Royal carried this cheerful quality into manhood as he grew into a person of great vision and varied interests. A friend said of him, "I never knew a man in all my life who had so much practical knowledge about any subject that you could bring up as had Royal Fillmore." Yet, following in the steps of his parents, the teachings of Jesus Christ as interpreted by Unity became his primary interest. He felt that through his efforts in *Wee Wisdom,* he could help instill the same love that he had for Jesus Christ in the hearts and minds of little children.

Royal left home upon graduation from high school to attend the University of Missouri at Columbia. There he was associate editor of the yearbook and a member of the varsity football team. Because of his huge build, it was necessary to order a special uniform for him. He and his mother corresponded often in those college days, and most of the letters heading toward Kansas City contained a typical college student request: send money. He wasn't always blunt about it, however. He would sweeten his mother with a remark such as: "Have a convert to Unity. Send lessons. Need $40, by Monday." He delighted in creating amusing salutations for his letters, such as: "Doctor Charlie," "The Philmors," and "Dear Mawdad and Co." Some letters were telegraph-brief: "Shall arrive Thursday. Kill the fatted calf. I mean go ape."

Mrs. Fillmore indulged her youngest son and sent him money in practically every letter directed to Columbia, usually reminding him, "You are no cheap boy." She never missed an opportunity in one of her letters to direct Truth to him. In reply to a letter in which he informed her that he was having difficulty with an instructor, she wrote: *"I am fearless and free!* Take this affirmation into the classroom and you will stand before your Goliath the way David did." Later, when he told her that the situation with the instructor was beginning to improve, she wrote: "Rejoice in your Greek study and love your instructor until he loves you, for love never fails."

After college Royal returned to Kansas City where he quickly became a major contributor to the success of Unity School. He traveled on behalf of *Wee Wisdom* and the school to various parts of the United States and Canada.

On one of these visits, to Merchantville, New Jersey, Royal met the girl of his dreams, Frances Sleater. They corresponded, he visited her in the east when he could and on one occasion the Sleaters visited in Kansas City. After Royal served as a lieutenant in the infantry during World War I, the young couple became engaged, and in 1920 they were married.

Just before the wedding on November 27, 1920, Royal wrote to his parents: "I never knew what a wonderful thing love was before. Fran and I are so happy. I wish you could all be here for the wedding. My heart will be with you all." After the wedding he wrote again: "In this moment of supreme happiness I must sit down and write you a line of thanksgiving. My heart is overflowing with joy and song, for God has given me the most wonderful spiritual companion that man ever had—excepting you and father. We felt you with us at the wedding. It seems that we have been married for years and our souls understand each other perfectly. I will bring home with me one who will be a positive factor in the Unity work—my life partner and wife—your daughter, Frances."

Frances wrote to Myrtle, too, saying: "My dear mother in Christ: I am just a child and make many mistakes, but am so thankful God has given me two of the most wonderful mothers and fathers in all the world to guide me, and a dream lover, which my mother in Christ gave to this world. I have prayed to God to give me all the knowledge I need to help Royal with his work for God. I have always loved Unity."

When Royal and Frances arrived in Kansas City after their honeymoon, they were greeted by boisterous and happy friends at the railroad station. Royal was captured when he stepped off the train, placed inside a makeshift lion's cage, and then hauled through the business district,

Royal Fillmore

followed by a parade of automobiles with horns blaring. Frances didn't know what to make of the scene and suddenly found herself husbandless. Soon the couple was reunited and at a gathering of all the Unity workers, Frances and Royal spoke a few words. One observer said of Frances, "She made us her friends, for keeps."

On the occasion of their first Christmas together, in 1920, he wrote in *Wee Wisdom;* "I had the most wonderful Christmas present this year that any boy ever had. Guess what it was. No, not a doll, or a new automobile, or a steam engine, or a horse. None of these things. Santa was better than this to me. You have heard me speak of the Boosters of Merchantville. Well, the chief booster Frances Sleater has come to Kansas City as my wife, and from now on Fran,

Frances Sleater Fillmore

as I want you all to know her, will be one with us in our work for good."

Royal and Frances had only a few precious and happy months together, for she soon became pregnant and shortly after their baby daughter entered the world she departed from it. Royal was grief-stricken and was forced to make difficult adjustments in his life-style without the one great love of his life beside him.

In the March 1921 edition of *Wee Wisdom,* Fran ironically had written about death, "Remember little Boosters, there is never anything really dead, but what seems so lives and will rise again to express God's love in some manner when the breath of love touches it."

Royal and Fran worked at the downtown Unity

headquarters, but they found time for many happy outings to Unity Farm as well. Occasionally they would stay overnight there in a tent, before structures were erected. They would describe their happy sessions at the farm for their *Wee Wisdom* friends. Each morning they would be awakened by an oriole or some other song bird, and then they would dress and walk to a nearby stream where they would sit by a little waterfall to listen and watch nature in its daily awakening. They both dreamed of being children again—Fran with dolls and her hair braided and Royal in knickers, romping and playing.

Fran was not strong, and she had a very difficult pregnancy. Nevertheless, her death a few weeks after a daughter was born came as a shock to Royal and the two families. The child, Myrtle Innocencia, named after the two grandmothers of the infant, was born on October 1, 1921. After the death of the mother, the child's name was changed to Frances in honor of the departed one. Little Frances was the first girl born to a member of the Fillmore family in more than a century. Myrtle took over primary care for Frances after her mother's passing, with Royal doing all he could as the only surviving parent. Grandma Fillmore later took more responsibility in raising the child because she had a maid and a cook to assist her and to help care for the young one. Eventually little Frances found a permanent home with Lowell and Alice Fillmore.

On November 9, 1921, only a short time before her death, Frances wrote a note (actually it was dictated because she was too weak to write) to Royal. The message revealed deep spiritual insight. It read:

"The same spirit that is in me is in the new baby.

"The mother soul is now in the full knowledge and understanding of all the conditions and wants to go on.

"Do not hold me because I can contact you and be

with you and baby from a much higher plane than you have yet contacted. The reward of sacrifice is greater than the desire of the human soul. Rise up and join with me in rejoicing that the battle is won. I am with thee and thou with me in Spirit, forever."

Royal could not recover from the loss of his new bride, the mother of his daughter. In addition to his grief, diabetes and high blood pressure caused him constant pain and eroded his strength. His excessive weight became a major problem, and his legs weakened. He became disinterested in caring for himself, and physical deterioration set in.

In September 1923, Royal finally agreed to be admitted to a hospital in Battle Creek, Michigan, specializing in body-building through proper diet and medication. A few days after his entry he wrote to his parents, "We shall all be together soon, and 'sweet' shall have a real, live daddy." He added that he needed treatment for courage, love, and joy. He died two days later, on September 9.

Royal's unexpected death was a tremendous shock to the Fillmores, their friends, and all the Unity workers. Royal, always bigger than life itself, was suddenly gone. He had been his mother's youngest, and, in many ways, favorite son. In the days immediately following his death, Myrtle went through the motions of living, but found her loss almost unbearably heavy. From deep within her, however, came the strength and the faith that were necessary for her to overcome this, the most serious crisis of her life. Eight days after Royal's passing, she poured her heart out in a letter to her sister Jane Munsell who lived in Nebraska:

"I've been a long time getting at telling you of this experience that is going deeper into my mother heart than

*anything I have yet had to meet. I suppose you already
have gotten news of it.*

*"The going of our glorious Royal boy. It was very
sudden at the last. He just went to sleep in his chair. The
dear boy has not been himself since Frances left the
manifest. He went about his business and did everything
required of him, but you could feel the gradual withdrawing
of himself from the outward interests. The spirit within him
seemed to be leaving his body temple for interests
elsewhere.*

*"At last we thought that if he went to Battle Creek
they'd compel him to quiet and with proper diet he'd come
out all right. He refused, they said, their medical treatment
and counsel. He was there just one week and then he went
to sleep.*

*"Blessed boy, he wrote me just a day or two earlier
that he'd be home in a few days. He was, but oh! Not as we
had hoped.*

*"Everybody loved him. The city must have given up all
its flowers. Loving friends crowded the chapel and
hundreds drove away that could not even find room
outside.*

*"I can't say more tonight. My heart is too full. But God
loves and blesses us all.*

*"I'm sure Royal is not idle, wherever he is. I am a
grateful mother. All my sons are treasures. Dear Royal is
still among them."*

A few months before her own passing in 1931, Myrtle
spoke of the memories of Frances and Royal and said:
"Why, I could almost touch them. The veil between must
be pretty thin, for they seem a part of life."

The sadness that she felt at the physical passing of her
son and beautiful daughter-in-law never departed

completely and she would always miss them, but Myrtle did not dwell in sadness. Whenever anyone mentioned their "premature" deaths, she would say: "We must forget all the sorrow and know that everything is straightened out. We know we can but think wonderful things have taken place for them in the Father's plan. It was wonderful to have had these two glorious ones in the family, and now we have our dear little Fran as a child of promise."

After Myrtle's death, a lock of Royal's hair was found among her personal effects—saved since 1908. A note attached read: "Clipped off by his mother, November 25, 1908. The barber missed it." Next to the tuft of hair was a note, now faded by time, signed R.F. (for Royal Fillmore) and directed to his mother: "For information as to the activities of your sons in business, let me explain, so that in the future you will not introduce me as the *office boy*. Lowell is in charge of office management. Royal does the purchasing. Lowell's official title is treasurer. Royal's official title is secretary." It is quite likely that Mrs. Fillmore read and reread this note with amusement many times, smiled a bit, and perhaps brushed away a tear, then blessed his Royal ongoing.

Charles and Myrtle Fillmore had three grandchildren, the eldest being Charles Rickert, born to Harriet and Rick in 1921. Myrtle was often described by friends as seeming to walk on air, so lightly did she weave her way through life, but she credited Rick with the same ability at the time of the birth of little Charles. "Rick is aloft," she wrote after the birth, "amid clouds of celestial regions. Harriet and Rick are among the proudest parents around." Baby Frances was born later in 1921, and Rosemary, Harriet and Rick's second child, arrived in 1925. From 1921 until 1931 Myrtle rarely wrote a letter to friends or family members in which

Fran and Charles R. Fillmore

Rosemary Fillmore

there was not a report on the grandchildren. She dearly loved the youngsters.

In Frances and Rosemary, Myrtle had the girls she had always wanted, and she was always eager to share news of their activities with her other loved ones. Charles Rickert helped her relive the happy days of watching her own three sons grow to maturity. These comments are typical of her reports on the grandchildren:

"Wee Rosemary has never seemed a baby. She is poised and independent and speaks with such authority, though she is very fair and sweet in her wishes, that those about her must invariably take notice, and it seems we must see someone of greater stature instead of the dainty little miss.

"Frances and Charles Rickert are very interested in

music. They have the story of Mozart and are very impressed by this wonderful man. Charles Rickert was greatly moved, and *disturbed,* because he had not started on his musical career as young as Mozart began his.

"Frances insisted upon helping the maid with the serving and would not eat with the rest of us, preferring to play true to form and eat in the kitchen. After dinner, Wee Rosemary, just two, said she wanted to do the dishes. And she really did wipe them. Every little once in a while she would come skipping in with some of the silver, to put it away."

Many happy memories skipped through Myrtle's mind in those last few years of her life. She especially liked to tell friends about Rosemary's independent attitude. On one occasion, Rosemary was reading from "The Night Before Christmas." When she hedged a bit on a word, her father prompted her. She stopped the show and turned to him, saying, "I don't need any help and I don't want any." Perhaps Myrtle's favorite story was about the time the little girl thought she had found out what it took to go to school. Rosemary had decided if only she could look like her brother, she could go too. One morning she was found in Charles Rickert's room, casually dressing in his clothes. Asked what she was doing, she cooly replied, "Getting ready for school." She was two years old. Actually, Rosemary never seemed to like being a child. Mrs. Fillmore observed when the child was only six months old: "Rosemary looks as if she ought to walk and talk. Rick says she feels bored because she still has to be a baby."

Charles Rickert, according to his grandmother, "quite holds his own in his Papa Charley's affection. He pays strict attention in Sunday school and answers questions with alacrity. I think his answers are sometimes rather startling. I think he will be an artist. He uses his pencil cleverly."

He delighted her at the poolside while he was still a toddler, and she told and retold a story that he insisted on holding onto a life preserver while he was learning to swim. It was obvious that he would never learn to swim with that bulky thing in his way, so eventually his instructor insisted that it be left at poolside. Charles Rickert refused, she related with glee, "to go into the pool without his doughnut."

All three grandchildren were showered with gifts by family and friends, especially the orphaned Fran. One time Fran got a life-size doll, which amazed Mrs. Fillmore. "It is smiling and has two teeth. I love it *myself,*" she told a friend.

Frances was raised by Alice and Lowell, whom she called Aunt Alice and Uncle Odie, but she often spent nights with Myrtle in the little arched home on the farm. Myrtle called her the dearest little companion one could have. Mrs. Fillmore always gave Alice the credit, however, for raising the little girl. "With Alice she has more freedom, and can play as lively as she wishes. And Alice is so good to Frances, and is teaching her many of the nice things we like her to know."

Eight days before her passing, Myrtle had a visit from a traveling salesman who was selling encyclopedias for children. Her answer to his pitch was a definite "no." "Perhaps I shall buy them later," she told him, "but sometimes I feel that the children already know too much."

Charles and Myrtle Fillmore's grandchildren married and raised families of their own. Charles Rickert married Anne Jones in 1943, and they have two daughters, Harriet, born in 1944; and Constance, born in 1948. Harriet married Richard A. DeBauge in 1967, and they have two daughters, Sarah DeBauge, born in 1968; and Leslie DeBauge, born in 1970. Constance married John Strickland in 1976.

Rosemary married Stanley Grace in 1947, and their children are Stanley Rickert Grace, born in 1948; and Rosalind Fillmore Grace, born in 1950. Rosemary later married Ralph Rhea, who is now co-director with her of Unity's Radio and Television Department. Stanley Rickert (Rick) married Maya Brandenberger in 1970.

Frances married Robert Lakin in 1945, and they have three children, Robert Fillmore Lakin, born in 1946; Charles Edward Lakin, born in 1948; and Frances Elise Lakin, born in 1952. Frances Elise married David Lenzo in 1976, and Robert married Susan L. Huston in 1977.

Busy as she was, Myrtle always had time for her husband, her sons and their wives, and her grandchildren. She never forgot her Page heritage either, and she kept in touch with her brothers and sisters until their deaths. On one occasion she wrote:

"Though I don't see you often, there's a spot in me that reaches out and finds comfort in kinship. You see you folks are about the only 'blood kin' I have left. I mean Page kin! I like to hear where you are, and what you are doing, and how big the world is. It may seem I am shut up here in a little corner, and up to my eyes in work all the time, but I like to peek over and see what other folks are doing. And the harder they play, the more I enjoy watching them and hearing about their good times."

Perhaps Myrtle's closest family contact through the years was with her sister, Jane Munsell, who lived in Funk, Nebraska. The two exchanged letters frequently. Jane was quite proud of her sister and in the late 1920s stated that fact in a letter: "It doesn't seem long since I was proud of my little red-haired sister and thought there never was so smart a child as she was—and that she took it all from our mother." In the later years, when Jane was in her 90s, Myrtle frequently sent money and bought her many gifts.

"Tell me please, not only what you need, but what you would really love to have. I would just love to send something that would make you feel lovely and grand," Myrtle wrote. Jane was obsessed with the thought of dying and looked forward to going to heaven. Myrtle wrote to her:

"We are speaking truths for you, dear sister, but you are so set upon going to that place you have so long believed in (heaven) that I suppose you will have to go there when a move seems promising. Well, you know I love you and yours, and it is a tie that can never be severed whether you decide to continue your present address or not."

Now and then in correspondence with Jane, Myrtle mused over what might have been:

"I think you are a wonder considering you have been brought up in a world full of wrong ideas of God. If only you and I had been born with the right concept of what is meant to be a child of God, we would have developed our divine possibilities, and so made God manifest, even as the Christ man, who could lay his life down or take it up and through whom the Father-Mind could do the perfect works. But instead we were taught to believe that Jesus was the only son and we were at the mercy of ignorant and superstitious beliefs.

"Why could we not have understood the plain teachings of Jesus and instead of considering ourselves aliens, claimed our right to dwell in the bosom of the Father, even as He did?

"Had it not been hidden—and forbidden—that we should know God intimately, as Jesus did, we too might have been farther on our way Godward."

When Jane died, Myrtle wrote lovingly to a niece, Jane's daughter:

"My arms are about you and my heart is warm

against yours. I am glad that our dear mother and sister has escaped her carnal imprisonment. I think she is rejoicing in the freedom of a spirit that has earned its release. Dear blessed soul. I have no tears to shed—and yet there is an ache in my heart. I think it comes rather from the old idea of separation and loss than from the true knowledge that there can be no separation in Spirit. We know life cannot die. Life lives on and on. We are finding that the Livingness of Spirit can take up the outer manifestation or lay it down, as Jesus Christ taught— through the practice of Truth."

Myrtle also kept in close touch with another sister, Mrs. Henrietta (Hettie) Page Gaston. She was the mother of the famed crusader against the use of tobacco, Lucy Page Gaston. The Chicago Tribune called Henrietta the power behind the throne in Lucy's anti-smoking efforts. When Henrietta died at ninety-three in Evanston, Illinois, she received a considerable amount of publicity. She had been friend of Carrie Nation, Frances Willard, and many other reformers of the day. On the occasion of her ninety-third birthday she was interviewed by a reporter. She told him in response to his question about her health: "I don't feel anything different today than I did ninety-three years ago. I couldn't feel anything then, either. But I've felt many things since." When asked about her views of young women in the 1920s, she responded: "If the girls did right, the boys would have to. They're equally guilty for modern loose morality. The girls weren't angels in my day, let alone today. I'll admit that there are more temptations nowadays. The fashions! They are perfectly all right if only they'd put more cloth on them. There seems to be a scarcity of material."

Before she died Henrietta asked that her coffin be rented to save money, and when that couldn't be done, she demanded a wooden box. Later she decided on cremation. Money was a problem for Henrietta in her advanced years because her daughter Lucy preceded her in death. Myrtle paid for Henrietta's nursing home expenses and provided her with spending money, and was glad to do so. Also, she visited Henrietta in the Chicago area as often as she could.

Myrtle kept in close contact with her two brothers—Daniel in Joplin, Missouri, and David in Clinton, Missouri. She lived in the same city with David for a number of years, and visited Daniel in Joplin a few times. David was a merchant. Not much is known of Daniel except he deeply loved his sister, Myrtle, and occasionally he wrote to her and included poetry he had especially dedicated to her.

In answering the questions posed at the beginning of this chapter: "What kind of wife was Myrtle Fillmore? What kind of mother? And did she have sufficient time for her family?" one can conclude that yes, indeed, not only did she have time for the family, but she also had a deep and abiding love. And of course she was loved very much by everyone in the family too.

VIII

The Personal Side of Myrtle

Almost all of Myrtle Fillmore's life was spent in the public eye, but she had a personal side too. Even there, Spirit was in charge, for she had only one great vision—that of an ever-closer relationship to the Father. After her passing in 1931, her personal credo was found in her own handwriting, undated:

> **To enjoy without possession.**
> **To see without coveting.**
> **To have without holding.**
> **To be without seeming.**
> **In short, to be myself, without desiring. Knowing that all this is for me, for my pleasure and the satisfaction of my immortal soul. To say that "I am monarch of all I survey. My right here is none to dispute." To be generous-hearted. What I see, others may see. What I enjoy, others may share also on equal terms with me.**

In the early days of the Unity movement, when there were appearances of lack, Myrtle would write letters to God. Each day she placed the needs of the Movement before God, and then she sat back in her positive, prayerful way to watch for results. She found it helpful to Unity, and the results were soul-inspiring to her. She expected great demonstrations, and then accepted them with a gracious heart. Of the letters, she said:

"Some of the letters I addressed to God and some to Christ Jesus. I wrote just as one would to a kind, loving, and generous parent . . . a parent whose delight it is to provide every rich and beautiful blessing for a much-loved child. Of course, I did not mail these letters, but put them in a drawer, and about once a week I would take them out and read them over, and bless God for His goodness and wondrous love."

Although most of these letters have been lost, a few have been saved. They tell more than many chapters could about the deep spiritual commitment that Myrtle had to God, to Jesus Christ, and to Truth. The following one was written in January 1913:

To Him my soul adores:
Holy One, I would do Thy will—I would give all that I am, all that I am capable of being into Thy keeping. I would think Thy thoughts after Thee. I would give my life in making manifest Thy will in all my words and works. I would be dependent on Thee alone for my inspiration and incentive. I would know or acknowledge no other source. Thou in me and I in Thee and they in us made perfect in one. Thou has sent me into the world. Thou only can direct and vitalize my effort. Help me realize this momently. There are none beside Thee.

Later in the same month she wrote another letter which she addressed to "The Lord of My Being." It reads:

Dear Lord of my Being, alone with Thee I am asking, What am I? Who am I? Where am I? In answer there comes from within, "I am not what I seem." Flesh and blood do not reveal me to myself. Back of personal estimate comes the consciousness that some way I am inseparately joined with Thee, and until my union is acknowledged and consumated through divine cooperation of Spirit, soul, and body, I am not content nor at-one with Thee in consciousness. "I am that I am." I am Thy all possibility. Where I am in reality is in Thy bosom. Where I am in the world of effects depends upon what I think I am.

Lord of my Being, I would be unentangled from the servitude and vicissitudes of the formed world. I would do all Thou wouldst have me to do. I would be "in the world but not of it." I would dwell in the gloriousness of Thy omnipresent companionship. I would always be still enough to hear Thy voice instead of the confusion and clamor of the senses. I would know and not assume. I would truly live and not exist. Give me, dear Lord, Thy conscious support and let me be filled with the love and zeal that give character and direction to the activities of mind and body. "I am in Thee and Thou in me and they in us, made perfect in One."

A third letter that she wrote to herself was dated April 16, 1916, and addressed to "The Ruling Lord of My Inner Being":

To the Lord of my manifestation: I heartily desire to purge myself of personality—I would know no man after the flesh, only Jesus Christ, and Him crucified. I would stand, so conscious of my oneness with Thee, that personal affection would have no power to move me. I would be so immersed in Thy love I could not feel the neglect—nor the withdrawal of human affections. I would be so far-seeing and wise that nothing on the plane of personal affection could make me unhappy or divert me from the consciousness of the Love that never faileth.

I would not be swerved by personality.

I would be so unified with the knowledge of my wisdom and strength and ability in Thee that I could always speak the Word with power, clearness and conviction.

I would know no authority, lean on nobody's thought or opinion.

I would stand fast in the knowledge that I am Thy thought going forth into unhindered expression.

Dear blessed Lord, strengthen me, in this blessed purpose and deliver me always from the adverse and personal sense of existence—I in Thee, blessed One, and Thou in me made perfect in harmonious Mind. Hold me to the knowledge that by divine inheritance I am beyond the influence of personal and external conditions—and that I do always recognize my inherent powers and assert my divinity in Christ. Witness this Spirit of Truth.

Myrtle's personal credo and these three letters clearly demonstrate her serious, thoughtful side, but she also had a light, fun-loving point of view. Perhaps the best insights into this attitude can be found in a booklet entitled "Confidences." The booklet is dated 1915 and apparently was used much in the same way autograph books are used today. Its owner carried it about Unity headquarters asking each worker to answer the questions posed on a variety of subjects. Here's how Mrs. Fillmore, in her own handwriting, responded:

My one extravagance—Movies.
My pet economy—Saving my breath.

My unacknowledged fear—Profitless conversation.
My "bete noire"—Copy for the printers.
My unconfessed weakness—Cookies.
My secret sorrow—A lazy pen.
My motto—Keep everlasting as is.
My favorite dish—A dinner of herbs where love is.
My favorite beverage—Adam's ale.
My unlucky day—One of fruitless effort.
My favorite superstition—A man is known by the thoughts he keeps.
My mascot—Omnipotent courage.

Not to be outdone by Mrs. Fillmore's honest answers, Charles also responded:

My one extravagance—Five-cent dishes at Unity Inn.

My pet economy—No Christmas presents, coming or going.

My unacknowledged fear—Meeting strangers.

My "bete noire"—People who talk poverty.

My unconfessed weakness—If I had one, I'd tell it on the housetops.

My secret sorrow—None, glad and happy always.

My motto—Everything is lovely and the goose honks high.

My favorite dish—Bean soup.

My favorite beverage—Missouri River water (filtered).

My unlucky day—None. All days look lucky to me.

My favorite superstition—That the star of my destiny is always rising.

My mascot—True words, rightly spoken.

Myrtle referred to herself throughout her ministry as an executive for God, and she ever sought to realize and manifest more of the perfection that an executive for God ought to demonstrate. People responded to her differently than they did to her husband or any other family member or Unity Worker. She was loved with an intensity that defies explanation, except in purely spiritual terms. This letter to her is an example from hundreds that are similar:

"My precious Mrs. Fillmore: You are precious, and you are mine. When I know enough to sell all I have and buy the pearl of great price, like the man of whom Jesus spoke, I shall include what you are in that purchase. Your consciousness, which radiates to touch all who will permit it, is like the warm pink glow of the priceless pearl, for the real of you which so many of us know, is such a beautiful and vigorous blend of life and love and substance. I'd better stop, though. I know you don't like to read of too much praise . . . "

The writer was correct. Myrtle did not like this kind of adoration. To praise her to her face was virtually impossible, so many persons who wished to tell her exactly what they thought of her were forced to do so in writing. Once at a public Unity session, a man rose to extol Myrtle's virtues for her good work, and she retorted quickly: *"It is not me. I had nothing to do with it. It is not the Fillmores. It is the Christ. All praise to Him. We are simply the channels."*

In addition to praising Myrtle, people sometimes felt a bit of envy toward her. Once, when a woman wrote to tell her of her own unfortunate position compared to Mrs.

Fillmore's station in life, Myrtle responded:

"I think I shall tell you that I, too, love beautiful things and that I appreciate the talents of others. But there were years when I did not have anything of beauty or loveliness around me—that is, nothing which the senses reported to be particularly desirable. There were times when I was obliged to do much more of the housework than I really felt physically able to do in comfort. There were times when I was obliged to wear clothes which others did not care for. Times when I did not have a dollar, with which to do the things I should have liked—not even to meet the expenses of the family. But do you think I worried over such things, or allowed them to hinder my healing, or my work, which I felt God was giving me to do? I was so full of knowing that God was my life, and that I didn't need to die, and of realizing that I could help others to feel and know the presence of God as their health and their supply, that I was kept busy expressing my new thoughts and blessing those who came my way."

Myrtle revealed much about herself in her correspondence with the thousands of people who wrote to her personally. She often compared herself with those who wrote to her. She might say, "I am working on that, too," or, "I know how you feel, because I have faced a similar challenge." Some persons compared her to an angel, but she would reply: "I am progressing, but I have much weeding to do in my own life. I am giving my own garden much attention now."

Letter writers referred to her as the Mother of Unity or, more personally, as "Mama Myrtle." They told her that she had the most wonderful smile of anyone they had ever known. "You are like a love-fairy," one writer said. "You showed us in your beautiful, impersonal way how lovely it is to be loving. I count it one of the greatest privileges I have ever experienced just to have been around you."

The love that so many had for Myrtle Fillmore was manifested in hundreds of gifts over the years. At first, she kept the gifts for herself and her own enjoyment, but eventually she changed her mind, explaining thus:

"I receive many beautiful gifts and treasure them in remembrances associated with them as well as their worth, and I used to keep all of these gifts—until it dawned upon me that I was making an idol of them. Now, an idol is something that has no life, no spirit, in it. And I thought, 'If I put things away that I can see no present use for, thus taking them out of the circulation of good, am I not making an idol of them?' "

On one occasion, after receiving an expensive and very ornate gift, she was criticized by the donor after it was discovered that she had given it away. She wrote to the friend who had sent the gift, *"Know this, dear, that I must be beautiful within, and in my fellowship with others, and in my sharing with them the good things of life, if I am to be beautiful without."* She added that selfishness cannot be a part of beauty and that by passing along the good that had been demonstrated, she expected to get more good things. *"Anything which awakens in me the loving desire to have others happy and adorned with beautiful things, and anything which helps me to express this loving desire in my own living, is sure to bring forth fruits in my life,"* she explained.

Just as she received many gifts, Myrtle also was asked by hundreds of people *for* gifts, usually of money, but occasionally for particular objects. Occasionally after receiving a particularly heartwarming letter from someone who appeared to be in desperate need, she would tuck "a bit of green" into an envelope and speed it on its way to the needy one. She rarely responded to direct requests for money, however. If someone asked for money, she reasoned that they were not recognizing their true Source. She would write them words of love and comfort and tell them not to look to her for a financial solution to problems, but to the Father. She might say:

"You see, it is this way. I receive a pay envelope just as all the rest of the workers at Unity do, and this money is to use for my personal expenses. I am not free to use Unity School's money that was given to the school by friends interested in forwarding the Unity work. It seems right now there are many, many places to use my regular salary and what I could spare has been used to put bread in hungry mouths to keep soul and body together. But with God as your unfailing, ever-present Resource, you are bound to receive the necessary funds that you need."

Much the same reasoning prevailed at Christmastime when hundreds of people sent gifts to Myrtle, many expecting a return gift and others simply writing to ask for help. "I know so many folks, and love them all," she would say, "and wouldn't want to leave anyone out—and at my usual speed it would take a year to go around."

Perhaps one of the most frequently received requests was for a photograph of Myrtle Fillmore. Literally hundreds of people wrote of their desire "to see what you look like." Both Mr. and Mrs. Fillmore tried to resist pressures for photographs and always stressed that it was not what they looked like that was important, but the work they did and the Truth they taught. In the late 1920s, however, Mrs. Fillmore had a change of heart. While she was at her ease on the porch of the Arches, a photographer took a picture of her. The result so pleased her that she had reproductions made and sent to her friends and to the hundreds of persons who had asked for a photograph. She explained to one of them:

"I have never been satisfied with what the camera gets when aimed in my direction. But on that one occasion, the beauty all about me on that little porch sort of enfolded me and included me! Many have asked for a picture, and now they shall have it!"

To one of her dear friends, she included this message with a picture:

"I want to come in and have a daily visit with you. I'm bringing my own "setting" with me, and I'll invite you to draw up the chair which is at my right. Now, let's just spend an hour here together in the sunshine and quiet of my little house in the apple orchard. Let's forget all that has pressed itself in upon us to make us sometimes feel that God the Good isn't all in all. Here in the silence, we shall know the presence of God, and see clearly just how we are to go about it, to live the life He is giving and how to bring forth the order and beauty and freedom and plenty which He has planned and which is but awaiting our understanding use. But let's don't get too far into the metaphysics of this wonderful thing—we're here together on the porch, just to rest quietly and happily in reality. Doing this, a transformation will be worked in us and for us. We'll reap the good fruits of all our years of study and affirmation and meditation. Words of Truth are living things, powerful, and working surely to bless those who think and speak them, just as fast as the way is cleared for manifestations. As we still our clamoring, the miracles of divine law are wrought."

The pictures Myrtle mailed to friends and correspondents gave them an idea of what she looked like,

but many still wanted to visit with her personally. Hundreds, even thousands made pilgrimages to Unity headquarters and Unity Farm, hoping to catch a glimpse of one or both of Unity's founders. Many of them had their hearts set upon spending a few minutes with Myrtle at her desk at Unity or on her porch at the Arches. Some who had the opportunity to do so never forgot it. Long after Myrtle's death, a 1928 visitor to Unity Farm described her as she appeared when she was eighty-three: "I was struck by the heavenly light in her eyes. They were young, clear, bright eyes and the light of God shone right through them."

In the early days of Unity, Myrtle paid little attention to her dress, other than to be neat, clean, and comfortable. Later, however, when she and Charles became public figures, she became more clothes-conscious. This was always true at Easter, and especially so in the late 1920s. In 1929, for example, she spent a great deal of time choosing just the right costume for Easter. "I know it is frivolous," she said, "and not at all practical, as compared with the creations I once thought quite the thing! But now I consider soft, silky things very commonsense."

Myrtle wore her last Easter outfit in 1931. She described the costume as suggestive of spring—a green and blue spray on a background of white, with a white satin flower woven into the cloth.

In the early 1920s, hair style became a matter of controversy when the "bob" began to grow in popularity. Charles Fillmore wanted Myrtle to get the new cut, but she refused. Instead, she stood by and watched as Charles encouraged Unity workers to "bob" their hair. By 1925, more than one-half of all women workers at Unity had taken the plunge, but Myrtle held out. Finally, in 1928, she too showed up at the office with her beautiful platinum hair in a bob.

After the deed was done, she wrote to a friend about "news that will make your jaw drop." She explained that it was not the pressure from Charles that had brought about the decision—although indeed he had urged her for years to do it—but instead it was for the health of her hair. She had discovered that she was losing some hair, so she told the beautician to shorten it. To her surprise, the hairdresser bobbed her! The editor of Unity News, an employee publication, was astounded, and wrote: "Will wonders never cease? Mrs. Fillmore has had her hair bobbed. She looks just like a beautiful young girl whose hair has turned white. That is just what she is, too."

Mother's Day for Myrtle Fillmore wasn't just a day of family gathering. Letters and cards for her poured in by the hundreds. Each year on the special day she would sit silently beside the many cards and letters addressed to her and radiate blessings both to those who had so honored her, and also to all mothers, especially those not remembered by their loved ones. She knew she was blessed among women to have so many loving expressions directed toward her not only on Mother's Day, but all through the year. "The Father has blessed me," she said, "in giving me the privilege of mothering my own fine boys, and of standing in the position so lovingly bestowed upon me by Unity friends."

Myrtle knew how much she was loved, because she knew her own capacity to love. But even a person such as she was had critics. Testimony that there was at least one such person was found among Myrtle's personal effects after her death. She may have read and reread the simple note many times, and one can imagine her smiling as she did so. The note read: "Wednesday evening your preliminary talk was very lengthy. Four rows back we could not hear all that you said and two men in front of us went to sleep. And one of them snored. While your husband, in back of you, also went to sleep!" It was dated December 17, 1926, and signed, "Your Friend."

But for every friend such as this one, there were thousands who wrote lovingly about Myrtle. For example, after receiving a letter from her, one worker wrote:

"How I wish that I might find a word that would tell you what I find written between the lines. I found it long before I ever came here. I found it in the book, *Wee Wisdom's Way,* and I felt it there. I saw it in the light of your countenance when I came here. I heard it in the love of your voice at the first noon silence I attended. There is only one word that means what I see, feel, and hear, and that is God. But there is another word, almost as precious to me, that brings God right into every part of my existence and blesses me and all mankind impartially with the light of Truth, and that word is *Unity.* Do you know how much I love Unity? You represent Unity to me. I wish that if we ever find ourselves at the farm it would be under that one word, *UNITY.* It doesn't need anything added. It stands for the Kingdom of God. Nothing can be taken from it. It is perfect in its simplicity."

Myrtle Fillmore committed herself to the Unity work, but she never put Unity above Truth or God. When someone told her that he couldn't get along without Unity, or her friendship, or anything else, she would remind him that he was limiting God. She emphasized that as long as anyone placed faith and trust in any outside source, including Unity or the Fillmores, growth would not take place as he would desire it. *"You would do beautifully without Unity,"* she would say, *"if you had never heard of us, but had awakened to the realization of the omnipresence of God."*

If any one attribute of Myrtle stands out more than the others, it is probably her generosity. She was filled with the spirit of giving which manifested itself as lavish gifts of her love, her material things, and her time. She demonstrated, a friend said of her after her passing, "the fulfillment of the Father's every promise."

Mrs. Fillmore herself put it this way:

"I really feel as if all that is worthwhile in life is serving one another and helping one another out of the pitfalls that strew the sense road, into the highway of spiritual knowledge. We only live as we advance and lend a helping hand to others."

In the early days of Unity, in 1897, she wrote what she called "My Faith." It was her personal statement of faith and love for God and her fellow man:

My Faith

I do not believe in evil. I believe in good.
I do not believe in sin. I believe in Truth.
I do not believe in want. I believe in
     Abundance.
I do not believe in death. I believe in
     Life.
I do not believe in ignorance. I believe in
     Intelligence.
There are no discords in my being. Being
     is peace.
My faith, understanding, and love are
     becoming one.
"What God has joined together let no man
     put asunder."

IX

She Traveled with the Truth

On a warm March day in 1928, Myrtle Fillmore stood in the garden outside her fairy home, the Arches, and watched as an airplane circled over Unity Village. She waved as the aircraft spiraled ever lower, and she shouted a friendly greeting to its occupants. Later, in describing the incident to a friend, she wrote:

"My, how I wished that I, too, were up there, sailing through the air, and seeing the beautiful earth from that angle. I felt that in Spirit I was living up there in the fresh air and sunshine and that I'd like to bless my body with the actual experience of being lifted up out of the fixed ways of doing things."

This remarkable woman, only a few months away from her eighty-second birthday anniversary, had turned her eyes upward and was yearning to take up wings and fly! And why not? In the 1860s she had traveled by wagon from her native Ohio through Indiana and Illinois along primitive pathways to Missouri; she had withstood the rigors of stagecoach and railroad coach rides into Texas, through Kansas and the Indian Territory (now Oklahoma), and later into Colorado; she had gone over the Rocky Mountains in a sleigh; and she had traveled by motor car, railroad, and even by water to many major midwest, eastern, and Canadian cities. Indeed, why shouldn't this progressive and innovative woman now consider transportation through the skies?

In May of 1928, Ernest C. Wilson, a Unity lecturer and author, astounded Mrs. Fillmore and everyone else in the Unity community. He had been in Los Angeles, and he needed to get to Missouri in a hurry. So, he simply boarded an airplane and in less than a day's time was in Kansas City. "Just think of that," Mrs. Fillmore mused.

If Ernest Wilson's feat wasn't enough to convince Mrs. Fillmore that flying was to be the latest vogue in transportation, something took place in October of 1928 that surely did. She told of the dramatic event in a letter:

"Yesterday, about six o'clock, the giant dirigible of this country sailed majestically over our heads and circled over Kansas City, signalling with lights. It looked as though we might almost throw a rock and touch it, but it was supposed to be a quarter-mile away. It is a city block in length, and has accommodations like a double apartment—several rooms. Its coming was so quiet and not much announcement had been made, so that many folks missed it. But it was quite a sight to all those who stood about, watching it. Someday perhaps we shall all be traveling about, over land and sea, in such great bird-like ships—only this one looks more like a great fat fish."

Flying was to be a subject of intense interest during the last three years of Mrs. Fillmore's life. She mentioned it often, both in personal conversations and in her letters. As an example, in answer to a request that she and Charles visit California, she wrote:

"Your description of your garden makes me want to see California, and especially some spots out there, more than I have wanted it before. But as yet, I haven't succeeded in getting Charles to consider a trip. It does seem as though I might go without him, doesn't it? Queer how we get so tied together that we refuse to do things as individuals—even though we are quite free to assert our individual opinions.

"Perhaps when airplanes are more numerous and making less expensive trips, we'll be able to flit out there for ocean bathing and to enjoy the fruits and flowers. I would like to be free sometimes to satisfy that in me which loves the ocean, lofty mountains—big, broad outlooks, so that my soul could feast itself upon the beauties of the manifest, as well as upon the inner Spirit."

Mrs. Fillmore talked of the possibility of flying to Cuba and she wondered how different from the United States that island nation would be; she glowingly described Arizona as a state "coming into its own," and she praised its climate and pure air as she talked of a visit there someday; she hinted to friends that she might just fly to Minneapolis and visit loyal Unity students and friends there who had so often asked her presence in their city; she often expressed an urge to visit such faraway places as Russia, Japan, and Germany, adding, "No doubt we'd be agreeably surprised with such countries were we to visit there." Of all her travel fantasies, however, especially in terms of a flying trip, California ranked first. And it happened that just such an urge forced her to make a decision: to fly or not to fly?

A friend in California persistently urged Mrs. Fillmore to visit her. In reply to each letter, Mrs. Fillmore deferred such a trip, but in one missive she added a postscript: "When you think of me, send an aeroplane along and I will come right over—I surely would love to be with you, and to live in sunny California, too. We could have lovely times together!"

The California friend responded by writing to Silent Unity, requesting prayers for funds to transport the Fillmores to California. When Mrs. Fillmore learned of the prayer request, she said, "It looks as if I might be obliged to pack my overnight bag and hop off, or withdraw my wish!"

The latter proved to be the case, because within a short time sufficient money was raised for an airplane trip for both of the Fillmores to California. Mrs. Fillmore faced the issue squarely, as she wrote: "It might be that if the plane were to drop down to take me, I'd back out. We're like that sometimes—think that we'd like to have a thing, until face to face with it, and then suddenly we've no use for it."

She never flew to California or, as far as can be determined, anywhere else. But she had the ability to create in her own mind the kind of warm and sunny climate California enjoyed wherever she was. She explained further to her friend:

"We feel it is up to us to stay right here, and to bring into expression the Christ ideas which will cause a beautiful sunny and warm climate and its blessings to manifest right here in Missouri. And you'd be surprised how much the climate has changed in the past few years. We don't notice the cold anymore, so why should we all seem to run away and crowd into a spot where some of these things have been accomplished? We'll make a California of our own."

Undoubtedly Charles and Myrtle Fillmore traveled more extensively than the average person of their day. After settling in the Kansas City area in the mid-1880s, they made several trips back to Colorado. In 1901 and 1902 they set up in Manitou Springs what they called "The Summer School of Metaphysics."

Sons Lowell, Rick, and Royal accompanied their parents to Manitou Springs in 1901, and Lowell later described their arrival in nearby Colorado Springs:

"Imagine our surprise to find the platform crowded with people, craning their necks and standing on every box

and truck to see us get off. We marched off (the train) while
the band played, and such crowding and pushing made us
think it was football season. But soon we found that all
the excitement was over the arrival of Vice-President
Theodore Roosevelt who was to deliver an address."

Even if the royal welcome at the railroad station
wasn't for the Fillmore clan, they enjoyed it just the same.
And despite the presence of such an important political
figure in the community, the Colorado Springs Gazette
found space enough to announce the new school the
Fillmores were starting:

> "Manitou is soon to have a new educational institution.
> The new school is to be of a religious character and anybody
> may have the benefit of its courses. Free will in all spiritual
> matters is one of the fundamental principles taught, so in-
> stead of having a stipulated sum for tuition, each person
> attending will give what may seem proper of his own free will.
>
> "The sessions of the school will be held in a large tent
> on Canon Avenue, which will be erected near Spencer
> Cottage. An able corps of teachers already has been en-
> gaged. The list includes Judge Clarkson of Omaha, Mr. and
> Mrs. Charles Fillmore of Unity, Mrs. Annie Rix Militz of
> Chicago, and Mrs. Grace M. Brown of Denver.
>
> "The school will be opened on Aug. 4 and will be con-
> tinued one month. The first address will be 'Practical Chris-
> tianity' by Charles Fillmore of Kansas City."

Two lectures were conducted daily, except Sunday,
and about forty students enrolled for the full program. The
school was considered so successful that incorporation
papers were filed, and the following year a similar course
of lessons was offered.

Mr. and Mrs. Fillmore enjoyed the mountains, and the
boys loved to climb. Mrs. Fillmore, now healed of the
tuberculosis that had threatened to drain her life away,

joined the young men one day and made the long trek up Pike's Peak. She later wrote back to a friend: "We picked our way over the boulders and rocks, upward, ever upward, as we do in our thoughts from material to spiritual." At four o'clock in the morning the tired but happy climbers reached the top and there they beheld the beauty of life and light in a golden sunrise.

In addition to conducting the metaphysical summer school the following year, 1902, Mr. and Mrs. Fillmore taught in Denver at the College of Divine Science for two weeks. The primary subject was regeneration. Unity and Divine Science, a movement founded by Nona Brooks, shared many common beliefs, and the Fillmore lectures attracted large crowds.

Mrs. Fillmore enjoyed Manitou Springs so much that she occasionally returned there alone for vacations. In early August of 1909, she went to Manitou Springs during one of Kansas City's torrid heat waves. Before she departed Charles asked her to send him a mountain breeze so that he might be cooled a bit from the scorching heat. She gaily responded that she would do so. On August 18 she wrote him that the view from her window "would delight your heart" and that a nice rain had brought cool mountain breezes into Manitou. "I trust you will get one of these breezes I promised you."

A few days later he wrote back:

"I do not see any prospect of coming to join you. The work is growing in every direction. The letters in Silent Unity are piling up—over one hundred on hand tonight. I shall not try to come for you—it would be neglecting too many important duties. The weather is cooler just now, and I shut the front door because of the cold air that is flowing in. It is 2 a.m. I suppose you have sent that cool breeze I told you to!"

Because Charles couldn't join Myrtle as he had hoped and as she had expected, it would mean that they would be apart on August 22, his birthday anniversary. But a resourceful Myrtle was not going to let the day go by without at least a present. On that day she wrote to him:

"I wanted so much to have something to send you that would express my appreciation of this date, and lo, it came about tonight that I could do so. The little package I am sending you is a demonstration and though you generally do not care for jewels, you will always love to wear this, for it is a genuine ruby and it is your birthstone and glows with the warmth and love of August, as well as symbolizes a love that never grows cold or faileth. From your old pard and lover."

Apparently she didn't get the mailing completed on the twenty-second, for on the back of the letter was scrawled in obvious haste, a clue to the "demonstration." It read: "I am writing this on a stone wall near the post office. I will be home next Sunday morning, leaving here on the 1:15 train and my finances need reinforcing right away. Send me as much as you want to."

In 1913, Myrtle and Royal traveled together to the East Coast, where they spent most of their stay in New York, New Jersey, and Pennsylvania. Then they sailed up the Hudson River to Albany and took a train to Buffalo. There they resumed their travel by ship onward to Detroit over Lake Erie, and then to Milwaukee and Chicago via Lake Huron and Lake Michigan before returning to Kansas City by train.

While in the East, Mrs. Fillmore and Royal visited the Curtis Publishing Company in Philadelphia. She described The Saturday Evening Post and Ladies Home Journal offices in a letter to Charles, calling the work "stupendous, past description." She was particularly interested in the printing facilities of the Curtis company, for the Unity printing operations were growing to the point that major improvements would soon be necessary. She conveyed several good ideas to her husband for modernization of the Unity facilities.

In New York City the mother and son walked along the sandy beaches of the Atlantic Ocean and beheld for the first time that great body of water. "It was a sight that delighted my soul," she said in a letter to Charles.

Although the visit was primarily designed so that Mrs. Fillmore could speak to Unity audiences wherever she visited, there was plenty of time for relaxation, too. In a letter to Lowell she described a dinner party she attended at the Plaza Hotel: "Everybody was in evening costume but me. I was modestly content in my black silk—I had no neck or arms on display."

In a letter to Rickert she wrote: "I wonder if I've ever worked so hard in my life. Surely my legs never did so much running up and down and traveling about. It was great returning from Staten Island. We sat where I could see it all. Liberty from her pedestal saluted me from a distance, and boats went up and down and sailed all about as we passed the bay. But I haven't had enough water yet. I love this exposure to water. Someday we'll cross the ocean, won't we?"

Myrtle loved New York City, and in the evenings after she had lectured to Unity students who thronged to hear her, she would take long walks in Central Park. Thousands of city dwellers sat on the grass and on benches in the park "getting the night air." Later when she returned to her room in the hotel where she was staying, the Martha Washington, she would sit quietly by herself in prayer and meditation. Before retiring she would write to Charles or to

some other family member or friend. In a letter to Charles
she joked about the view from her hotel room. "From my
room on the twelfth floor," she wrote, "I can look over and
see the Vanderbilt Hotel. The very top part of it is the
Vanderbilt city home. You see, I have to pull down my
blinds to keep them from watching me dress in the
morning!" Almost as an afterthought in the same letter, she
confided that she still had plenty of money, but added: "It
goes like water. My room is $1.50 per day and taxis are 75
cents."

Before Mrs. Fillmore left Missouri, she and Charles
had a long talk about the opulence of New York City. She
told him she felt that since New York was the finance
capital of the United States, the city must have an interior
center which, once found by those of spiritual mind, would
open up avenues of abundance to those who would use it
for the furtherance of God's kingdom.

It was with this thought in mind that Mrs. Fillmore
called upon Emma Curtis Hopkins, who was now located in
New York City. It was the first time the two spiritual leaders
had met personally since the Fillmores studied under Mrs.
Hopkins in the 1890s and early 1900s. They had
corresponded regularly, however, and Mrs. Hopkins
had kept a close watch on the spiritual fortunes of Unity
and the Fillmores.

Few details are known of the conversation between
Mrs. Hopkins and Mrs. Fillmore, but it is known that Mrs.
Fillmore told her about the feelings she had that perhaps
part of the great wealth of New York City could be
channeled into spiritual purposes if the right person made
the right kind of contacts. That evening as Mrs. Fillmore
wrote to her husband, she recounted the events of her visit
with Mrs. Hopkins, and added:

"After a long and most wonderful silence in which she

held my hands, she said some wonderful things to me which I will not put on paper. But I will say she felt *I was* the one sent to touch the button. She didn't word it that way. I am really sent here to *help* open up the inner way."

In 1916 Mrs. Fillmore returned to the East where she spent two weeks lecturing and visiting friends. Again on this trip, she attempted to see Mrs. Hopkins personally, but connections could not be made. They corresponded in notes between hotels and telephoned each other several times.

Mrs. Fillmore made two trips in 1921, one to Denver for a brief vacation and lectures, and a second to Chicago where she and Mr. Fillmore presented a two-week series of lessons. In Chicago they found people very thirsty for the Truth as they taught it and they encountered standing-room-only crowds at each lecture. The Fillmores visited Chicago on many occasions during their lifetimes, attending classes with Mrs. Hopkins in 1889, 1890, and 1891, and again in 1903, 1905, and 1906. Mrs. Fillmore made several more journeys to Chicago to visit her sister Henrietta Gaston in the 1920s.

Mrs. Fillmore occasionally traveled to Funk, Nebraska, by train to visit her sister Jane. On one occasion in 1915, she addressed a postcard back to "Charles Fillmore or any of the Fillmores who can decipher this." In it she told of her long but lovely train ride through the Nebraska countryside and of her arrival at the farm, including details of how her sister killed a chicken for dinner and fried a lot of bacon for breakfast. Strict vegetarian that Mrs. Fillmore was, she added, "Not on my account, though."

In 1923 Mrs. Fillmore and Royal spent another memorable two weeks in the East and in Canada. It was a wonderful time of togetherness for this devoted mother and son despite Royal's declining health. He died only a few weeks after their return.

In a letter written to Charles from Montreal, Myrtle told of their plans to take a steamer to Quebec City. While in Montreal, Royal attended to some business, and his mother took a sight-seeing trip. Despite the fact it was July, the weather was so raw that she had to wear a warm sweater and overshoes. She wrote optimistically about Royal and promised to return home very soon with many blessings and a lot of love for all those at home.

Charles accompanied Myrtle to the East in 1926 and they took along their orphaned granddaughter, Fran. They left the child for a stay with her grandparents in Merchantville, New Jersey, and continued on to lecture in several cities in the near vicinity. Everywhere the Fillmores spoke, every seat was filled and many persons stood. Offerings piled up and overflowed containers. Upon their return to Kansas City, Mrs. Fillmore wrote glowingly about the speaking tour, especially in New York City: "We had a very generous welcome from the Unity Center there and were shown all kinds of lovely attention by those who have long known us through our literature. People flocked to hear us, and we were glad to see the interest taken in the Truth."

Myrtle's last known trip outside of Kansas City took place on a weekend in late September 1931, just days before her death. Charles and Rick and Lowell and their wives accompanied her on an automobile trip to the Missouri Ozarks, a region dear to Mrs. Fillmore's heart. Although she had traveled extensively, she considered Missouri her home state and was very proud of it. On the occasion of a previous trip into the Ozarks in 1928, she wrote:

"I was especially impressed with the way in which folks

have cleared their rough, rocky land of the dense undergrowths, and have succeeded in finding just what will grow and yield best on the soil, so these acres are giving them an abundant harvest of good things. Way down in these mountainous regions, we found regular little flappers and children looking and acting much as our city children do. Little frame school houses are all along the way, making it possible for them to educate themselves and take their rightful places in the world. Folks don't need to refer to Missouri as a backwoods state anymore! We are proud of our state. And others are learning to appreciate it more and more."

The demands on Charles and Myrtle Fillmore's time were enormous. They received hundreds of requests every year to make personal appearances and lectures in every part of the country. Their devotion to their duties at hand, with Unity, kept such visits to a minimum.

Often in begging to be excused from personal appearances, Mrs. Fillmore would say something like this, taken from a 1929 letter:

"Neither Charles nor I feel ready for the trip just now. We are in a sort of cocoon stage, getting ready for our wings. And when they come in, in all their strength and radiance, we'll fly and visit from place to place just as the butterfly gaily flits from flower to flower. There's no hurry, you know! We're all just going from glory to glory, throughout eternity."

Sometimes when there was pressure to visit a friend somewhere, either locally or in some distant city, or the need to make a number of hospital calls, or to accept a speaking engagement, Mrs. Fillmore would say:

"Sometimes I am reckless enough to think I would like to take God's place in omnipresence, just for a day or two, to see all the folks!"

X

Home: A Sacred Trust

Myrtle Fillmore believed the home to be the most important factor in national life and homemaking to be a sacred trust. She often said, *"If you want love and justice, then establish such rules in your home."* She was firmly convinced that war and all other forms of conflict are purely and simply the result of inharmonious and unhappy homes. She herself had little time for housekeeping because of her wide-ranging duties with Unity, but she loved the many places where she lived—from log cabins to tents to apartments to stately houses to her "fairy home" which later became known as the Arches.

Charles and Myrtle Fillmore and their children especially loved two homes in Kansas City. Perhaps the most nostalgic was a large dwelling on Wabash Avenue where Myrtle accepted her healing and Charles found God in the silence. It was there that they began the work that came to be known as Unity, and it was there that their three boys grew to manhood. The second of the dearly-loved Kansas City homes was on Elmwood. Mr. and Mrs. Fillmore left there in 1924 when a comfortable and spacious apartment was prepared for them at Unity headquarters at Ninth and Tracy. Myrtle found the move to be a sad one because the Elmwood home was full of precious memories. She wrote her sister Jane: "Well, I 'spose I am to give up our

Wabash Avenue

438 Elmwood home the first of June. It's a big struggle for me and no one knows nor have our folks any idea what that place means to me. Of course, I'll have as good or better place. And Rick is having me a 'fairy home,' as he calls it, put up for 'mother' at the farm."

The prospect of leaving the beloved Elmwood home was so distressing to Myrtle that she jokingly began calling the new apartment "Gasoline Court" even before moving day. There were several reasons that she didn't relish moving to the new quarters. Entry was from an alley, the only access was from a steep stairway, the rooms were above the furnace area, and the view from the windows was somewhat obstructed by a parking lot, a garage, and automobiles—hence the "Gasoline Court" tag. It wasn't long, however, before Myrtle was very much in love with

438 Elmwood; Royal (left), Lowell, and Myrtle

the apartment. She could overlook the garage area to a beautiful little park nearby, and she greatly enjoyed a huge tree that cast shade near a south window. She found the stairs to be "some climb," but after all, she was only seventy-nine years old in 1924, so she could negotiate them without difficulty. She was, as she told everyone, a "good climber," and she could never understand why people many years her junior had a problem with the steps. She found the apartment pleasing in another respect too. She could slip away from her desk and her busy schedule to take a cool bath on a hot day and maybe nap for a few minutes.

Unity Farm was being developed at this time, and Rick had his mother's home under way. The little home was to have three names within the next few years, but more important, it was to be for Myrtle a dream home, a retreat away from the pressures of the Unity business operations, a place where she could be alone with the nature she loved so much, where she could take dear friends for long and pleasant talks, and where she and God could be alone together.

One of Unity's most interesting stories concerns this little home. Legend has it that Myrtle did not like to cook, so the house was built without a kitchen. As with all legends, there is some truth in it. There is ample evidence, however, that the home without a kitchen was Rick's idea, not Myrtle's. In fact, when she was first permitted a tour of the new home, she was surprised to find no kitchen. Amazement might best express Charles' impression. He set about immediately to find a way to have a kitchen added, but to no avail. Myrtle liked Rick's idea and accepted it completely.

Friends and relatives were startled when they found out that their beloved Myrtle was to live in a home without a kitchen. In one letter to a friend, Myrtle responded: "Mr. Fillmore and I have not come to the place where we do not eat, although we find more and more the substance in the bread of heaven." She added, "I dearly love to get into a kitchen and cook but I suspect I have gotten so in the habit of letting someone else do it that I'd almost get hungry before I'd plan and prepare regular meals."

A letter to her sister, Jane Munsell, perhaps best explains the matter:

"You are wondering how I get along in a house without a kitchen. Well, you see, Rick had that all provided for me when he planned this sweet, lovely little resort.

"He knows how I have lived so long with others in my home, and how eating and all its accompanying preparations were such a big factor in his grandmother's

The Arches

calculations of housekeeping. Well, to relieve me of this
burden, he said, 'Mother, I'm going to build you a fairy
home without kitchen or care.' And this arrangement is the
result.

"If Mother Fillmore is able to get about, she will look
after the cooking. She is a splendid cook. Of course, we'll
always have somebody to do the work, if she can't. Mother
Fillmore lives in the transformed old farmhouse. The boys
have done everything to make it pleasant and convenient
for her. I call myself her city boarder. Mr. Fillmore and I
always come out Sunday afternoons, and we have our own
swell sleeping apartment in the little house."

The fairy home was just that. It included Old English,
Irish, and many other kinds of architecture—to keep one
guessing, as Myrtle described it. Rick's ingenuity made the

fairy home a curiosity-seeker's delight. Myrtle told her friends that it was a home the likes of which could not be found anywhere else. She was happy, however, that it had a wall and a gate that would shut it off from the sight of passers-by. "Seems it is to have a gate with a lock and *I'm* to have the key. So, you see, I can control admittance. There are so many sight-seers coming and going that I think I'll have to keep the gate locked most of the time."

Before the time came to occupy the fairy home, however, a mystical occurrence took place. Rick took his mother to the farm in June of 1924 to view the little house when it was virtually finished. After he had shown her through the building and they had walked outside, he excused himself and asked his mother to go back to her downtown apartment with the driver. He said he didn't feel he should leave yet.

Rick stood alone outside the home, drawn to it in some mysterious manner. He walked around the house, confused by the strange feelings within him. And then it happened! Inside the little house a flare of light could be seen. Rick dashed inside and discovered a raging fire. Rags which had been thrown into a corner by painters had burst into flames from spontaneous combustion, Rick extinguished the fire and was firmly convinced from that point forward that the little home he had built for his mother was under the law of divine protection.

After living in the home for a year, Mrs. Fillmore decided that it needed a name, something more formal than the fairy home. So, after much consideration, she christened it "Orchard Crest." However, the architectural focal point of the little house soon brought about a change in name. The name Orchard Crest just never caught on with anyone, and workers preferred to call the structure the Arches. Sometime in 1929 Myrtle yielded lovingly to the demand and also began referring to her little house as the Arches. It is a name the home still bears today while it houses a Unity executive, Otto Arni, and his family.

During the last seven years of her life, the Arches was the *special place* where Myrtle could relax and enjoy the beauty of the farm, either by herself or with devoted friends and family members. She loved the porch and the comfortable swing that hung from its ceiling. "I am always happy," she told a friend, "there in the little house, surrounded with the presence of love, which my many dear ones have created." And her friends felt the same way. One of them wrote to her after a visit: "I think I shall never forget those moonlit, fragant, sweet nights on your porch. I haven't had much of the material things of life for many years, but I have found much beauty, even if I had to create it, but looking back along the way I can see no dream or memory sweeter than those nights."

Myrtle loved all there was to see and touch and feel in and near the Arches. There was no excuse for work or worry there, and although her neighbors were sometimes noisy, she loved them, too: "The front of the home opens out upon a south porch most as big as the whole house—of stone arches and cement floor. This lets you out into the orchard and oh, such birds as have homes out there. The mockingbird makes a stage for his opera on our high chimney. I hope that the nice family of robins who built their country home on my front porch last summer will come again this year. They are such lovely neighbors, and are so successful in handling their sturdy, bright-eyed youngsters. And I am sure that a man would soon become a millionaire who could invent an alarm clock to chirp like their early morning calls on the lawn."

Even though she said before moving into the house that she would probably have to keep the front gate locked because of curious people who wanted to see the house, this wasn't the case. The door latch at the Arches was always open. "Come curl up on my swing," she would tell a visitor. "We can talk and if my conversation encourages you to do so, you can take a nap."

The Arches was her last home, and it was her favorite.

XI

"No Murdered Thing"

"No murdered thing" was Myrtle Fillmore's philosophy concerning food during the last thirty-six years of her life. She became a vegetarian in 1895 at least partially because of Harry Church, Unity's printer, explaining, "The appetite left me without my even thinking about it and I am sure I outgrew the demand for murdered things." Charles Fillmore became a vegetarian about the same time, although the precise date of his decision is not known. Before his death in 1948, however, he did begin consuming small portions of fish on occasion.

Charles and Myrtle loved simple foods: fresh green onions, lettuce, radishes, asparagus, cabbage, beans, peas, cheese, fresh fruits, nuts, whole grain cereal, honey, an occasional baked potato, and sweets in limited amounts. Mary Fillmore, Charles' mother, was an excellent cook and served delicious meals to her son and daughter-in-law and other family members and friends. Mrs. Fillmore often observed of her mother-in-law, "Grandma likes everyone to eat beyond the polite point." When Charles and Myrtle didn't eat at Mother Fillmore's home, they dined together in the Unity Vegetarian Inn, one of Kansas City's most popular eating places in the 1920s, or they took simple, nutritious meals in the Tea Room at Unity Farm when it opened in the late 1920s. They had a kitchen and "snacking facilities" in their apartment on Tracy, but even there Mary Fillmore did most of the cooking. At the Arches on the farm there was no cooking, of course, because there was no kitchen.

Generous Unity students and friends sent literally tons of food to the Fillmores over the years, especially at Thanksgiving and Christmas. Baskets of fruit and vegetables arrived daily, along with fruit cakes and pastries and candies. Most of the food was given away to family members, friends, and workers, but sweets were rarely passed along until they were at least sampled.

"Our sweet tooth has never been extracted," Myrtle would explain as she nibbled a piece of gift fudge or cake, or as Charles sampled a bite of a gift chocolate Easter rabbit.

Being vegetarians was not without inconveniences and challenges. When Royal was attending the University of Missouri in 1909, he notified the family by mail that he intended to be home for Thanksgiving and would be accompanied by several classmates for the traditional dinner. He demanded turkey, although he well knew his parents' views toward any kind of flesh-eating. Myrtle was not to be cowed, however, and in a letter of response she said very simply, very directly, and very conclusively: "Suppose, dear boy, we cut the turkey out for Thanksgiving and have better things. It doesn't seem quite consistent for people who believe as we do, in the sin of taking the creature life, to dish murdered things up on our table. You know we'd have plenty of delicious things."

There was no turkey on the table that Thanksgiving in the Fillmore home—or any other year. And soon Royal was back in the vegetarian fold after having backslidden briefly into flesh-eating habits at the university. He wrote just a short time later: "Many people have discovered that their minds are clearer and their bodies healthier if they do not eat meat. Vegetables and fruits are really our natural foods, and besides, none of us wants to take the lives of animals, do we?"

In those early days of the twentieth century, it was not uncommon for city dwellers to raise pigs and chickens in their back yards to provide food for the table. One such neighbor of the Fillmores raised pigs, and Mrs. Fillmore could hardly stand it when she heard the squeals which signified that another little animal was about to be butchered. So she sat down one night and spoke the word for the safety of the remaining pigs. This incident, seemingly insignificant, became her *"pig experience"* which she later spoke of in hushed tones, if at all. The next morning after her prayers for the pigs, the animals were missing. No one ever found out what happened to them— they simply disappeared. Very few persons ever heard about the pig experience—but those who did also got a lecture on "the power of the word."

Once after Mrs. Fillmore wrote an article about vegetarianism, she got a letter from a small girl in Australia, a portion of which is a tribute to Mrs. Fillmore's cause, and a testimony to the little girl's persistence. It read:

"I am a vegetarian and am trying to teach our cats to be vegetarians but find it a very hard task. I took a bird from between the cat's claws. She was just going to kill it and eat it, and when I took the bird from her, she scratched me. This cat is going to be the hardest to teach to be a vegetarian. I am sure to win at last. I feed our cats on bread and milk and oatmeal."

Of course, Mrs. Fillmore never proposed that cats and dogs be forced into vegetarianism, but undoubtedly other persons experimented, as this little girl did.

Charles shared Myrtle's aversion to "murdered things" and partially in jest and partially seriously, he made the rounds at Unity employee picnics in search of meat or a sandwich that might have been brought onto the grounds surreptitiously. On one occasion he came upon a worker about to bite into a hot dog, and with much fanfare and laughter, he ceremoniously nailed the bit of meat to a tree. The following year, before the annual Unity picnic, he announced that this year there would be no meat products taken to or consumed at the picnic. The workers, most of them vegetarians themselves, knew that he wasn't serious, and of course, the non-vegetarians brought their meats along as usual. But just to show the violators that he was consistent, he again made a mock search of the grounds and discovered a worker about to bite into a ham sandwich. With similar fanfare, he attacked the sandwich and pierced it to a tree.

Anytime the Fillmores found themselves away from familiar surroundings, food became somewhat of a problem. Vegetarianism outside of Unity wasn't very common. Before any trip in which they were to be house guests, it always was necessary to lay certain dietary ground rules. On one such occasion Mrs. Fillmore wrote: "I dislike having people to go to the trouble of making dishes for us because we are *peculiar* people. I hesitate going anywhere, for really, I can't bear anything with animal grease in it."

In 1903 Lowell edited *Wee Wisdom* for a month while his mother was absent on a trip, and he had some fun at the expense of his parents and vegetarianism. He wrote:

> "Myrtle left the large boys, took the small one, Charley, with her to Nebraska for several weeks' vacation. In Nebraska the little boy fed the pigs, chased the chickens

and geese, and made them run and cackle and squawk,
but he didn't hurt them, for he is a vegetarian."

In the same article Lowell made it plain that Charley
was really his father, Charles Fillmore, and that it was all a
joke. But many readers of *Wee Wisdom* either didn't read
the entire article or were so shocked at reading of a "fourth
child" that they sat down immediately to write the editor,
their dear Mrs. Fillmore, and asked some very probing
questions. The letter response was so great that Mrs.
Fillmore was obliged in the following issue to comment on
Lowell's joke. She explained that she really had only three
sons and that in reality "Little Charley" was her husband.
"Maybe," she said, "there are others who do not appreciate
that these three boys have all outgrown their papa in size
and they like to call him the smallest of the Fillmore boys, or
'Little Charley.' It is all in such loving, rollicksome fun that
their papa enjoys it and is a boy among them during fun
time."

Neither Charles nor Myrtle used intoxicants nor
tobacco and they felt these two substances to be
responsible for many of the world's challenges. Mrs.
Fillmore was particularly concerned with the practice in
many homes of adults drinking and smoking in front of
children. "It is too bad," she said, "that dear little ones must
come into contact with such foolishness in the homes of
their dearest friends and relatives. I am so thankful for our
Unity ideals and living habits, that our little ones may grow
up without the many frivolous things which verge on
dissipation."
She admitted to be uncharacteristically critical of
smoking and she was often teased about it, especially by
her sons. Once when she and Charles were invited to a gala

community-wide dinner, she was told by Lowell and Rick
that she would be very uncomfortable there. She recalled
that they told her: "Why, Mother, they'll hand you a ham
sandwich, a cup of coffee (which she didn't use either), and
you will eat in a cloud of tobacco smoke." But she went
anyway and maintained that despite it all, she had a good
time.

Hundreds of people through the years asked Mrs.
Fillmore either personally or in writing for her opinion
about smoking. She had an opinion, and she never wavered
on it. It was:

*"I know that the charming Christian men and women
who smoke are good and lovable. But I would that they
could be happy without it. Someway I just can't see it, that
what I call a real Christ-like person would waste time and
energy in smoking. I can't quite see the picture of the Christ
with a cigarette or cigar hanging from His mouth, or even
between His fingers. I can't see a cloud of smoke
enveloping His head, or pouring from His lips. And I can't
quite imagine Him laying a cigarette on the table, or tossing
it to the ground, before stretching forth His hand to bless
and to heal one who comes to Him in faith. I know very well
He wouldn't criticize or condemn smoking, but I don't
honestly think He would take it up Himself."*

She realized that some Unity workers and students
were smokers, but even on this point she was rigid.
Workers who smoked were hired only if it could not be
avoided. "I only regret," she said, "that we must resort to
hiring them because we don't find enough of the good and
capable workers who are free and satisfied without
tobacco. I am sure that as these workers grow in
understanding, they will give it up."

Mrs. Fillmore's advice to hundreds of persons who
wrote to her about health problems usually included: watch

your diet! She encouraged eating what she called "spiritual foods which wash out the accumulations in the tissues, clear up the brain structure, and soothe and quiet." She pointed out that the spirit will more readily handle the flesh when the body is denied the foods which make it heavy and dense and which irritate the stomach and cause it to crave more food. As far as she was concerned, fresh fruits and vegetables were all that was required to build strong and healthy bodies. Most other foods, she declared, were a burden to the organs.

In 1928 Mrs. Fillmore met Dr. Bengamin Gayelord Hau-ser of New York's Hauser Institute. He spoke in Kansas City at the request of the Fillmores in a series of lectures on nutrition. He attracted huge audiences, and many were turned away at the clogged doors of the halls where he lectured. Unity was beginning its building program at the farm at the time, and Dr. Hauser used this analogy: "How is Unity going to build those new buildings at the farm—by thinking them only? No, indeed, you are getting the very best building materials and placing them together according to the blueprints. And we must get the very best building materials, suited to the body's needs, and place them together according to the blueprints of our health and perfect bodies. But we can eat the right foods and have the proper rest, and yet not have health, if we still indulge in some foolish mental habit."

Mrs. Fillmore was intrigued with this thinking. She had watched her diet carefully since that day in 1886 when she began her healing process, but in 1928 she was eighty-three years old and was beginning to feel some of the pains that often accompany the aging process.

Because she had had such wonderful health in the intervening years since her healing, she was determined that she was not going to permit herself to be "put on the shelf" in the near future, if ever. She was an extremely active woman, putting in many more hours of work than the average Unity worker who was years younger. But in this year of 1928, on two occasions she was forced to spend time away from her duties because of health challenges. Even then, however, she took work home with her and answered correspondence while sitting on the porch of her beloved Arches. The fresh air and Mother Fillmore's cooking combined on both occasions to refresh her and hurry her back to full-time duties. After the second healing challenge ended in late August of 1928, Mrs. Fillmore wrote:

"I have just had an unusual experience. I feel that I have truly been reborn. There were days of suffering, and days of bringing my body into the realization of the new strength and peace that welled up in my soul. I have glimpsed a new world, am better acquainted with my own soul and body, and have a greater desire to keep them together—to really live from within, including my body, the ideas which come. I have always demanded of my body that it keep going, doing the bidding of my mind, regardless of whether it was really wisdom which prompted, or only human desires and belief. I am consecrating myself anew."

Even though she credited overwork for her two illnesses, that did not deter her from going back to her duties at the same pace as before, or at an even more hectic one. In her determination to help others in their time of need, she violated the very advice she had so often given, which was:

"It may be, blessed friend, that you are overtaxing that body of yours, and have been giving forth more than you have taken the time and the quietness to receive. The physical man in us is a willing and obedient servant, and does just what we tell him to do, but we mustn't be a heavy taskmaster, and try to drive him beyond what he has developed the capacity to endure. In my very own experience, I find that it is always best to listen and obey when I receive the hint to take things easier. At such times when I've disregarded the hint, I've received the *kick*."

After receiving the *kick* twice in 1928, Mrs. Fillmore took better care of herself, rested more often, and felt on top of the world for the next two years. Then in 1930 at the age of eighty-five she began to feel ill again. She wrote to Dr. Hauser:

"You see, after a certain amount of wear and tear, especially after we're living on 'borrowed time,' as the world would call the passing of the three-score-and-ten mark, we find ourselves worn a bit and in need of very practical help, for we have no intention of allowing ourselves to be placed on the shelf.

"There will come a time when we can draw forth the universal mind stuff, just the elements we need in the right proportion and relation, to maintain the proper balance in our organisms. We shall be able to draw chemical substances from the fourth dimensional realm, down into our physical body. But in the meantime, we need to make practical all the knowledge we have concerning bodily renewal, through using intelligence and discrimination in the selection of our food.

"And so I am asking your help, and shall be glad for anything that you can tell me, to help along the work of bodily transformation and renewal."

Mrs. Fillmore seriously considered, after Dr. Hauser so suggested, going east for a time to study at the Hauser Institute. But, she finally concluded, her duties at Unity were so heavy that it was not practical for her to leave them, even if it meant continuing health challenges. Instead she determined to stay at home, follow the suggested dietary plan Dr. Hauser offered, and do a lot of earnest prayer work. She wrote back to Dr. Hauser:

"When I really became open and receptive in the 'secret place' within, and took the proposition of going east to Spirit for light, I felt an inner conviction, a definite leading. So it came to me that my place is right here. The Spirit of Him who 'feedeth the ravens' will see to it that I have just the right food elements in their proper relationship to each other, and I feel sure that everything is working itself out in a satisfactory way. I shall meditate upon the innate life and substance of the Word. 'Man doth not live by bread alone.' And, if there is a soul hunger back of the seeming need for food, that hunger will be satisfied by the spiritual life and substance of the Word."

Within days a Unity worker observed: "Mrs. Fillmore looks and acts like she feels like a billion dollars; she seems so sweet and so happy."

And that's the way her life was—sweet and happy—for the remainder of her time on this plane of existence.

XII

Sounds of Unity

Charles and Myrtle Fillmore were pioneers in radio broadcasting and realized the virtually unlimited possibilities in spreading Truth by this medium. As early as 1922, Unity lecturers were transmitting Truth viewpoints. The first Unity messages were broadcast from a window in a downtown Kansas City store by Francis J. Gable. Curious passersby gathered on the sidewalk to watch Mr. Gable speak into the microphone. Few persons had radios in those days, and anyone who did could expect to have a lot of house guests when it was time to tune in to favorite programs.

The broadcast of the first Unity Sunday talk also came in 1922, from the Tracy headquarters chapel. But it was not until 1924 that Unity plunged wholeheartedly into radio. Unity purchased WOQ (the oldest station in the Middle West) operating with five hundred watts, and relocated it on Tracy. By the time of its dedication in 1925, the station was operating with one thousand watts.

Mr. Fillmore found radio a fascinating means of disseminating his views, and when he wasn't otherwise occupied in the Unity operations, he almost certainly could be found in the transmitting room. Mrs. Fillmore had a program each Wednesday morning called "God's Half Hour," and other family members and workers also took their turns at the microphone. WOQ's range was quite extensive, and wattage was frequently boosted. When weather conditions were favorable, Unity broadcasts could be received in every state east of the Rockies and in Canada. A story in the Kansas City Journal in 1926 told of WOQ being received in Nigeria, Africa. Many passengers on ships at sea, often far out in the Atlantic, reported to Unity that they had heard WOQ quite clearly. A Vermont woman wrote to the Fillmores and praised them for the religious programming on WOQ, especially its late night broadcasts. "We set our alarm clocks and it is well worth our time to stay up until 3 a.m. to listen," she said. Mr. Fillmore preferred to broadcast after midnight, as the air waves were very clear at that time since most daytime stations had gone off the air.

During a trip to Winnipeg, Canada, Lowell Fillmore wrote home, "They get WOQ better here than many folks do in Illinois." A woman in Illinois reported: "I am a night hawk, so I amuse myself with the radio. Imagine my surprise to find your oasis in a desert of jazz. You will never know what you have done for me." The Fillmores estimated that the Saturday night WOQ healing service in which Charles, Myrtle, and Lowell all took part might have attracted as many as two and one-half million listeners in the late 1920s.

Mrs. Fillmore called the radio a symbol of omnipresence and often pointed out that anyone who tuned in to WOQ's wavelength would receive Unity messages. So it follows, she said, that those who tune into infinite Mind receive wisdom, understanding, and the blessings of the one Mind. She explained that Unity workers keep in touch and in tune with infinite Mind by raising thought patterns to the perfect standard of God and by excluding error thinking and static that are caused by dwelling on the personal side of life.

However, there were many persons who could not receive WOQ, and they sometimes complained in letters. Mrs. Fillmore gave each one the same answer: *"Don't worry if you aren't picking up WOQ. We'd rather have you with us in Spirit anyway—you receive us best then, and there is nothing to blur the love and power and light we share with you."*

Mrs. Fillmore had a system of transmitting that she felt was far superior to radio anyway, and she often described it, *"I keep in touch with all my friends through the spiritual radio."*

Another very practical reason that Mrs. Fillmore preferred the use of the spiritual radio was that the use of transmitting equipment in WOQ's studio was not a very ladylike endeavor. Giving a radio talk required enormous stamina and the ability to withstand high room temperatures, especially in the summer, as the broadcasting had to take place in a closed and soundproof room. Air-conditioning was unheard of then, and fans were too noisy. Mr. Fillmore seemed to relish the task, however, and he often sat for hours in a tiny airtight room, until he was soaked with perspiration, doing the thing he felt ought to be done. Mrs. Fillmore was not prone to worry about anything, but on occasion she did feel it was necessary to caution Mr. Fillmore to get more rest, instead of sitting up all night at the microphone. She indicated such concern in a letter to her sister in 1925: "Charles has gotten himself so tied up to casting messages over the radio that it leaves him no time for leisure or relaxation."

WOQ was a religious broadcasting enterprise and was never intended to be anything else, but the Fillmores were very flexible, and perhaps the best testimony to this fact came about in 1928. Another Kansas City radio station had announced that it would broadcast a baseball game between the St. Louis Cardinals and New York Giants. As game time approached, a scheduling conflict was discovered that made it impossible for the station to carry the game. Executives of the other station hurriedly contacted Mr. Fillmore and asked him if WOQ would save the day. Mr. Fillmore yielded to the argument that thousands would be disappointed if the game weren't broadcast, and he agreed that WOQ would do it. The other station transmitted the program it was committed to, and announced from time to time that WOQ was handling the baseball game. The Fillmores received many positive letters and verbal responses to this action, and undoubtedly the action won some new friends to Unity.

WOQ ended its existence under Unity management in 1934 in its tenth year of service. The federal government ruled in response to a lawsuit that the frequency could better be used on a commercial rather than religious basis. For some time a Wichita organization had been sharing time with WOQ on the frequency. The government ruled that although both stations were doing a good service for their communities, it would serve the public interest best for the frequency to be reassigned.

Although the decision was disappointing in some respects, it was met with affirmations of divine order—and Unity went right ahead with its broadcasting in a different manner. Within a few months arrangements had been made with more than fifty radio stations in the United States, Canada, Australia, New Zealand, and Cuba to transmit Unity programs. More people than ever before became acquainted with the Unity viewpoint after WOQ signed off for the last time.

XIII

"A New and Perfect Order"

Myrtle Fillmore was not a politically-minded woman, but neither she nor Charles was ignorant about politics or economics. It made little difference to either of them whether a Democrat or a Republican was elected as President or to any lesser position of power and authority. What counted most was the caliber of the man or woman seeking office. From Mrs. Fillmore's letters, however, it is obvious that in the presidential campaigns of 1924 and 1928 she supported Republican candidates.

She was quite fond of both Calvin Coolidge and Herbert Hoover. Of Coolidge she wrote: "We feel sure that if he had the time for it, President Coolidge could give us some splendid Truth articles. And what a joy and help it would be to have more of such messages coming out through our magazines and newspapers, in place of some of the personal history that occupies so much space in current literature."

She urged her friends both before and after his election in 1928 to support Hoover. On July 26, 1928, she discussed the upcoming election in a letter to a friend:

"Wouldn't it be splendid to have a man come into the President's chair without any ugly reports? And wouldn't it be royal of us all to really feel that because he was God's

own son, and doing the Father's work, that he was sure to be wise and considerate and loving and steadfast—really capable and impersonal in handling the affairs of state and nation—even the things of international interest? And wouldn't we get the greatest satisfaction, no matter how he was chosen, and by so doing, hold him and ourselves to the high ideals and the course of action best suited to our needs?"

New York Governor Alfred Smith was Hoover's opponent in 1928. Myrtle wrote of him: "Gov. Smith doesn't stand very well around here. But then there may be many loyal supporters who say nothing and do much. We are holding that God is taking care of these affairs, and that the Christ Mind is ruling in all, and discerning and placing the right men in their right places, that all may know more of peace and progress and freedom and ability to use that freedom." Despite favoring Hoover, Mrs. Fillmore confided to a friend that the real winner of the election would be the Christ Spirit and that Jesus Christ had been and would continue to be the head of the national affairs of the country. She added:

"We have been praying earnestly for weeks for this country, for the government, for the men who are seeking office, for those who are helping in the campaigns, for those who are voting, and for the awakening, and harmonizing, and establishing of a new and perfect order throughout the land following the election. We have been, and are continuing to declare, that God has appointed a ruler, a counselor, a governor—and upon His shoulders shall our government be! Jesus Christ is the head of our national affairs. And the Christ in all those who are awake is alert and doing that which is for the highest good of all.

*One thing I am sure of—the earnestness of the people will
make them (Mr. Hoover and Mr. Smith) more receptive to
the inspiration of Spirit, and the ultimate will be real
growth."*

On the day before the election in 1928, Mrs. Fillmore
organized a workers' meeting to stir up enthusiasm and to
encourage everyone to go out and vote, and she made no
attempt to disguise her feelings that Herbert Hoover was
her choice. Later, on the day of Hoover's inauguration, all
the Unity workers went in a body to the Unity auditorium to
hear the new President's address.

After his election, however, despite anything he or the
United States Congress could do to prevent it, the country
began to slip into an economic depression. Mr. and Mrs.
Fillmore and the Silent Unity workers never let a day go by
without prayers for corrections and adjustments in national
and international affairs. Mrs. Fillmore's devotion to
Hoover never wavered, even a full year after the crash of
1929 and when the country was in its worst depression in
history. She wrote of him:

"Herbert Hoover is a fine man. We stand back of him
with our prayers for guidance, protection, and success. He
is doing the very best he can under such trying
circumstances. Christian metaphysicians have a stupendous amount of work to do to help the world see the
Truth that makes men free from ignorance, superstition,
and fear."

The advice she offered for righting the depressed
conditions is as valid now as it was then. She said:

*"This period of adjustment the world is going through
cannot last very long. Some think that people have bought
too much on credit, and are now paying off their debts 'on
the installment plan,' but when they get out of debt they*

will be on a more secure foundation financially than before. The thing to do in times like we have been having is to remain positive and not let any of the negative, outer thoughts sink in, but let them slide off like water on a duck's back. It is not a time to fall into the current of race thought, but to hold fast to the principles of Truth that are bound to demonstrate abundance of good."

Both Myrtle and Charles Fillmore were firmly in opposition to war and to spending billions on military operations and defense. In 1926, Mrs. Fillmore wrote: *"I wish Uncle Sam might see the need of saving our youth from their worst enemies, instead of putting his millions into defense against an imagined one. We are praying for the glad day when the warships shall be turned into schoolhouses and love shall become ruler in the hearts of men."*

But the Fillmores were realistic, too. They watched two of their three sons—Rick and Royal—march away to World War I and the third, Lowell, would have gone, too, but he was past the age of acceptance. Many persons wrote to Unity asking about such military service, and the answer was always the same: it is necessary for all Truth students to take an impersonal view of war. If called, go, and if necessary, serve in the trenches. But know that it is because there is a particular work to be done.

Although the prayer vigil at Silent Unity has always been steadfast and unceasing, the intensity of the affirmations for peace was greatly heightened during times of conflict such as World War I.

Mrs. Fillmore never visited a foreign country other than Canada, but her correspondence with people all over the world made it possible for her to understand both the better and the less desirable aspects of other nations and other forms of government. She knew that Americans enjoyed many advantages that people in other lands seemingly did not have. She knew of the hardships that people were forced to endure in lands where dictators ruled. All in all, she simply loved all people in all nations and wished that everyone could make a personal declaration of independence from suffering and hardship.

In July, 1901, in the pages of *Wee Wisdom,* Mrs. Fillmore declared:

> "We as a nation have declared our independence from the rule of other nations and other powers, yet as a people we are abject slaves. To what? Just ask anybody and see if he is not wanting freedom from something.
>
> "We will declare ourselves as no longer yielding to the servitude of fear and anger, of impatience and selfishness, and bad habits, but we will know the Truth that makes us free, and we will let love be the goddess of our liberty, and kindness the father of our country. Then, pain and disease, sorrow and want, can never find a foothold and we will be glad people, and our patriotism will vent itself in remembering 'where the Spirit of the Lord is, there is liberty.' "

XIV

An Eventful Year

Three events—two of them happy ones, another sad—took place in the early months of 1931, the year of Myrtle Fillmore's passing. The unhappy occasion was the death of Grandmother Fillmore, Charles' mother. The gay and festive events were the fiftieth wedding anniversary of Charles and Myrtle, and Myrtle's selection as Queen of the May.

Grandmother Fillmore was loved by everyone who knew her. Her name was Mary Georgianna Fillmore, but she was known by practically everyone as Grandmother or Grandma—except by Charles and Myrtle, who called her Mother Fillmore. Charles had made a home for her in Denison, Texas, and she lived at first with him and later with the whole Fillmore family for almost fifty years. She was apart from the family only during brief vacations, and she filled the roles of housekeeper, babysitter, cook, dishwasher, shopper, counselor, and all-purpose friend and confidante for the Fillmores.

At Unity Farm she lived in what is now the golf clubhouse, just a few yards from the Arches where Myrtle and Charles often stayed. The absence of a kitchen in the Arches made it necessary for Myrtle and Charles and their guests to dine at Grandma's house. She was a robust woman and enjoyed excellent health most of her life. Near

Mary Georgianna Fillmore

the end, however, she had a number of serious health challenges. One of them left her unable to walk without assistance, so her cooking and serving days came to an end, and a full-time cook had to be engaged. Even so, she supervised kitchen operations from her rather unusual wheel chair. The rockers were removed from her favorite chair, and it was mounted on small wheels. As a result, she had what Myrtle described as a "roller-skate motor chair." Myrtle said she was the chauffeur, the engine, the gas, and the whole works, including back-seat driver.

On March 12, 1931, Grandma Fillmore "took her flight," as Myrtle described it:

"She left us just like a babe dropping off to sleep in its mother's arms. She was 97. She has slipped from the sight and touch of the sense consciousness only, for we know that in omnipresent love, there can be no separation. Mr. Gable was out of the city, so our Mr. Ernest Wilson conducted the services. It seemed she was there, very much alive, enjoying it all. Perhaps when her precious soul comes again into the visible into a new body temple, she will be able to make the permanent union of mind, soul, and body in eternal life. A lonesome place is left in our lives, but we take comfort that she is free from pain and distress, and mortal strife and conflict."

Although it seems fashionable in some quarters to joke about mothers-in-law, and worse yet to scorn them, Myrtle Fillmore always showed the greatest respect and consideration for her mother-in-law who "lived-in" almost fifty years. Myrtle probably seemed more like a sister than a daughter-in-law, because she was only eleven years younger than Mary.

Near the time of Grandma Fillmore's passing, Myrtle was beginning to think of her fiftieth wedding anniversary. She confided to a few close friends that March 29, 1931, was the happy day. She told each of them that she preferred the date go unnoticed and that she did not want gifts. But that was not to be the case. Somehow even the Kansas City Star heard of the upcoming anniversary and wrote a story about it. Local radio stations also paid heed to the noteworthy event.

On the anniversary date, a Sunday, Mr. and Mrs. Fillmore walked into the Unity chapel and were called to come forward out of the audience. The new minister, Dr. Ernest C. Wilson, then proceeded to marry them again. The

Myrtle and Charles Fillmore (*circa* 1930)

wedding was witnessed by an overflow crowd at the church and the event was described on radio station WOQ to thousands of listeners. Myrtle told her admirers that day that the first half-century knot had held quite tightly, but that she and Charles had obeyed the new minister like good children and had let him tie the knot for another half-century of happiness. She pledged that the next fifty years would be even richer and more beautiful than the previous ones—and she wondered aloud at how thrilling it would be at their one-hundredth anniversary celebration. Whatever Charles said on the occasion has gone unrecorded, but if he was true to form he would have felt both amused and blessed by the festivities, and no doubt he made major contributions to both the seriousness *and* the good fun in the situation.

Silent Unity workers conducted a prosperity session for Charles and Myrtle in observation of the anniversary, presenting them with a huge bouquet of golden roses, and each worker filed past to give the celebrating couple a personal message.

The family did not overlook the gala occasion either. Rick and Harriet had a reception which was attended by many friends and relatives. The three grandchildren amused and entertained the guests with readings and music. Myrtle was obviously pleased with the recognition and appreciation, but she tried to minimize the milestone by saying, "After all, fifty years is not very long when one is living in eternity!"

Unity workers again showered Mrs. Fillmore with love in May of 1931 when, much to her surprise, she was selected Queen of the May. For several years the queen title had gone to one of the beautiful young secretaries or clerks in the Unity business office. But it was pure joy for

Mrs. Fillmore that she was chosen, and she made the most of the situation by announcing, "I wouldn't be at all surprised to receive an offer from Hollywood." She told of feeling as if she were "in the footlights" in a letter to a friend: "Our Mr. Ingraham crowned the May queen, and I had several tall and stately young ladies as maids in waiting. Everything would have been perfect, but my crown of sweet peas weighed about six or eight pounds and was many sizes too large, and came down too far over my ears! The one who crowned me said in his speech that after considering all the candidates for queen, they unanimously decided to choose the youngest and the fairest and the most loved, and so I was chosen. It was a very sweet and lovely tribute from our blessed workers, and I certainly appreciate the spirit of it."

Afterward, she asked to know the names of all the girls who were in the contest with her and later she personally wrote to each one, thanking her for her kindness. She knew she had taken a chance from one of them to win the coveted title, but they in turn were happy that a deserving and gracious lady had been honored.

XV

A Beginning, Not an End

In the late summer of 1931, Myrtle Fillmore came to the realization that her work on this plane of existence was nearing an end and that the transition commonly known as death was about to take place. She confided this conviction to several close friends and family members and no one could dissuade her from her determination to make the change. On October 6, at peace with herself, with God, and with her family and thousands of friends, she quietly slipped into the next dimension. Although there was great sadness at her departure in bodily form, everyone realized that God had simply summoned her home for a while, and because of this knowledge there was rejoicing, too.

Mrs. Fillmore faced her death the way she had faced life, with courage and spiritual assurance. During her long years in the ministry when anyone raised the question of death, she was always quick to respond that death is like sleep. It is a sort of rest, she would add. *"But, just as we awaken with the morning, and desire to take up our round of activities, so do we awaken from the longer sleep, and desire to take up life's activities. Then comes the necessity for reimbodiment that the soul may have a temple in which to dwell, or a vehicle of expression."*

Although she definitely believed in reincarnation, she was opposed to putting off until later the growth that should be taking place now. She once wrote: "I have never been able to work up any enthusiasm over past incarnations, or even to feel that I knew anything about my past. The present is enough for me!"

Mrs. Fillmore was eighty-six when she died, having passed the three score and ten Biblical "allotment" to man by sixteen years. When she was seventy years old, she declared that age to be a "mere childhood" and said that the soul is just getting a well-rounded knowledge of the world in which it lives after only seventy summers. Charles Fillmore, on the occasion of his seventieth birthday, was a bit more dramatic. He announced his age in the Unity employee publication and added, "No one has sent me lilies yet."

Frequently in the 1920s and early months of the 1930s, friends of the Fillmores would inquire about their health. Mrs. Fillmore on one occasion replied in a letter:

"Mr. Fillmore and I are 'growing young' as fast as we can and we have all eternity in which to grow. We should help others to get away from the old race beliefs about life—that we are born, grow to maturity, have children, rear them, and decline and die. We can and must help others catch the higher vision of living—the development of soul qualities which make life a beautiful and helpful experience. There is so much to be seen, and learned, and done, that surely one can't get all of it in three score years and ten."

She had the opportunity to counsel many people through the years on the subject of death, and she often was able to provide loving comfort to those in bereavement. Once she wrote such a person:

"It is that our loving Father has only let a sad soul in a pain-racked body slip into a haven of rest; just out of

sight, but not away from those it loved; veiled from the senses, but not from the hearts that held it dear; lost only to sight and sound, but still waiting to be known to you as the living friend you have loved, but not lost. So, you are to realize that there is no loss or separation in Spirit."

Occasionally she would get a letter from someone asking her if she would like to explore the inner realm thoroughly and not return to earthly conditions. Once she responded:

"Sometimes I do feel that I'd like to just slip away from all this that is going on about us. But when I feel this way, it is because of some negation, some boiling to the surface of some old subconscious ugliness, or some remnant of belief in the reality of suffering and inharmony. So I know full well that God is not 'calling me home.' I would like to rest and see the goodness and the beauty of God revealed all about me and within me. But I am beginning to realize I can rest here, and see these beautiful realities if I will do it!"

Both Myrtle and Charles Fillmore entertained the possibility of eternal life in the bodies their souls were presently inhabitating. Through their lives of consecration and prayer, they both made efforts to demonstrate it. Neither one made it, but they both lived to advanced ages—Myrtle to eighty-six and Charles to ninety-four—and they had fulfilled lives in every respect.

Despite the fact that Mrs. Fillmore eventually accepted her death and talked freely about it, earlier she had written much about eternal life in the body. In 1928, for example, she told a friend: *"We are now entering into the place in our unfoldment where we must help these dear souls to stay with their bodies, and to lay hold of the life more abundant which quickens, and heals, and restores and perfects."* Mrs. Fillmore seemed somewhat preoccupied with death in that year, but if so, she was even more concerned with health and life. She had experienced two short illnesses and was watching her food intake more diligently than ever before. She wrote then: *"Seems to me my life is divided into three or four parts, and each part clamoring for more time and attention than I am humanly able to give. Sometimes it seems I will have to rest. But God is so good to me, and the moment I let go, there comes a new inflow of fresh life and substance, and I am strengthened and cheered on."*

She prayed that Spirit might show her the way to a more quietly active life and that she could be freed from those things that were not important, so that she could concentrate upon those things of eternal importance. It appeared to many of her friends and family members that Mrs. Fillmore started preparations to die about this time. She confided to several persons that she thought she had accomplished everything she could in this life plane and that the time was near for her to pass on. She said she would know the exact time when God revealed it to her. That time arrived in 1931.

A few weeks before her passing Myrtle stopped at the desk of a co-worker and told of her impending death. She explained to him that she felt it would be easier for her to do the work ahead of her from the invisible plane. Despite all the worker's protests, Myrtle declared the matter closed.

On the Wednesday before her death, Mrs. Fillmore helped her husband lead the Wednesday night prayer service. On Thursday she was at her desk in the Unity office, writing letters and receiving callers. She was in a very relaxed and happy mood that evening when she traveled to the Arches to spend a weekend resting and writing. Friday and Saturday were spent in walking around on the

grounds, sitting on the porch of the Arches and listening to
the songs of the birds in the nearby orchard where, in fact,
she even helped pick a few apples. On Sunday she had
company, her dear friends Tesla and Herald Landon. Mrs.
Landon recalls that Mrs. Fillmore told her that day that she
intended to die in a day or so. "She was so calm, so
peaceful, and so beautiful," Mrs. Landon remembers. "She
told me her work was done on this side and it was time to
go." Two days later, on Tuesday, Mrs. Fillmore died.

Over the next few weeks, the hundreds of persons
with whom Mrs. Fillmore had corresponded were
informed:

> "For some time Myrtle Fillmore has felt that she was
> ready for a change. It was difficult for us to share this opinion
> as she had been enjoying good health and seemed to have
> an abundance of energy. However, with the idea in her
> mind, she peacefully passed out of body Tuesday evening,
> October 6, 1931.
>
> "Your love for her and the Unity work has been felt
> throughout the years, and we wanted you to know of this
> change for our dear one, and to have a copy of the enclosed
> article (a clipping from the Kansas City Star). Mrs. Fillmore
> never considered that in her work at Unity she was founding
> a personal service, but rather that she was teaching others
> and encouraging them to carry on the work in which she
> was a pioneer.
>
> "Mrs. Fillmore's all-embracing love and devotion to
> this work can never leave us, and her presence abides as
> a living force. Join us in knowing our Unity with the Spirit
> of Life and Love in which there is no separation, but con-
> tinuous unfoldment."

The editorial column of The Kansas Citian magazine
recognized the major contributions Mrs. Fillmore had
made to mankind: "Nothing is more beautiful in retrospect
than an unselfish life earnest in its devotion to the cause of

suffering humanity and the general betterment of
mankind—a life that knows no death because of the wealth
of tender memories that will be forever cherished in the
hearts of the beneficiaries thereof. Such a life was that of
Mrs. Myrtle Page Fillmore."

The death of Mrs. Fillmore was reported in two places
in the Star. The obituary column insertion was brief:
"Fillmore, Mrs. Myrtle, age 86 years, passed away Tuesday
evening at her residence, Unity Farm. Survived by her
husband, Charles Fillmore, and two sons, Lowell Fillmore
and W. Rickert Fillmore of Unity Farm. For further
information call D. W. Newcomer's Sons."

The news columns of the Star, under the headline,
"Her Faith Won Millions," carried the following story about
the life and death of Unity's cofounder:

> "More than forty-five years ago a Kansas City woman
> turned to a new application of Christianity for a solution
> to many months of illness and financial despair in her
> family.
>
> "Tuesday night that woman, who had inspired a
> school of religious thought that circled the earth, passed
> on. She was Myrtle Page Fillmore, vice-president of the
> Unity School of Christianity.
>
> "Mr. and Mrs. Charles Fillmore moved to Kansas
> City with their three children. [This was an error since Royal
> was born in Kansas City in 1889.] Previously the family
> had lived in Texas and Colorado, seeking a cure for tuber-
> culosis of the lungs from which Mrs. Fillmore was suffer-
> ing. As a boy Mr. Fillmore had suffered a hip disease and
> curvature of the spine."

LOST HIS FORTUNE

> "Mr. Fillmore was successful in the real estate busi-
> ness here, accumulating $150,000. That was swept away
> in the collapse of a boom and the family was destitute and
> in need of nourishment and medical attention. To quote
> an article that appeared in the Star five years ago, this

was what happened when the family was in the depths of despair:

" 'Then just when it seemed that there was nothing left to life, there came an extraordinary change over Mrs. Fillmore. During the many months of heartbreaking trials, she had reasoned out that there must be a supreme power operating upon fixed divine law, and that this law, applied in faith and faithfully, must of necessity set aside all negative or destructive agencies. And she applied her theory with remarkable success. Her tuberculosis vanished, as did the ailments of her children. She treated her friends similarly. Sickness and poverty became only as bad dreams. In their place health and the ability to work reigned. And Charles Fillmore, grasping the full meaning of this divine law, began to help her in her ministrations, reaping much benefit physically, mentally, and materially.

" 'It was in 1886 that Mr. and Mrs. Fillmore began to devote a part of their time to demonstrating the new doctrine conceived by Mrs. Fillmore. In 1889 they decided to devote their lives to it.' "

STARTED WITH ONE PUBLICATION

"They started with one publication and in an old residence at 1315 McGee Street. From this modest beginning, their work grew into what now is known as the Unity School of Christianity.

"The school is neither a church nor a sect. It has no membership, but it is known that at least 30,000 persons in Kansas City are followers or are interested in varying degrees. 'Millions' is the only word that the school's officials can use in speaking of the followers all over the world.

"From the McGee Street residence, the school has grown into an institution that has extensive holdings on Tracy Avenue between Ninth and Tenth Streets, and the 1,200-acre farm on U.S. Highway 50. Starting with a small composing room in which type was set for one publication, the school now has a printing plant that issues seven publications. Fifteen bound volumes from the plant now are in print and countless leaflets and booklets have been issued."

NOW EIGHTY WORKERS

"The Silent Unity work started with one worker to assist Mr. and Mrs. Fillmore. Now there are eighty workers in this department alone. On the Tracy Avenue land there is a vegetarian cafe and the school's radio station, WOQ. The school employs about four hundred persons.

"Five years ago it was estimated that more than two million persons were following the teachings of Unity. Today there are more than one thousand Unity centers and study classes.

"In the bare outline those are the things that have grown out of a woman's attempt to end the despair in her family. The discoverer of a religious doctrine that has gone over the world, Mrs. Fillmore seldom went away from the city. She went to Denver and Chicago a few times, but most of her activities were in Kansas City.

"Mrs. Fillmore was 86 years of age. She was born in Pagetown, Ohio. A graduate of Oberlin College, Oberlin, Ohio, she taught school in Clinton, Missouri, and Denison, Texas. She and her husband celebrated the fiftieth anniversary of their marriage recently."

ACTIVE UNTIL THE LAST

"Mrs. Fillmore was active in the work of the organization until a few days ago. Last week she was at her desk at the Unity headquarters and on one day last week she found entertainment in picking apples on Unity Farm.

"She never dropped the writing of letters, which she started at the founding of the school. Much of her correspondence was with followers in foreign countries."

Dr. Ernest C. Wilson presided at a memorial service for Mrs. Fillmore on October 9, 1931, in a funeral home chapel. More than twelve hundred persons attended the service and hundreds more milled about outside and circled the block in their automobiles. Following are the remarks Dr. Wilson made in Mrs. Fillmore's memory:

" 'And God shall wipe away all tears from their eyes;

and there shall be no more death, neither sorrow, nor crying, neither shall there be any more pain: for the former things are passed away.' This was the vision of one whose sight was very clear, and the great work to which the life of Myrtle Page Fillmore has been dedicated was conceived in similar vision.

"It may seem to some of us to be a far vision—the doing away with death and pain and crying and sadness— but surely the very beginning of that great overcoming is in our own minds and hearts, by the clearing of our own vision.

"This is a very unusual occasion. I do not suppose there is anyone present who has ever been at a service of this kind, marked by so many unusual qualities as this one. We have come together to honor one who, forty-five years ago, was given up to die, and who, by a quickened vision of Truth set aside that sentence, and brought to the world a message that has quickened the lives of millions of people! Surely, there have been few women in the world whose influence has been more widespread and more wonderful than that of Myrtle Fillmore, and it is a very hallowed privilege to have had an association with her; to have listened to her inspired words; to have shared the quickened vision that she so abundantly expressed. I know that today, just as my own mind is so filled with memories that my lips fumble for words, so your minds too are filled with beautiful and tender and loving memories, wonderful and priceless associations. Yet we should not let those memories blind us to her living presence now. We should not forget that living presence. We should not forget the teaching to which Mrs. Fillmore dedicated her life, and to which she still dedicates her life.

"This service is unusual in another respect: for surely there are very few people who have seen their way so clearly and made their decisions so definitely as Myrtle Fillmore did. Her transition was such a decision. A number of those who have been very close to her know this, and

firmly believe that Mrs. Fillmore need not have slipped out
of the body if she had not wished to do so. But she did wish
to do so. She spoke of it to a number of those who are
present here today. She spoke of it to me some time ago,
when clearly there was no least shadow of illness upon her
to suggest such an idea. Nor was there any reason at the
time of her passing why she should need to do so. She
could, I am sure, have remained with us as long as she
might wish to, and I think that is what she did. Not that she
did not wish to be with us, but that she had some very clear
and definite ideas about work that was just ahead of her to
do, and she felt that this change had a part in that work.

"Mrs. Fillmore's vision, like that of Mr. Fillmore, is
unusual. Perhaps many of us do not see, quite so clearly as
Mr. and Mrs. Fillmore do, that this phase of expression
that we call physical life is, after all, only a very small part
of life. Life seems to begin when we enter the body, and to
many it seems that life ends when we lay aside the body;
yet it was very clear to Mrs. Fillmore that life neither
begins at birth nor ends at death; that in our 'father's
house' there 'are many mansions,' and that there are
many planes of life. Not forgetting Christ's ideal of the
great final overcoming, the triumphant quickening of the
body that will displace death, we nevertheless see that on
the way to this overcoming there are many avenues of
expression, and many steps to precede that final one.
There are many ways of ministering, and it may be that
Mrs. Fillmore was quite right in her vision—as I am very
much moved by faith in her to think that she was—
and that at this time, and under circumstances that may
have been clearer to her than to us, it was the right and
wise step for her to take.

"How much we need to have faith, and to know that
there is a loving, guiding Presence that works through
our life, and that calls us in its service, often in ways that
we cannot quite understand, and whose wisdom we cannot always see!

"It was a very great mark of courage and of understanding, and of faith, too, that she should express a desire to take this step. Since she expressed that desire, we who love her would not have it otherwise; we would not have our love bind her or limit her in any way. If she were speaking to us now, I know that she would tell us that very thing, and that she would want us to have that feeling about her just as she has it about us.

"I am sure that we are not going to feel that Mrs. Fillmore is away from us. After just a little, when our sight becomes clear again, we are going to be conscious, as always, of her radiant presence as the great mother-spirit of Unity; the great, loving spirit that we can best honor not by fear, or sadness, or too much dwelling upon past things, but by our own self-dedication to the great ideals that she taught and demonstrated so lovingly to us. This is the best tribute that we can pay to Mrs. Fillmore, and I pray, as I know you do, that we may be true not only to Mrs. Fillmore's ideals of the spiritual work of Unity, but to our own highest vision of that work.

"Mrs. Fillmore has been called an idealist, and it has been thought by some that her vision was not always very practical, because in many respects it went so far ahead of the ways of the world. Yet how wonderfully her faith has been demonstrated! How wonderfully, through Unity School, in the last forty odd years, that great ideal has shone, like a beacon of Truth indeed! Unity's ways have not been the ways of the world; and we pray God that they shall not be the ways of the world, unless the ways of the world become the Unity way—the great loving, freeing, healing, radiant spirit of Unity that is not limited or bound by selfish commercial standards, or by anything but a desire to serve God, and to serve Him as understandingly, wisely, and lovingly as we know how to serve.

"So this gathering is not only a recognition of our love for a great, fine leader, but also, if our love be really love, it marks our own rededication to the high vision of practical

Christianity to which she devoted her life. What a wonderful and beautiful picture is presented by this woman of clear vision, who so definitely knew beforehand the course that she wanted to take, and who took it in faith and courage and understanding—even though it led into the unseen! Took it even in the face of the negative thought of some who will not understand! We all can help, in the great work that she has still ahead of her, by our constructive faith and understanding of this experience.

"So interpreted, this service becomes one of peace and of happiness, even of joy, joy that by our prayer and faith we can help one whom we love to fulfill in her own way what she wished to do. Let us then be conscious of the presence of this dear one, who is quite near to us, surely; for we realize that nearness is a matter not of time nor space but of love, and that we are closest of all to those whom we love most. In that sense we are very close to Myrtle Fillmore today, and she, I am sure, is very close to us; not that we would bind her to us, but close to us by reason of abiding affection. Confident of that, we can turn to the presence that she so clearly recognized—the presence of a wise and loving and all-understanding God— and take to Him any little shadow that rests upon our heart, and let His presence dissolve it.

"Dear Father God, it is to Thee that we turn now. We ask that we may understand this experience and behold it with illumined vision. If there are steps for us yet to take before this experience becomes quite clear, O God, give us faith and love to be steadfast and strong and worthy of the high vision of this one who is dear to us. Quicken the hearts of those who feel resting upon them even the slightest shadow, and make them to know the reality of Thy abiding; to know that there is no separation in Spirit, that there is no distance that love cannot cross. Help us to see in this transition the working out of a purpose whose every step may not be quite clear to us, but whose goal or ultimate most surely is.

"In the light of the Father's presence we greet and bless you, dear Myrtle Fillmore. We behold you not identified in any sense with inactivity, nor longer hampered with this fleshly garment that you have so sweetly and understandingly laid aside, but we behold you as always you have asked us to do, with eyes of Spirit, as full of grace and Truth, as radiant with that eternal youth and life which are of God, as a mighty power in His good service. We should like you to know that, though we want you to be near us in your thoughts, we would not have any limitation of our thought deter you from your onward way. But, if in the sight of God it is well, we should like to feel that our thought of you and our love for you will be to you an added source of strength and peace and understanding in this new adventure that you have elected to begin.

"We cannot say farewell to you, but, rather, reaching across this seeming distance that is not real, reaching into the great heart of God in which you and we are one, we say to you: God bless you and God keep you. God give you the strength and the inspiration and all that you need, as indeed we know that He does, to carry on the great work to which we know you are dedicated. In Christ's name. Amen."

Charles and Myrtle Fillmore had shared the speaker's platform at the Unity Chapel on Tracy since the building was dedicated in 1906, and for years before that they had shared their lives. On Sunday, October 11, Mr. Fillmore yielded his responsibilities to guest speakers. A week later, on October 18, Mr. Fillmore was alone on the platform. His beloved Myrtle, who had spoken the words of the Lord's Prayer and had given the meditative messages for more than twenty-five years at the headquarters chapel, was gone. He stepped forward at the point in the program in which Mrs. Fillmore normally led the meditation, and he offered these words:

" 'But we would not have you ignorant brethren, concerning them that fall asleep; that ye sorrow not, even as the rest, who have no hope. For if we believe that Jesus died and rose again, even so them also that are fallen asleep in Jesus will God bring with him.'

"Dear friends and co-workers in Christ: It is not our custom here at Unity even to mention the visits of the 'last enemy' whom we have resolved to finally overcome, as taught by Jesus.

"But there are certain conditions under which we should exchange sympathy and give thanks for that universal unity which these days of stress and strain have brought. I feel your sympathy and I thank you from the bottom of my heart for your many expressions of comfort in thought and word. This occasion is so pregnant with the absence and the presence of the one who has for years stood in my place at this point in our Sunday morning lesson that I am constrained to speak a few words of consolation and comfort, not only for you but for myself.

"Personality sorrows and grieves when the bodily presence is withdrawn, but the sense of absence can be overcome when we realize that there is a spiritual bond that cannot be broken. We do not look at life as a night between two eternities, as do those who, Paul says, have no hope, because they live and have been educated in a foolish fashion, looking at life as a transitory material thing; but we who are following Jesus Christ in the resurrection know life as a spiritual thing, and that we live spiritually, if we understand the law of life, and that we shall continue to live in Spirit, whether in the body or out of the body. And we know that this spiritual bond is the only bond that will really endure.

"We know that we shall endure as minds, and we shall know one another in our souls after we have left the body; but have we any assurance that our earthly ambitions are eternal? No; if our consciousness is founded on the things of the world, that is personality, and personality will

The man of her life,
Charles Fillmore

perish. But there is a bond that is of the absolute—the
things that are true and real; that bond will endure; and to
this end I want to call your attention to a little allegory that
appeared in an old number of our magazine UNITY, which
as I remember Mrs. Fillmore selected some years ago as
representing the relation that existed between us. It is
called 'The Enduring Bond,' and was written by Olive
Schreiner."

Once there was a woman who loved a man, and he died; and she sought some way to reach him where he was, and could not.

And one came to her, an angel, and said,

"I have been sent to help thee, for thy crying has been heard; what is thy need?"

And she answered, "That I might find the soul of my husband, who is dead."

And the shining one said to her, "That may be done only if there is a bond between you that death could not break."

And she said, "Surely there is a bond! I have lain in his boson; I have kissed his dear hands over and over, for love of him."

But the angel shook his head and said, "There is no bond."

Then she raised her head proudly and said, "Surely there is a bond . I have held his children in my arms; with their innocence have they bound us together. By the sorrow in which I bore them, there is an enduring bond."

But the angel said very sadly, "Even this will not suffice."

Then the woman paled, but she said, "My spirit and that of my husband were one; in naught were we separate. Each answered each without speech. We were one. Does not this hold?"

But the angel answered very low, "It does not hold. In the domain of death all of these bonds of which thou speakest crumble to nothing. The very shape of them has departed, so that they are as if they never were. Think yet once more before I leave thee, whether there is one thread to bind thee to him whom thou lovest; for if not he has passed from thee forever."

And the woman was silent; but she cried to

herself desperately, "He shall not go from me!"

And the angel withdrew a little way. And the woman thought a thought with deep inward communing: and after a space she raised her pale, drawn face, and gazed with timid eyes at the pitying angel.

And she said, though her voice was as the last whisper of the dying waves upon the shore, "Once, but long ago, he and I thought of God together."

And the angel gave a loud cry; and his shining wings smote the earth, and he said, "Thou hast found the bond! Thou hast found the bond!"

Thus the word of Mrs. Fillmore's passing was conveyed to the congregation of Unity Chapel and to residents of the Kansas City area. But another task lay ahead. Thousands of readers of *Wee Wisdom* and UNITY magazines had yet to be informed. The Fillmores had spoken frequently in the pages of these magazines about eternal life. Now it was necessary to discuss death. It was decided that *Wee Wisdom,* consecrated to *life,* would simply overlook the death of its founder. The children who were reading *Wee Wisdom* in 1931 weren't really acquainted with Mrs. Fillmore, as she had all but ended her active association with the magazine several years previously. But UNITY magazine was another matter. Because of printing schedules, the passing could not be reported in the November or December 1931 issues. So, in the January 1932 issue the following account was published in the pages of UNITY:

"Myrtle Fillmore, one of the founders of Unity School of Christianity, passed on to the invisible side of life Tuesday, October 6, 1931. Forty-five years before, medical science had given Mrs. Fillmore up to die. Through sheer faith she set aside that death sentence and began to help others by the exercise of that simple, beautiful faith in Christ's teachings to which she attributed her own healing. Except for her devoted love to her family, she gave her entire time, thought, and energy to the ever-growing work of the school that grew out of her pioneer work and that of her husband, Charles Fillmore.

"Those who knew her intimately and to whom she had expressed a desire to make the change believe that she might have remained in the body indefinitely had she so chosen. Every phase of the change was made in divine order. As was customary with her, she closed her work at her office in Kansas City on Thursday, after a day spent in writing letters, in receiving callers, and in helping with the regular healing work of Silent Unity. After leaving her office, she spent the evening in picking apples at Unity Farm.

"Not long before her passing she climbed four flights of stairs to reach the writers' office, where she made a sunny, smiling visit. As always, she was in the best of spirits, a characteristic that made her visits to various departments of the school a delight and a benediction. During her visit she remarked that she wanted to make a change.

"That's fine," the writer answered. "What kind of a change?"

"I believe that it would be easier for me to do the work that is ahead of me from the invisible plane," she said.

"Oh, you mustn't do that. We need your help, your inspiration, your spiritual guidance, here," he answered.

"You know that you will have that anyway," she said smilingly.

"We have faith in Myrtle Fillmore, faith in her clear spiritual vision, faith in her allegiance to the guidance of that Presence which she so faithfully served for so long a time. We believe that she was following the guidance of that Presence in making the change that she chose to make. We cannot permit our love for her to be less generous than was her dear love for us. If she wished to step into the invisible, we would not have it otherwise. We would not have any personal thought of ours retard her progress, or cast a shadow upon the serenity of her faith and work.

"Therefore we shall carry on, striving to make our loyalty to the high principles of Truth, which she taught and lived so beautifully, our tribute to her. And just as we shall be very near to her in our thought and love, we know that she will be very near to us. It cannot be otherwise.

"Souls are near to one another not in proportion to proximity, but by reason of their common purposes, their love for one another, and for something greater than any one of them. We have faith that our common love of Christ will keep us close to one another and to Myrtle Fillmore.

"In accepting this change, we do not desert the ideal of overcoming death as did Jesus by quickening the body to a fourth-dimensional expression. But we are mindful that death is the last enemy to be overcome, that we take a very big step in that overcoming when we overcome the fear of death, and that there are many steps to take, many high adventures in God's glorious service, before that final overcoming. We 'suffer it to be so,' in the calm of assurance that life neither begins at birth nor ends at death, that in our Father's house there are many mansions, and that if it were not so He would have told us.

"A great man of old said that he was as a little child, not knowing how to go out or how to come in. Most of us have not yet learned to master birth and death, to make our comings and goings serenely and in order. Myrtle Fillmore had evidently made that great overcoming. She gave seven-day-a-week service to the work she loved best, and when she made up her mind to make the change she did it beautifully and graciously, preparing her associates for that change, teaching them lovingly and sweetly as always, even in this last gesture. As was her custom, she went to her lovely country home to spend the weekend with her family, where she quietly and peacefully lay down to rest, and serenely slipped out into the realm that lies just beyond the senses.

"Surely Myrtle Fillmore must take her place with the illumines of mankind. Her life no less than her teachings inspired faith and courage, and understanding, in the lives of millions, and, through the great work that she established, will continue to inspire others so long as that work serves

God's wise and loving purposes. Millions have risen, and
shall rise, to call her name blessed, and to reverence the
dear Christ whom she taught them to serve."

Although Mrs. Fillmore's death had stunned Unity
workers and members of the family, it did not slow the work
that she had started. There was a determination to go
ahead doing the work that needed to be done and not to
dwell on sadness at her departure. Perhaps best illustrative
of the mood of the Fillmore family after the death is an
exchange of letters between Dr. H. Emilie Cady, author of
Unity's basic textbook, *Lessons in Truth,* and Lowell
Fillmore. Six days after his mother's death Lowell answered a piece of correspondence from Dr. Cady. His
letter contained the usual information about Unity's
progress, his concern that Dr. Cady remained well and
happy, and his beloved flower garden's status. But he did
not mention his mother's passing. On November 5, 1931,
apparently after learning of the death, Dr. Cady wrote to
Lowell again:

"I have only just learned of the beautiful transition of
your dear mother and my dear friend. How I rejoice with
you who are left behind! I am so glad that it is she to whom
hath been given just now this larger, fuller life than any of us
seem to realize while here, except for a moment at a time.
When I look at your last kind letter to me, and see that it
contains no hint of anything unusual having occurred, in
your life or in the Unity household, I again rejoice with you
and in the strength of character and faithfulness to principle
shown by you in a matter which lay very near your heart.
To me it is beautiful and dear Lowell, may I ask that any
similar event in my own life, should such come at any time,
be treated this same way?"

Lowell Fillmore answered Dr. Cady's letter on November 17, 1931, and said in part:

"Your beautiful letter about Mother made me very happy. We are not letting ourselves indulge in the thought of what we might term our personal loss, the loss of dear Mother's physical presence. We want her pathway toward the Absolute to be free from even the tiniest shadow of negative thought.

"Mother had spoken many times during the past year of wishing to make the change in her life, and two weeks before she left she mentioned it to several friends. Naturally, we tried to dissuade her. We told her how much we needed her here, how much the Unity work needed her, but she said: 'How do you know I mightn't do better work from the other side?' You see, she had a vision of a greater work to be accomplished, and we, who may not fully grasp her spiritual outlook, could but withdraw our argument and stand by with thoughts of love, and strength, and joy, so that her beautiful soul may have freedom in Spirit to continue its chosen work. We have loosed her, dear friend, and let her go.

"Would you like to know about the service we had for her at the chapel? It was so beautiful, so unlike any other service I have ever attended. Mr. Wilson's address was a talk to her friends. The idea of joy and love was stressed. She was dressed in a dainty lavender dress which she had worn last May Day when she was crowned Queen of the May of Unity School. She was so radiantly happy that day and she loved her lavender dress. Those who looked upon her body as it lay in the casket can never doubt her joyousness in making the change in her expression of life. It was as though she had put her house in perfect order and closed its lips with a sweet smile. About her face was a glow of happiness radiating, and all who looked upon her there were glad that they had done so, for instead of causing them to mourn and grieve, it stirred within them a corresponding glow of happiness."

The physical life of Myrtle Fillmore had ended, but the work which she had started was to go on, and on, and on....

XVI

So We've Come Up to Here!

Myrtle Fillmore's passing in 1931 did not slow the growth and expansion of the Unity movement. There was grief, to be sure, that the physical presence of one so loved was no longer in the visible realm, but there was joy, too, that she had gone on to another phase of eternal life where her soul unfoldment could continue.

Charles and Myrtle Fillmore planted vital Truth seeds in the 1880s and they nurtured Unity through its formative years. By the time of Myrtle's transition the movement was already well established.

Unity is what it is today because Myrtle caught a glimpse of the sublime—the Truth—and she and Charles were the perfect partners to carry out that Truth under the banner of Unity. They tuned in to God, received and acted upon divine ideas, and shared their good with all humanity.

Today Unity is worldwide in its scope. When the Tracy property was sold to the Salvation Army in the late 1940s, and a huge new administration building was erected at Unity Farm, the Unity School of Christianity consolidated all its activities at the rural site now known as Unity Village. Within the 1400 acres of the village are formal gardens, fountains, forests and orchards, lakes and recreational facilities, and the necessary buildings conducive to carrying out the activities of spiritual expansion.

Rickert and Lowell Fillmore reviewing plans beside a scale model of the new administration building (1947)

Several buildings have been erected at Unity Village since 1949 when the headquarters was moved from the Tracy property. One of them is Unity Inn, a modern cafeteria which carries on the tradition of quality food and service which was established at the Tracy site.

A second new structure, a new chapel, more formally called the Activities Center, contains seating for 1100 persons. Services are conducted twice on Sunday and once on Wednesday night. Many other activities take place in the center both day and night throughout the week. Its auditorium can be divided into three separate soundproof rooms, each with its own sound system, lighting, and temperature controls.

Also housed at Unity Village is the world headquarters of the Association of Unity Churches, an organization that serves more than 300 churches all over the globe. Most of the ministries are located in the United States but increasing numbers are being established in such countries as Canada, Australia, the Dominican Republic, Puerto Rico, Jamaica, Germany, Great Britain, Nigeria, and a number of other nations. More than 325 ordained ministers and hundreds of licensed teachers serve these churches and scores of small study groups. Unity's seminary, the School of Ministerial and Religious Studies, graduates and ordains approximately thirty new ministers each year—a figure that has more than tripled since the 1960s.

The Unity Institute for Continuing Education attracts hundreds of persons each year to the village for study of Truth principles. Graduates are licensed as teachers and work with study groups or assist ministers in churches. Still another educational facility is Wee Wisdom School, a preschool and kindergarten which trains children with the most modern techniques available.

Unity Village has a Retreat Department which welcomes additional hundreds of persons each year to participate in Truth lectures, panel discussions, meditations, and workshops. Ample time is provided to retreatants for rest and recreation and many of them take advantage of recreational facilities such as swimming, golfing, tennis, and hiking. Motels, cottages, and hotel rooms on the village grounds can accommodate up to 200 persons.

One of the largest religious publishing houses in the midwest issues three periodicals—UNITY Magazine, *Daily Word*, and *Wee Wisdom*. Almost two million persons subscribe to these publications.

Unity issues several new books each year, too, adding to a list of some seventy-five titles already in print. Much of the Unity literature is printed in as many as twelve foreign languages, some materials are available in large print, and a considerable amount of literature is produced in Grade 2 Braille for the sightless.

Brochures, booklets, prayer cards, and pamphlets are published by the millions. During the course of a year as many as one-hundred million pieces of literature are distributed to individuals.

Forms of communication such as radio and television and tape cassettes also help spread the Truth message. The Cassette Department issues tapes on seminars, lectures, and interviews with Truth leaders and ministers, and makes *Daily Word* available on tape to persons with visual handicaps. The Radio and Television Department writes and produces *The Word,* a one-minute inspirational message broadcast on 1300 radio and television stations. Many celebrities participate in taping these messages.

What is believed to be one of the world's largest collections of metaphysical books is housed in Unity's Library. More than 30,000 volumes are available for study and research. The Heritage Room, part of the Library complex, contains items of historical interest and a complete collection of Unity magazines, books, pamphlets, and booklets.

Silent Unity continues to be the heart of Unity and more than 200 persons work in this worldwide twenty-four-hour ministry. More than two million persons contact Silent Unity each year, about one-quarter of these by telephone where workers pray directly with the callers. As in the beginning, there is never a charge for prayer, but many persons respond generously with free-will offerings to help keep Silent Unity active in its work of prayer support for the millions.

A Counseling and Resource Center located in the administration building complements the work of Silent

Charles R. Fillmore

Unity by direct contact with individuals. Hundreds of persons visit the center and are counseled by trained personnel. The latest service in this respect is the Unity Help-Line telephone system in which crisis calls are handled by volunteer counselors. Again, no charge is made for counseling, but offerings are accepted.

In all, more than 500 persons are employed at Unity Village—a far cry from the handful of workers who started Unity in the 1880s. Some 250 persons live at the village, which has its own fire department, security force, and "town" officials.

The continuing story of Unity's growth would not be complete without mention of Unity Temple on the Plaza in Kansas City. It is considered the founders' church because it grew out of the original Unity Society incorporated in 1903 by the Fillmores. The first Unity Society Building was dedicated in 1906, but the facility was outgrown rather

Rosemary Rhea

quickly. The Fillmores chose the site at 47th Street and Jefferson in 1929. Work was delayed on the new structure for several years, and when it was started, some fifteen years were required for completion. The building was first occupied in 1948.

Charles Fillmore, who in 1933 married Cora G. Dedrick, a longtime Unity employee, was still living when the first service was conducted in the new temple. Charles passed on shortly afterward, on July 5, 1948. Church officials dedicated two chapels in the temple to the memories of the two Fillmores.

Lowell Fillmore succeeded his father Charles as president of Unity. Rick, who had designed and constructed Unity Village, was secretary. In 1972 Lowell yielded the presidency to Charles Rickert Fillmore, Rick's son. Rick passed away in 1965, and Lowell made his transition in 1975.

Frances Lakin

There have been many changes in Unity through the years, but one thing has remained constant: Unity has no strict creed or dogma and continues to emphasize individual growth and soul unfoldment. The idea that God is within each person, and that He can be reached through prayer and meditation, is foremost in the mind of every Truth student.

In 1951 a bridge over the fountain between the Administration Building and the Tower at the Village was dedicated to the memories of Charles and Myrtle Fillmore. It was named The Bridge of Faith—and the affirmation that was spoken that day aptly sums up the idea of Unity that Charles and Myrtle Fillmore envisioned and demonstrated:

"We are not only dedicating a bridge today, we are rededicating Unity, for Unity is a Bridge of Faith. It is a bridge from the old race beliefs to a new understanding of Truth."

Myrtle Fillmore often told of her vision for Unity in these words: "Unity is a school of religious investigation and experimentation. We have incorporated into our teachings all the good we have found in all the religions we have studied. We have taken Jesus Christ as the head of the Unity work, and are seeking to demonstrate Christ principles as He demonstrated them."

And then she might add, with a smile, "When folks come poking around here, reading the things we read, saying the words we say, and singing the songs we sing, they just catch the thing we have and never get over it!"

A Look at Unity Village Today . . .

The Tower

**The Peace Chapel
in the
Silent Unity Building**

The Light that Shines for You

The Silent Unity Building

**A Door to the
Administration Building**

**The Charles and Myrtle Fillmore
Bridge of Faith**

The Administration Building

Food and Fellowship
The Unity Village Inn

Christmas at the Activities Center

The Myrtle Fillmore Grove

A View of the Rose Garden

The Publishing Building

Myrtle Fillmore's Favorite Home: The Arches

Blossoms in the Orchard

Children on a Nature Walk

What Myrtle Fillmore Said About . . .

Affirmation: Affirmation of good is a word of Truth. We must be faithful and orderly in speaking these words of Truth. To speak Truth faithfully is a healing stream. Affirm the now as your only active eternity.

Age: The belief in old age is something we must get rid of in our understanding of eternal life and youth. It does not belong in God's creation. Age is not a piling up of years, but a period of unfoldment. Growth and unfoldment go on and on in ceaseless progression. Let's make an agreement here and now that we'll never use the word *old* anymore. Why, it even makes our clothing grow old and wear out. Let's use the words that build up and keep everything new in our world.

Amusements: Jesus Christ directed His followers to be in the world, but not of it. If you can take a happy part in any amusement without getting bound so that you take on care and anxieties that fill you with responsibility, which makes for heaviness or wastes the precious substance needed in body-building—it could not be called wrong.

Astrology: Unity does not teach that the horoscope has any power over anyone, except as one endows it with power through his own thoughts and words. We know that God is the only real power in the universe. Why give the controlling power to things of the manifest earth when Jesus tells you the kingdom of God is within you? There is so much to study and to learn in getting the understanding of our own faculties and their expression that we see no time for you to waste in studying astrology.

Beauty: Beauty and appreciation are inborn, and so are all the qualities that make for the transformation in the outer world. Emerson teaches that those who have capacity to appreciate beautiful things have more enduring title to them than those who hold material ownership of them.

Blessings: One who is living the Christ life attracts blessings of all sorts, and he need never worry about financial matters, though he will give enough thought and attention to them to keep his part of the law.

Body: We must know the chemistry of the body. We must feed the whole man. We have to have this outer man and have to make the mortar that builds him up. Sometimes the soul gets so anxious about what it wishes to do that it tends to neglect the body. This is not fair to the body or to those who must take care of the body when it is neglected. Your first duty is to bless your body. Get your thoughts right down into it, and praise its wonderful work. Learn what it needs and arrange for supplying those needs.

College: It is our experience that boys and girls sometimes come out of college not any better fitted to take up their life work than before they went in. And many of them lose God in the maze of men's minds, which they are supposed to depend upon for their light. We do not imply that there are not many splendid things in college; but we do feel that those who attend should know so well what they are going for that they are willing to go to the Father and learn how to bring forth the necessary supplies.

Condemnation: One who is working in the Jesus Christ consciousness condemns nothing! You may say that Jesus Christ condemned some things. Well, we are sure that Jesus was not fully understood in His efforts to bring men into the light of Truth, and we feel sure that He was not expressing the Christ ideas when, or if, He condemned others in their shortcomings. He made nothing of impurity and talked very little of the negative side of daily life. He simply saw the real self of each one and called that forth.

Consciousness: The more you think about God's presence of life, purity, love, strength, and health in every fiber of your body temple, the stronger will become your consciousness that your organism is the temple of "Christ in you." God is already in every part of your being, so it is just a matter of being conscious of oneness with Him.

Change: It is much more important to change and to do that which is really best for our progress and our health than it is to be smugly consistent or to make the excuse that we have always done thus and so it is too late to change now. The moment we discover anything undesirable in our minds or our lives, we should seek to make the changes necessary to bring about that which is desirable.

Christian Science: Mary Baker Eddy maintains that matter does not originate in Mind; we agree with her there, but cannot follow her in giving matter the power to crowd Mind out of our universe. We have no war with matter. When we, here at Unity, heal human bodies, we do not set up the theory that the bodies do not exist, as in Christian Science, but we hold that the mind that believes in the body is unified with the real, spiritual substance.

Christmas: Would it not be well for us to consider individually and collectively the question of how we can observe Christmas in the spirit of its true idea? We have enslaved ourselves with the burden of giving at Christmas. We have lost sight of the real spirit of giving when we spend ourselves and deplete our purses for the sake of conforming to the almost universal custom of exchanging gifts with our friends. It would be much more in conformity with the Christ Spirit to use the time in sending out to our friends the joyful thoughts that come spontaneously from the Christ love. The gift is but the symbol of what we desire for our friends.

Church: I have spent literally years in church. And I enjoy attending church and taking part in services more than anything else I do.

Cruelty: When the harshness of others seems to crush you, you can send forth love, the power that not only blesses you but goes forth to redeem the adverse conditions in the outer. When petals of the fragrant rose are crushed by cruel hands, they send forth their sweetness even more than before.

Death: Jesus Christ promised repeatedly that those who believed firmly enough should never see death, and we also believe this to be true. Death has no part in God's eternal plan, and we are rejoicing with you that you are incorporating the truth into your consciousness.

Demonstration: People often ask how long it will take to make a desired demonstration. The time element does not enter into spiritual healing. There is no time in Spirit, and all answer to prayer is instantaneous. "Before they call, I will answer, and while they are yet speaking, I will hear." However, time enters into man's mortal concept of things; therefore the time required to bring about the healing in the outer depends upon one's ability to realize truth and to bring it into manifestation, through faith and the spoken word.

Denial: We boldly deny evil. We deny sin, sickness, and death. These things are not put away by denials. They are only there as a false sense. Denials put away the false sense and we see as we are seen by the great spiritual Father of all. We find we can dissolve the earthly house of false beliefs by denial and enter into "the house not made with hands" by affirmation. Every denial should be followed by an affirmation.

Disease: What we call disease is lack of harmony in the organism. When we touch the Christ state of consciousness, harmony pours over us, and that which is called illness—a condition resulting from inharmony within ourselves—is corrected by an adjustment of mind.

Dogma: The church will find out someday that the Christ man was not made to fill its creeds and dogmas. That was the great lesson Jesus the Christ came to teach, but only those who are free to think for themselves have discovered it.

Dreams: Dreams reveal to us the character of our thinking.

Employment: It surely is not good judgment and wisdom to keep at a thing, year after year, which brings no appreciable returns, and which does not cause the soul to grow and expand and radiate through the body as ever-renewing health and youth. It is foolishness to devote oneself so wholly to a given line of action that one's own consciousness is neglected, so that one fails to learn how to keep in health and strength and how to bring forth the things needed for daily comfort and peace of mind. It is not always best for one to continue doing that which he likes to do, or that for which he has been trained, or that for which he is paid best. We need to round out, to develop the rest of our faculties and powers, to do that which brings us close to humanity and that which increases what the world needs most.

Eternal Life: In the true thoughts of life, years have no power to take from life that which God has given it. Years have no power to take from life that which God has ordained shall be endless, permanent, enduring, eternal life.

Evil: Where good is, evil cannot exist. Pure reasoning from the axiom, "God, the causing power is all," reduces evil to zero and the problems of life are resolved to the simple equation: all good equals satisfaction.

Faith: We appreciate your faith in us, but we want you to have faith in yourself—for God is in you and working through you, just as much as He is in us—and just as much as He is in Jesus Christ.

Fear: Sometimes we fear that we have not the ability to do a thing that we ought to do; we fear that there are obstacles in the way. If there are obstacles, we have made them. God never put anything in the way of our progress. When we get rid of our fears, we find out that the way is clear for us to go the Lord's way.

Flowers: I love flowers and the dear girls here in Silent Unity keep my office supplied with their beauty. I bring flowers from my fairy home garden to help make all of our offices beautiful when I come in each morning.

Food: You may have gotten the impression that Unity gives a lot of thought to the matter of diet, because of our having the Vegetarian Inn and because we occasionally publish something concerning diet. But we really give little thought to diet. We endeavor to furnish ourselves with the good fresh foods from forest and field and orchard. We like to know something about the body's construction and its physical needs and how to supply these. After that we leave it with our own inner intelligence to demand what is needed and to take care of the assimilation.

Forgiveness: Forgiveness is the act of putting something else in place of the thing forgiven. You put the positive realization of the Truth of Being in place of the appearance of negation and adversity which your senses and your intellectual training report. It does not matter that there is no immediate transformation; you have made use of your God-power to erase the appearance and to establish Truth. Such an attitude invites only the best from other souls.

Future: The future is what we make it. But we are learning that we are developing God-given faculties and powers,

276

coming into consciousness of sonship. So, after all, the future is in God's hands, and it will reveal in our life the state that Jesus called the kingdom of God or the kingdom of Heaven.

Gifts: Many of the most important and necessary things in life are free gifts from God, and we may have them constantly without any thought of doing any definite thing in return for them. The air we breathe, the sunlight, the beauty of nature, the out-of-doors for recreation and inspiration. For these we should be thankful to God.

God: Though personal to each one of us, God is IT— neither male nor female, but Principle. God is not a cold, senseless principle like that of mathematics, but the Principle of life, love, and intelligence.

Good: We find that we must not only be good, but *good for something.*

Habit: Drop out of your mind that a bad habit is a terrible thing. When you think of it as a terrible and powerful thing, you keep giving it as much or more power than you allow the Christ.

Healing: Sure healing is attained by him who ever keeps the portal of his thought guarded by these two angels: denial and affirmation.

Heaven: The state we call heaven is awaiting those who are ready for it: the peace and harmony and order that come from living in tune with infinite good.

Hell: The word in the original language, which the Bible

translators have called "hell," means a provision for a place of purification. In the country which used such means for purification, there was a long ravine in which a fire was kept burning all the time. Here the people brought their trash and garbage and dead animals to burn them, so that they might keep their cities clean and sanitary. Sometimes these folks, in speaking of the effects of spiritual training upon their lives, referred to a process much like their material efforts to keep their cities clean. So, when the translators came to their writings about the valley where there was a fire burning all the time and which fire consumed everything undesirable, they just incorporated it into their religious version of these writings. And our preachers have sought to frighten their people into being good, by describing this state of torment and burning as a condition which they would face after death.

Holy Spirit: The Holy Spirit is the activity of God-Mind in the consciousness of men.

Home: Every home takes on the quality of the prevailing thought held in it.

Housework: I'm going to lecture you a bit. You just look around and see if there aren't a number of things you've been doing that you can let go undone. I'll just venture you are one of those old-fashioned housekeepers—always cleaning, straightening, and fixing. And I suspect you'd feel disgraced if you should wear the same housedress until it got soiled. Just forget some of those old habits, dear, because we are living in a new day, when there is so much more to do and so many interests of more import than the details of housework.

I AM: When we learn to be still and to know the I AM (God's perfect idea of us), we lack nothing. We can become like Jesus Christ if we abide in this secret place of Spirit.

Ideas: All of us must hitch our faith to the divine ideas that make for abundance of manifest good. Then we have a foundation upon which to build our castle of health, happiness, and prosperity. The eternal realities upon which to build are discerned by the eyes of faith and spiritual understanding.

Jehovah: The Lord God, or Jehovah, is the individual consciousness of God, the Christ mind unfolding the ideas of God-Mind.

Jesus Christ: Two thousand years ago there came a manifestation of human life so conversant with the great causing Power of life that He called that Power *Father,* and it was said of Him, "The Word became flesh." He was a fearless teacher of Truth. He spent His ministry freeing mankind from delusions. With the sweeping proclamation, "Call no man your father on the earth: for one is your Father, which is in heaven," He emancipated the race from the limitation of mortal parentage.

Knowledge: The things that we have thought to be beyond our ken are gradually coming into our knowledge. We are gradually coming to know that we are one with Him who knows all, one with the one perfect life.

Life: Life is our gift from the Father, a gift that is never withdrawn, never lessened, never limited by the Giver.

Liquor: What is this liquor habit anyhow? Seeing with clear vision, we learn that back of the false appetite is a yearning for God, a hunger and thirst after righteousness.

Love: Love that fulfills the law is the great sense of unity that prompts the soul to seek the understanding and practice of that which is for the welfare not only of the beloved but of all humanity.

Mind: As you study, you will learn that your mind receives from two sources: the universal Mind of Being, which has its outlet through your consciousness, and the intellectual activities of the individual minds about you, which have both conscious and subconscious phases of expression. That which you receive from the Mind of God is always good, always helpful, health-inspiring, and peace-inspiring. That which you receive from the reports of your senses or from the minds of others, may be true and helpful, or it may be false and harmful. The study and practice of Truth will help you discriminate between the false and the true.

Mothers: Sometimes mothers are apt to feel that they have been "placed on the shelf" and that they are in the way. They begin to think habitually along these lines, and negative thoughts, together with disappointments because of the seeming indifference of their cherished ones, undermine their health, peace of mind, and strength. Mothers have given their heart's best to the children they have reared, and the love of these children means to them almost everything that is worthwhile.

Motion Pictures: We are praying that some good producer, and someone who can dream dreams and see visions and do lovely things, will bring out some truly beautiful and living and peace-inspiring and joyous pictures. We'd love to see a film setting forth everyday life, as God has planned it for His children. I think most of us could contribute some happy features to such a picture. I can't see how folks get into such habits of going to "bum" shows so often, and yet not taking in a church show once in a while. Why, the really up-to-date ministers have more good jokes, more really clean, clever ways of entertaining than the shows have. And all the time they're helping us to see ourselves and others in a better light.

Nature: I was almost accused of being a nature worshiper when I was a little girl. And I have always loved what I see in nature, as well as in all artists who are so close to the beauty side of God. Nature is surely the glorified face of Good. See the beauty about you and you do see the manifestation of the infinite Mind.

New Thought: Instead of thinking and saying "New Thought," would it not be better for you to think and speak God Thought? New Thought lets one in for all sorts of conjectures and experiments and isms. To identify oneself with New Thought is to open the mind to the winds and waves of the new race thought which is being built up. While to identify oneself with the Jesus Christ standard of thinking, which is made known in the individual mind and heart through the action of the Holy Spirit, keeps one poised and free and filled with light.

Now: Keep your soul open to the shining light of Truth by denial of past or future claims upon you, for you live in the *now.* Affirm the now as your only active eternity.

Opinions: The opinions of others cannot get you down or lift you up. You have the power of God within you to raise yourself up to where you know you are His child, with ability along all lines and with freedom to do whatever you really wish to do.

Order: Divine order will be expressed in your work when you have faith in God. Your hours will be filled with good, profitable work.

Ownership: Whatever is your own under the law of good comes to you; whatever does not belong to you is taken away to find its right place.

Parenthood: There is no secret sin or petty deception practiced by the parent so deeply hidden but it will find its way to the surface through the child. Example is greater than precept. We cannot successfully train our children in honesty and uprightness when we are lacking in those qualities ourselves.

Past: The past recedes from us if we do not embrace it and the light that the changing perspective throws upon it makes it a pleasing background for present activities.

Pleasure: Outer pleasure is like moonlight: sometimes it is very beautiful, but there is no element of growth in it. It does not help the power within us to come forth.

Prayer: Set aside regular periods every day for prayer. Use words of Truth during your silence periods. As you change your thinking and bring it into line with Truth principles, a transformation will take place in your consciousness. Your mind will become keen, awake, alert, and illumined, and your body temple will be filled with new life. You will be inspired with practical ideas that will enable you to succeed in a larger way.

Problems: Your problems do not exist except in your own mind. And they are there only because you have made them. As soon as you withdraw your thoughts and feelings from the things which you have invited and built up, they will fall flat and dissolve.

Procrastination: Again the old habit shows itself. Didn't get to do it. Just so much doing that had to be done. Some of these days perhaps we'll become so at-one with order and system that we won't have our affairs pushing us all the time. We will be masters of our time. Won't that be lovely?

Prosperity: When we are endeavoring to listen, to understand, and to follow our divine guidance from the spiritual center of our own soul, we find that every wind that blows (whether it appears at first to be good or ill) does fill us with the spirit of plenty—because the winds are evidence of God's ideas and substance, and plenty is the one reality. So we may rejoice in our prosperity and use it day by day, in full assurance that it will never fail.

Regeneration: When once the ideal man is conceived in the mind as a possibility, and the requirements of Law are complied with, the regeneration of mind and body is under way.

Religion: I had years of searching for something which I did not find in the religion of my parents. And now, after we find the Truth, we are really glad that we had not accepted the old limited beliefs of those who did not know the indwelling God, aren't we?

Restlessness: Our restlessness represents a power that is crying out to be expressed. It may take the form of appetite or of ambition, but rightly directed it will be a wonderful something within us that will transcend all the desires of the outer senses. When our powers are placed aright, we shall direct our aspirations and ambitions toward God; we shall know that we can be satisfied with nothing that earth can give.

Results: Do not be concerned if you do not always get from your study and your prayers the results that your senses take cognizance of. Your spiritual awakening is the important thing.

Salvation: Our salvation is in our living by the Christ pattern—not only the teachings of the man Jesus Christ but by the Christ mind within us.

Santa Claus: We can learn a most important lesson from the faith of the child who hangs his stockings by the fireplace for Santa Claus to fill with the gifts he has been asked to place in it. Instead of trying to lessen the faith of the child in the unseen helper, it would be vastly beneficial to us if we learned from him how to ask, stretch forth the empty hand, and find it filled. Of course, it is not necessary to lay stress upon the Santa Claus personality. The teaching should be that there is a loving Helper who answers our prayers, an ever-ready Provider for all our needs.

Satisfaction: You will never find the peace and satisfaction which your longing soul calls for if you are looking to Christian Science for these things, but neither will you find them by looking to Unity. Cease trying to find an anchor for your thoughts in the beliefs of others, and turn within to the

284

holy sanctuary of your soul, for it is there that you are to find and to know God. Until you do this, you cannot know what body of individuals you are most in harmony with. Freed from the beliefs and traditions of others, the glory of the Lord will be revealed to you.

Scientific Healing: I hope those doctors who have finally admitted that spiritual healing is scientific will be as ardent and insistent upon throwing over all the atrocious methods of treatment which they have employed in the past as they have been in imposing them on the lazy and long-suffering public.

Sickness: This influenza business isn't all that it seems to the medical world, flesh appearance rather than the inner workings of the mind. We consider it a sort of housecleaning—getting rid of some of the kinks in consciousness which don't measure up to the standard of peace and purity and freedom and plenty for which we have taken a nationwide stand. When we identify ourselves with Christ ideas, we must be willing to dig up and throw out everything which does not measure up to Christ-likeness. And if we don't seem to know how to do this gracefully— why we are likely to develop something which the doctors are eager to name and experiment with, and which the neighbors like to talk over.

Silence: The silence is a kind of stillness, a place of retreat into which we may enter and having entered, may know the Truth. We go into the silence by observing the instructions, "Be still and know." The only way to really *know* is to become perfectly still, to get away from the outer and from looking for things, into the inner quiet where we are alone with wisdom. In the silence, wisdom is given for every need.

The silence is like the sun: it is always shining. It brings forth the best in us.

Sin: We should remember that man is always punished by his sins and not for them.

Soul: God never sends a soul into the world without providing for its needs.

Success: The three essentials to success in the study of spiritual science are understanding of its fundamental principles; pure and unbiased reasoning; and ability to prove that the principles are workable.

Supply: There is an inexhaustible supply, and we are God's beloved children for whom He is ever providing and to whom He has given His own life and wisdom and power and substance.

Teaching: I know that teachers do become attached to their pupils and really do feel the wrench when the pupils leave for other fields, but my, the satisfaction I have had in seeing my students go forth to make use of what I had given.

Thanksgiving: Show me a family where thanksgiving and praise become a habit and I will show you a healthy, harmonious and prosperous household. For surely as the filing wings its way to the magnet, so surely does our waiting good fly to meet the needs of the praiseful, thankful home. Show me the seeds you sow and the thoughts you think and I can foretell the manner of your harvest, for it is the same in our mind world or in the soil world.

Thought: Every thought molds from the etheric essence a form symbol, which symbol has a certain degree of temporary life and by virtue of that life impresses itself upon the body.

Time: It matters not if one has been in this work one year or one hundred, if his heart is in the work and he has the understanding of Truth to back up his efforts. We know that Spirit does not recognize time and that years are only a false conception in the mind of man, so we take no cognizance of the passing of years.

Truth: When we use the word *Truth,* we mean that which is true of God and true of God's children. This spiritual Truth is that you are God's own beloved child and that God is ever giving you His own wisdom, love, power, life, and substance.

Understanding: If you would grow in understanding of spiritual things, become as a little child and let the universal spirit of good teach you. Do not strain your intellect in trying to understand the mighty questions of life; wait until you have developed faculties which can comprehend them.

Unity: Now where did you get the idea that you should follow Unity? Don't we repeatedly tell our students that they are to turn within to God Mind and to their own Christ consciousness? Don't we explain that we do not wish the individual to accept what we say, *because* we say it; and to try to live by it, because they find it in Unity literature? Our prayers, and our lectures, and our literature are to point the individual to the Source of his light and life and every good, within his own spiritual consciousness.

Universe: If you would know the perfect relation of all things in the universe, cultivate the soul. It is intelligence itself and will reveal to you, in the silence of meditation, glories and beauties of which you have not dreamed.

Vision: Study and practice daily, keeping your mind and heart, your vision and your emotions fixed on God—God in you. "Christ in you"—is your "hope of glory."

Weather: The time will come no doubt when man will master the weather conditions and it will be the weatherman's job to furnish everybody with just the right climatic conditions, and to bring rain when it is needed. Let's hope that he will be able to please everybody.

Wisdom: Wisdom is justified of her children, and none of us ever gets fooled. Some people may get fooled out of their health, their wealth, and their joy, but not us, because *we know.*

Work: I should like to straighten out an idea in your letter where you say, "I have to work in order to live." Now that is getting the cart before the horse. We do work and we love to serve because of opportunity it gives the industry of Spirit to express through us; but we do not look to the work for our supply, but steadfastly to God.

Yesterday: The restrictions of yesterday have no power to overshadow our lives today. When we realize that, we are in the eternal now.

Her Poetry

SONG OF PROSPERITY
(Undated)

Our Father God, to Thee,
Throughout eternity
Thy name we praise.
Thou art the Source of all,
Thou lovest great and small;
Thy Life sustaineth all;
Thine be the praise.

I am Thy child of health;
I am Thy heir of wealth;
All Thine is mine.
Joy and prosperity
Are ever mine in Thee,
Wisdom and harmony
And Love Divine.

MOTHER GOOSE'S NEW DEPARTURE

(Written at turn of century)

Goodby, old Goosey-Gander Goose!
Goodby, old spinning wheel.
You've served me long but now I feel
Such new life stir, I want a wheel
That I may ride and spin and whirl
Like any Twentieth Century girl.
I've been an old Goose long enough,
I'm tired of all the oldtime stuff;
The newest thing I want to be,
In all this brand new Cen-tu-ry.
This old cap will never do
For bright new thoughts to shine out through.
So off it goes, down goes my hair;
Away with wrinkles, age and care.
See! Mother Truth holds up her glass.
Why! Here's a young and comely lass.
I see as plain as plain can be,
Just as we think, just so are we.
The newest thing that we can find
Is a new thought within the mind.
All's new without when new within
Come let us take a little spin.

THERE LET ME REST
(Undated)

Give me Thine hand, Lord, in mine own,
Take me unto Thy breast.
Glad is my heart, and sweet the way
When in Thy love I rest.
Bright are the hours with Thee so near—
My faith on Thee is stay'd,
I know no doubt, I feel no fear, how can I
    be afraid?

Thou art so tender Lord,
Thou art divine;
I want in all this world
No love but Thine.
Thou art my all in all,
Dearest and best.
Take me, fold me, in Thine arms,
There let me rest.
There let me rest in Thee and find,
Dear Lord I love Thee so!
The secrets of a happy mind,
The joy that cannot let go.

I have no joy in life but Thee,
No faith but in Thy name.
Folded in love, my heart would be
Forever Thine, the same.
Thou art so tender, Lord.
Thou art divine,
I want in all this world,
No love but Thine.
Thou art my all in all,
Dearest and best.
Take my love, take my heart,
Take all the rest.

THANKSGIVING
(1901)

We count our blessings and they grow;
We deny our evils, and they go.
Such is the blessed law of good;
We could not break it if we would.

CHRISTMAS
(1901)

Drowsy little sleepy head,
Downy little pillow,
Make a voyage far away
Through the night, so still, Oh!

Far away where Christmas Babe
Lies on manger pillow,
Where the wise men's perfume sweet,
All the air does fill, Oh!

Hear the choir of heaven sing—
"Peace on Earth, Good Will," Oh!
See the Christ-Babe smile on them,
Sleepy head and pillow.

Hasten home, O voyager!
Through the night, so still, Oh!
Find the Christ Child in thy heart,
Sleepy head on pillow.

LOVE AND YOU
(1901)

One little word to tell it,
Four little letters spell it—
   L-O-V-E

One little heart to know it,
Two hands and feet to show it—
   Y-O-U

One little word to cover
A great world's sadness over—
   L-O-V-E

One little tongue to speak it,
Sweet willingness to seek it—
   Y-O-U

In kindness let it bubble,
'Tis the cure for care and trouble—
   L-O-V-E

When it sparkles into gladness,
There's no room for pain or sadness—
   L-O-V-E

All the hearts about you glowing
With the warmth that love is showing—
   Y-O-U

For the world is healed with feeling,
One glad heart itself revealing—
   L-O-V-E

EASTER RECITATION
(1902)

Soft the winds of Spring are blowing,
Like my thoughts the streams are flowing;
Bud and blossom, bird and bee,
Share in happy life with me.

Who am I that I know
Why the buds and blossoms grow?
Who am I that I see
Life alike in bird and me?

I am I, I am He;
I in Christ, and Christ in me
Life and living, two in one—
God the Father, God the son.

Like the lily, pure and white,
Blooming in the sun's glad light,
Father in Thy light are we,
Like the lily, pure and free.

Seed and shell only mean
Life is waiting to be seen;
Bird and blossom only tell
Of glad life that bursts its shell.

There's no sadness, there's no gloom,
There's no weakness, there's no tomb,
When the Living Christ in me,
Is by loving thoughts set free.

Glad our songs shall ever rise,
Warm our hearts as Easter skies.
Only good with us can bide,
Life, glad life, is Easter-tide.

APRIL
(1902)

A game of hide and seek they play,
This sun and shower of April day.
And while one seeks and while one hides,
Or one upon the other glides,
In romping steps of shade and sheen,
The brown clods turn to living green.
There's burst of color everywhere,
There's trill of gladness in the air,
There's swish of wing, there's hum of bee,
There's fairy legions come to see
This April game of seek-and-find,
This symbol of our happy mind.

AN EASTER EPIC
(1902)

Humpty Dumpty was round and white,
His heart of gold was hidden from sight.
Over him brooded, soft and warm,
A biddy hen, in Tommy's barn.
Long in the silence, warm and still,
Humpty Dumpty felt a thrill.
Felt a quiver, coming, going,
Humpty Dumpty began a growing,
Began to feel his golden heart beat,
Began to be feathers and eyes and feet,
Began to long for room and light,
Began to peck at his walls of white.
One telling stroke, and the deed is done.
Humpty Dumpty steps out in the sun.
All the king's oxen and all the king's men,
Can never put Humpty Dumpty back again.

UNTITLED
(Undated)

All the birds turned out to sing,
All the bees to humming,
Butterflies like flowers with wings,
In every hue were coming.

Little rivulets with joy
Swift and swifter running.
Spread to water-folk the news
Of the mothers' coming.

Everything with touch of life
Thrilled with new-felt pleasure;
Earth and heaven together drank
Their bowls of green and azure.

But Mother Goose look'd sadly 'round,
And Mother Truth looking longing,
For not a "human flower" was there
In all that happy thronging.

"Where are the children, Mother Goose?"
Cried Mother Truth: "You're wronging—
For earth and all that is in it
Are children's sweet belonging."

"I've summoned all," said Mother Goose.
"Alas your invitations
Excluded all who ever hurt
The least of God's creations."

"Summon again!" commanded Truth,
"All hearts have love inlaying;
Bid all the children come and find
That Love's the Queen of Maying."

UNTITLED
(1905)

Always do your best.
Half-heartedness is sin;
Put your whole mind into it,
Then you'll always win.

THANKSGIVING
(1905)

O Giver of our good,
We thank Thee every hour:
Thy blessings wait our word.
Thy richest dower
Is ours before we ask.
Like fruit upon the tree,
Ours is the task
To gather-in from Thee.

CHRISTMAS
(1902)

I wish one and all, Merry Christmas!
A season of unhindered cheer!
I hope that the good old "Saint Santa"
(Who is papa the rest of the year)
Will get 'round on time with his reindeer,
Do the chimney act safely and well,
Cram the stockings till every gaunt dangler's
Too full its sweet misery to tell.

Then I wish each slumbering dreamer,
May wake Christmas morning to find
That the Christ-Child has made it a manger
In the sweet loving thought of each mind.
That the Giver of gifts with old Santa,
Has viewed for the generous part,
While full to the brim is each stocking,
Overflowing with Christ in each heart.

REALIZATION
(Undated)

Last night I was thinking of Christ's love,
    was thinking
And it seemed that His promise, "Lo, I am
    now here"
Like a loved voice addressed me, sweetly it
    blessed me.
And quickened and gladdened my soul with
    its cheer;
And quickened and gladdened my soul with
    its cheer.

It seemed Christ the living, the loving,
    the loving,
Like a warm glowing presence pervaded my
    breast,
While a soft whispered blessing my soul was
    caressing,
Thrilled me and stilled me, with peace and
    with rest;
Thrilled me and stilled me, with peace and
    with rest.

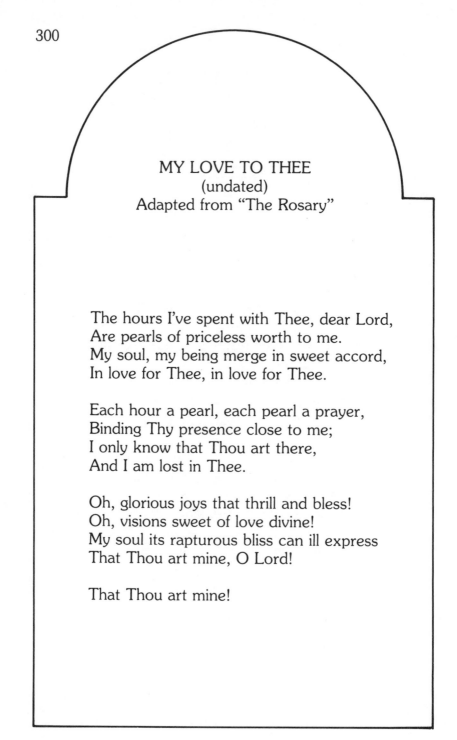

MY LOVE TO THEE
(undated)
Adapted from "The Rosary"

The hours I've spent with Thee, dear Lord,
Are pearls of priceless worth to me.
My soul, my being merge in sweet accord,
In love for Thee, in love for Thee.

Each hour a pearl, each pearl a prayer,
Binding Thy presence close to me;
I only know that Thou art there,
And I am lost in Thee.

Oh, glorious joys that thrill and bless!
Oh, visions sweet of love divine!
My soul its rapturous bliss can ill express
That Thou art mine, O Lord!

That Thou art mine!

JANUARY
(1904)

About the year,
    that's here
        my dear,
With love and gladness,
        health and cheer,
With life that's free
        from care and fear,
Comes the New Year,
        my dear.
For the old year,
    gone by,
        don't sigh.
In love's safe garner
        there doth lie
The grains and fruits,
        in rich supply
Planted and reaped, by you and I.

MAMIE'S THANKSGIVING
(1904)

Dear Lord, I am thankful, so thankful,
That You are never away.
I'm sure I don't know what would happen,
If You would go off and stay.

For Life would be sure to go with You,
And then nobody could live;
And the flowers and grass would wither,
And the sun no light could give.

There would never be anything doing;
There'd never be anything done.
Without You, O Lord, there is nothing—
Not anything, under the sun.

So I'm thankful dear Lord, so thankful,
That You are with us today,
For I know all the good and blessings
Wherever You are must stay.

MY VALENTINE
(Undated)

Do you want a Valentine?
You can share this one of mine.
It is full of love and truth,
Full of health and full of youth;
Like the ring that has no end
Is my *Valentine,* my friend—

Round and round and round and round
Its unfailing love is found;
Always just the same to you,
Beautiful and strong and true;
Giving, giving, giving, giving
Life and breath to all things living.

Oh! You guess my *Valentine.*
You accept this gift divine,
You confess through smile and nod—
'Tis the *omnipresent God.*

A HAPPY IDEA
(1905)

"What do they do with all the Old Years?"
Queried Wee Ned.
"Do they melt 'em up over
And run 'em anew,
Like Johnnies' lead?"

"Wise little man you have given the clue.
Why waste the years?
We'll melt 'em all over
And run 'em anew
And leave out the sorrow and fears."

PRINCE MARCH
(1905)

The story of the Sleeping Princess
Most anyone can tell;
How she slept within her castle
Held there by a magic spell.

Till a Prince came, brave and daring,
With a loving kiss
Broke the spell and won the Princess
(You've all heard of this).

We have seen a Sleeping Princess,
Bound by Winter's spell;
Shut within her cold brown castle,
(You all know her well).

And the Prince, so brave and daring,
With a sturdy smack
Wakes the Princess with his wooing,
Calls her color back.

Life thrills all her sleeping pulses—
March awakens Spring;
Earth is filled with stirring impulse,
Birds are on the wing.

DAILY WORDS
(1910)

Monday:	If you want the good to grow, watch the little words you sow.
Tuesday:	If you want life's blossoms rare, pull out thoughts that wear and tear.
Wednesday:	Loving good is always brought into sight through loving thought.
Thursday:	If you want to meet a smile, take one with you all the while.
Friday:	Kind and loving deeds attract, and like the echo, come right back.
Saturday:	What we give, we surely get; love for love, and fret for fret.
Sunday:	This sweet law, dear Lord, I know; I will reap the good I sow.

Most of Myrtle Fillmore's poetry was written for and published in *Wee Wisdom*.

Unity Books
Unity Village, Missouri 64065

Atom-Smashing Power of Mind, by Charles Fillmore
Be! by James Dillet Freeman
Be of Good Courage, by Frank Whitney
Be Ye Transformed, by Elizabeth Sand Turner
Beyond a Miracle, by Sue Sikking
Both Riches and Honor, by Annie Rix Militz
Charles Fillmore Concordance, The
Christ-Based Teachings, The, by Donald Curtis
Christ Enthroned in Man, by Cora Fillmore
Christian Healing, by Charles Fillmore
Consent, by Newton Dillaway
Dare to Believe! by May Rowland
Dynamics for Living, by Charles Fillmore, arranged by Warren Meyer
Emerging Self, The, by Ernest C. Wilson
Focus on Living, by Winifred Wilkinson
God a Present Help, by H. Emilie Cady
God Is the Answer, by Dana Gatlin
God Never Fails, by Mary L. Kupferle
Gospel of Emerson, The, by Newton Dillaway
Great Physician, The, by Ernest C. Wilson
Guidelines for a Healthy Marriage, by David Goodman
Guidelines for Parents, by Anne Lee Kreml
Halfway Up the Mountain, by Martha Smock
Happiness Now, by Mary Katherine MacDougall
Healing Letters of Myrtle Fillmore, The, compiled by Frances W. Foulks
Healing Now, by Mary Katherine MacDougall
Health, Wealth, and Happiness, The Prayer Way to, by Lowell Fillmore
How I Used Truth, by H. Emilie Cady
How to Let God Help You, by Myrtle Fillmore, compiled by Warren Meyer
How to Use the Power of Your Word, by Stella Terrill Mann
Inside Me, Outside Me, by Elizabeth Searle Lamb
Jesus Christ Heals, by Charles Fillmore
Keep a True Lent, by Charles Fillmore
Know Thyself, by Richard Lynch
Lessons in Truth, by H. Emilie Cady
Let There Be Light, by Elizabeth Sand Turner
Light for Our Age, by Robert P. Sikking
Like a Miracle, by Sue Sikking
Live Youthfully Now, by Russell A. Kemp
Magic of the Word, The, by May Rowland

Magnificent Decision, by James A. Decker
Make Your Dreams Come True, by Stella Terrill Mann
Master Craft of Living, The, by William L. Fischer
Meet It with Faith, by Martha Smock
Metaphysical Bible Dictionary, The
Mind: the Master Power, by Charles Roth
Myrtle Fillmore: Mother of Unity, by Thomas E. Witherspoon
Mysteries of Genesis, by Charles Fillmore
Mysteries of John, by Charles Fillmore
New Age Understanding, by Donald Curtis
New Unity Inn Cookbook, compiled by Alice Rinehart
Only Believe, by Sue Sikking
Open Your Mind to Prosperity, by Catherine Ponder
Patterns for Self-Unfoldment, by Randolph and Leddy Schmelig
Practical Christianity for You, by James E. Sweaney
Prayer: The Master Key, by James Dillet Freeman
Prospering Power of Love, The, by Catherine Ponder
Prosperity, by Charles Fillmore
Prosperity Now, by Mary Katherine MacDougall
Revealing Word, The, by Charles Fillmore
Revelation: the Book of Unity, by J. Sig Paulson and Ric Dickerson
Secret of Health, The, by Richard Lynch
Story of Unity, The, by James Dillet Freeman
Talks on Truth, by Charles Fillmore
Teach Us to Pray, by Charles and Cora Fillmore
Thoughts for a Friend, by Foster McClellan
Today and Every Day, by Elizabeth Searle Lamb
Turning Points, by Martha Smock
Twelve Powers of Man, The, by Charles Fillmore
Unity Way of Life, The, by Marcus Bach
Way of the Christ, The, by Donald Curtis
Week That Changed the World, The, by Ernest C. Wilson
What Are You? by Imelda Octavia Shanklin
What God Is Like, by James Dillet Freeman
What Will You Have? by James A. Decker
Wonderful Child, by Sy Miller and Jill Jackson
Working with God, by Gardner Hunting
You Can Be Healed, by Clara Palmer
Your Hope of Glory, by Elizabeth Sand Turner

Printed in the United States of America
137F-15M-10-77